"*Food Gift Love*'s recipes are a double pleasure: First there's the pleasure of making them, and then there's the pleasure of sharing them as gifts, boxed and bowed, bottled and beautifully beribboned. From cookies and jams, marshmallows and extracts, to cordials and curds, Maggie's book is filled with delicious ideas to help you share the foods you love best with the people you love most."

—DORIE GREENSPAN, author of *Baking Chez Moi*

"Maggie has truly inspired me to make every single recipe in this lovely book. I wish I had written this book—I love everything about it. Who doesn't want to make or receive a homemade food gift? But this book is the best food gift by itself already."

—YVETTE VAN BOVEN, author of *Home Made*

food
gift
love

Make and show something
special. xox

~M Bather~

food gift love

MORE THAN 100 RECIPES TO MAKE, WRAP, & SHARE

Maggie Battista

FOUNDER OF EAT BOUTIQUE

Photography by Heidi Murphy

HOUGHTON MIFFLIN HARCOURT
BOSTON · NEW YORK

Design by Laura Palese

Styling by Catrine Kelty

Hand lettering by Kristen Drozdowski

For information about permission to reproduce selections
from this book, write to trade.permissions@hmhco.com or to
Permissions, Houghton Mifflin Harcourt Publishing Company,
3 Park Avenue, 19th Floor, New York, New York 10016.

www.hmhco.com

Library of Congress Cataloging-in-Publication Data

Battista, Maggie.
Food gift love : more than 100 recipes to make, wrap, and share /
Maggie Battista, founder of Eat Boutique ; photography Heidi Murphy.
pages cm
Includes index.
ISBN 978-0-544-38767-6 (paper over board) —
ISBN 978-0-544-55640-9 (ebook)
1. Snack foods. 2. Gift baskets. I. Title.
TX740.B394 2015
642—dc23
2015004480

DOW   10 9 8 7 6 5 4 3 2
4500591828

Printed in the United States of America

to my mother

THE BRIGHTEST STAR
IN EVERY ROOM

contents

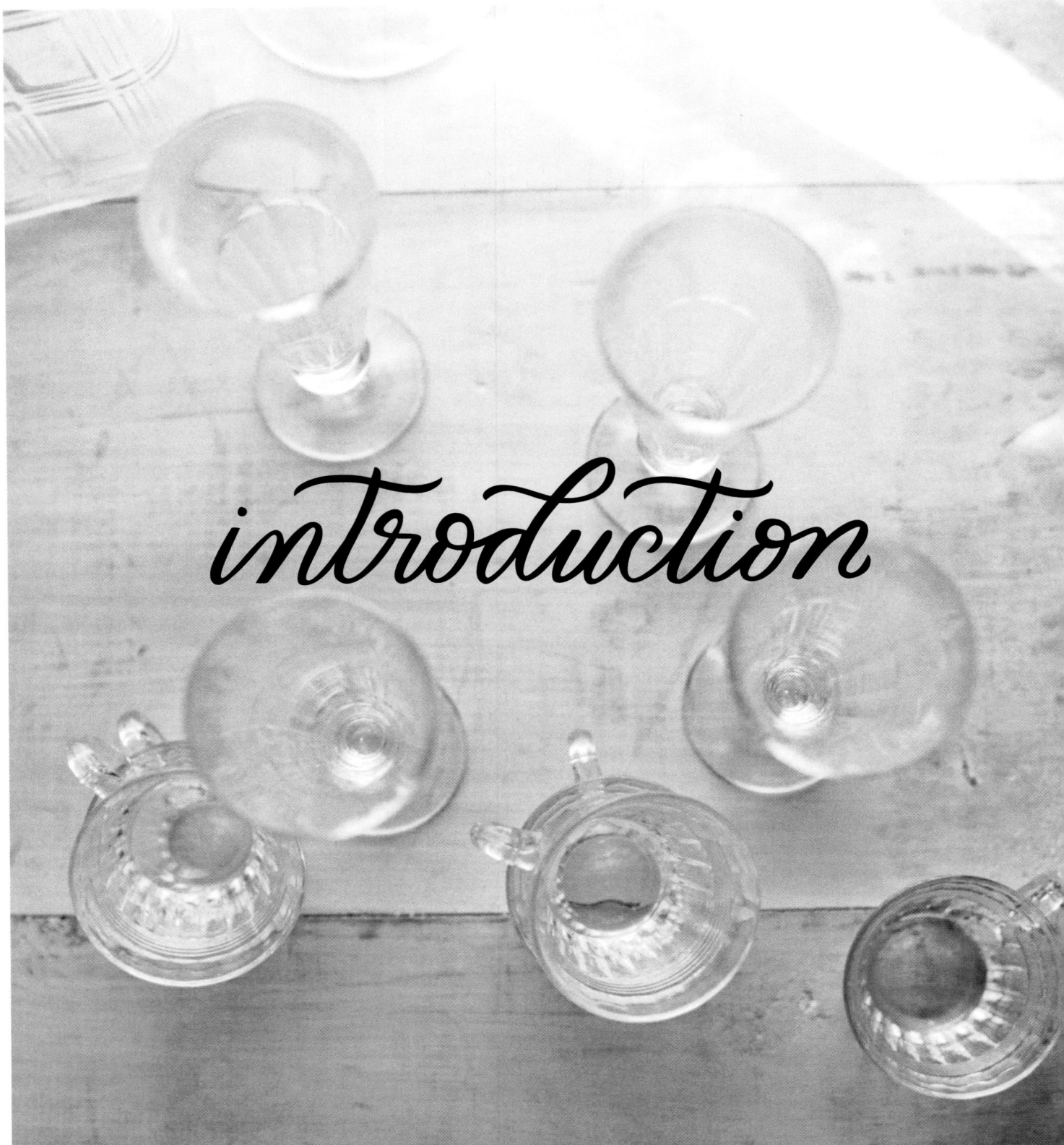

introduction

food is a gift

My mother is naturally gifted. She can scout out a fresh batch of candied orange rinds anywhere in my home. She can start a party in the drollest of rooms with a wink or a nod. She remembers every single birthday and prompts me to send thank-you notes. And she is the consummate gifter.

An exotically beautiful woman from Central America, my mother fell for an American boy and was determined to be the exemplary American housewife. She was a mother to her two daughters but also a caretaker to her brother's three children for many years. She was quite happy focused on domestic life and found joy in figuring out how to perfect the minute steak and string bean plate every housewife of that era had to master, crossing it off some implicit checklist.

Ever my biggest fan, my mother urged me to do well in school; to begin working as soon as I could (at age 14); to go to a good college, get a good job, and make a good living (whatever "good" meant); to wait as long as possible before walking down a wedding aisle; and to, eventually, do everything she never could.

While still working a technology career, I began to build a professional life in food, and during my figuring-things-out phase, I realized her influence from random significant moments in my childhood.

I remembered that my mom became a honeybee on the weekends, attracting everyone to our cozy house. When she convened with her extended family, she was a star, instructing the creation of Latin dishes, generating on-the-fly dance parties to old melodies from the record player, and teaching all of us kids to keep the good times going by chanting in unison *no te vayas* (don't leave) when someone was ready to skip out early on her party. I never understood, until recently, how much I envied her talents.

My mother was also driven to charity and ran food drives with our local church, collecting extra canned goods wherever, whenever. She maintained a list of folks in the community who needed the extra food and personally delivered it. With boxes packed to the brim and one of her daughters reluctantly in tow, my mother would visit each recipient. Really, visit.

Her visits were often long and drawn out: she'd enter their homes, sit down at the kitchen table, and take a cup of tea. As a little kid, I was restless and felt like we were imposing by taking anything from someone with so little. But my mother knew this exchange of hospitality was the most sensitive way to offer what she could: extra food and an empathetic ear.

My mother was marvelous in these moments. She delivered a gift of food and, in the same instant, delivered a world of love, compassion, and old-fashioned hospitality. I am nowhere near the person she is, but I keep trying with every gift I package.

The recipes in this cookbook developed through my building a business but also through unknowingly trying to be exactly like my mother. They're assembled in chapters from easiest—recipes that you can pull together on the way to a gathering or made fresh and gifted in moments—to most ambitious—recipes that require a bit more patience but yield great reward (yes, I mean the spirits). And while you should give whatever you want at any time of year—because food is almost never an inappropriate gift—I've also suggested uses and gifting occasions within many of the recipes.

As you work your way through the chapters, you'll discover how natural it is to craft food gifts to store in your *Food Gift Love* pantry for whenever the need may arise or to offer for specific occasions to your loved ones or to the neighbor down the street who just popped in to share tomatoes from her yard. In fact, gifting food with food is like a double rainbow—transformative and remarkable and entirely too rare today. Let's go change that.

about eat boutique

While the gifting of boutique food eventually became a habit for me, my business Eat Boutique did not happen overnight. In fact, it came to life over many years of writing and living in all sorts of food places.

Born as a blog in 2007, Eat Boutique became my path toward a life in food. A couple years in, I crafted my first gift box of small-batch food from mom-and-pop-style makers across New England and sold out of it instantly that holiday season. The moment Eat Boutique was featured in the *Wall Street Journal* in 2011, I started shipping food gifts year-round. I also began hosting pop-up retail markets, gathering makers and their food fans in a single space for shopping, sampling, and a bit of cheer. In 2013, Eat Boutique won the International Association of Culinary Professionals award for Best Culinary Brand; it was a significant moment because there I was, reveling in it all, standing with Alice Waters. When anyone asks at what point it felt like a real business, I joke that it was probably the moment I cried in front of Alice Waters. But it was likely years earlier when I had put Eat Boutique on hold to travel regularly to Paris for work.

"Boutique" is originally a French word used when referring to a small shop. I didn't fully understand its meaning until I lived in the city of light and enjoyed legendarily good food on-and-off for months at a time, exploring the delicious nooks and cobblestone crannies of Paris. Coming from the country of big-brand retailers who use the term "boutique" so liberally, I found Paris to be charming and focused on small and special in a way that was new to me.

Every other day, I picked up a baguette two blocks from my apartment. I got to know the man who kneaded the dough and timed the baking in such a way that yeasty aromas drifted down the avenues as the workday ended. I also learned to savor one super-soft passion-fruit caramel a few times each week, rather than gorge on a bag of manufactured candy at one sitting as some of us are wont to do.

During all those Paris visits, I sampled at least twenty different types of croissants, from the average Monoprix version to the richly layered croissants of each neighborhood mom-and-pop-style bakery. I ate artisan French jam right off a spoon on a fairly regular basis, not able to wait mere moments to get it onto the toasted baguette. I enjoyed so many culinary pleasures, filing them away in my brain for my future sourcing.

When I returned to the States, I saw food through a hypercritical lens, seeking out superior fare and talking to food makers and shop owners to understand the vision and techniques behind what I was putting into my mouth. If I was spending more to buy craft-intensive food as I had in Paris, I wanted to know the person stirring the big pot of fruit and sugar, or even tapping forests of maple trees for my weekend pancakes.

I also wanted to taste before I brought anything home. I sampled so many maple syrups until I found the version that resonated with my palate, my wallet, and my heart. I tasted spoonfuls and spoonfuls of marmalades and jellies before I found my favorite textures and flavors. On many occasions, I would attempt to recreate the preserves to verify the ingredients or test certain techniques—and this detail-oriented process has felt like an unofficial PhD program in tasting. Eat Boutique has grown into a food-gift blog and business that introduces people to the food products I discover and helps them make food gifts on their own.

I also learned some valuable fundamentals about cooking, like real caramel is soft not hard. Sweet dishes that are also bitter or tart make the sweet part all the better. High-proof spirits will preserve the essence of almost anything, and almost anything can be dipped (and gifted) in chocolate if it's tempered. And just like time improves relationships and wine, it also improves flavors.

Through it all, I've come to treasure the boutique life. I cook and share meals made on a small-batch, handcrafted scale in my neighborhood and in far-flung destinations—and that's how I choose to experience the world. I believe a great meal is worth driving an extra mile (or thousands) for, especially if the host pops out to say hello or the cook shares a creative recipe. Boutique makers who cook in small batches produce foods that are fresh, unique, and special. Eat Boutique has grown into a business that is my expression of love for the gift of pure food and the people who dedicate their lives to making it.

I've helped thousands of regular folks send *Food Gift Love* all over the country and the world through Eat Boutique. I've also been lucky enough to meet thousands of food makers, and as they share their craft and vision, they encourage me to want to eat better and cook well. The spirit of a maker is within you, too, so you know all those things you've wanted to make? You should go make them.

about this cookbook

WHAT IS *FOOD GIFT LOVE*?

Over the last eight years of building Eat Boutique and working closely with a community of food makers, chefs, home cooks, and restaurateurs, my mind was consistently blown by their gifts to me: they'd offer advice, favorite recipes, a visit to the kitchen to watch a specific technique for rolling pasta, a glass of something strong from their personal bar, or the simplest of food gifts like a bowl of homemade butter or a vial of their favorite spice blend. The food gifts were effortless and natural, less about perfection and more about sharing a little bit of themselves. In those moments, they supplied good old-fashioned hospitality, educated me, and fostered my love for gifting food.

Traditionally, we know food gifts as a batch of cookies or a jar of marmalade—and there's nothing wrong with that—but as my community has shown, there are so many other ways to give gifts of food. *Food Gift Love* challenges that classic notion with a variety of foods that nourish, delight, help, and inspire.

This collection of more than 100 recipes tested by more than 80 recipe testers spans all types of food, from something you might give in the moment, like a fresh batch of lemon-flecked Ricotta Cheese (page 73) or a warm loaf of Roasted Banana Bread (page 148), to a delicious sweet treat like little cups of Panna Cotta (page 78) and Quick Strawberry Jam (page 185), all the way to gifts you may make a few weeks in advance in time for a holiday, like Vin d'Orange (orange-infused wine, page 224) or a tart Rhubarb Cordial (page 231)—all of them easy to wrap with ribbon and present with a short note.

Food Gift Love is about cooking, wrapping, and gifting pure simple food. It's about the kindness, support, and love that goes into sourcing wonderful ingredients, then crafting them into something delicious, and offering it to a neighbor, family member, colleague, or friend. And, filled with my tips and advice, this cookbook supplies the skills and encouragement to make food-gifting part of your lifestyle.

THE RECIPES

The recipes included in *Food Gift Love* are personal reflections of my experience as a food-gift business owner combined with my personal food-gifting style. They range from simple and classic in nature, like a basic way to make butter and some flavor variations, to very specific and creative in nature, such as kumquats soaked in honey. I've included many traditional recipes with simplified steps and amped up flavor as well as recipes discovered during my travels and honed over many years of gifting.

Recipe Testing

Food Gift Love came to life in no small part due to the amazing team of 80 recipe testers from across America, Canada, Italy, Germany, the Netherlands, and the United Kingdom. They were chosen from more than 200 applicants to represent a diverse range of skill, from cooking newbies to home cooks who make fresh food daily, to professional food makers and chefs who consistently cook for large groups. I wanted to be mindful of all the unique setups that exist from kitchen to kitchen—the difference in ovens, equipment, available ingredients, and climate—and how they may affect your personal success. My testing team shared rigorous notes to support my recipe development, and I hope you'll enjoy the results in these detailed recipes and your final dishes.

food gift love pantry

A *Food Gift Love* pantry is meant to be a modern kitchen larder, filled with the basic ingredients to make food gifts; any special equipment required; gift-wrap materials such as containers, boxes, ribbon, and tape; and the food gifts themselves, ever-ready for presentation on a moment's notice. Let's discuss all of these essentials in greater depth.

KITCHEN BASICS

Ingredients

These are the basic ingredients to keep on hand in order to create food gifts on the fly:

Baking powder

Baking soda

Butter, unsalted

Carrots

Celery

Chocolate, milk, bittersweet, semisweet, and dark

Cocoa powder

Coffee beans

Cornstarch

Dried fruit

Eggs, large

Extracts

Flour, all-purpose

Garlic

Herbs, dried and fresh

Honey

Lemons

Maple syrup

Olive oil, extra-virgin

Onions, white, red

Nuts, unsalted, raw, and ground

Rolled oats

Sea salt, fine, coarse, and flaky

Seeds

Spices, ground and whole

Sugar, granulated, confectioners', dark brown, and light brown

Vanilla beans

Vinegar, apple cider, balsamic, distilled white, and white wine

Yeast, active dry

Yogurt, Greek-style and full-fat

Equipment

To create these food gifts, you'll use some of the standard equipment already in your kitchen and also some specialized equipment. I believe you have the basic equipment available in your kitchen today, and I have not called them out in the recipes. The special equipment is helpful for specific recipes. Before starting a recipe, look to the Special Equipment section (if any) to make sure you have what you need on hand.

BASIC EQUIPMENT

Aluminum foil

Baking dishes, all sizes

Baking sheets, all sizes

Blender, standard

Bowls, all sizes

Cooling racks

Cutting boards

Food processor

Forks and spoons

Grater

Kitchen scissors

Kitchen timer

Kitchen towels

Measuring cups and spoons

Parchment paper

Pie plate

Pizza cutter

Plastic storage bags

Plastic wrap

Plates, all sizes

Rubber spatulas

Sharp knives

Silicone pan liners

Slotted spoons

Strainers and sieves

Tongs

Vegetable peeler

Wax paper

Whisks

Wooden spoons

SPECIAL EQUIPMENT

Bottles, all sizes with airtight lids

Bread pans

Cheesecloth

Cherry pitter

Coffee filters

Double boiler

Funnels, narrow-mouth (for narrow-neck bottles) and wide-mouth (for jars with wide openings)

Glassine bags

Grinder, for coffee beans and spices

Hammer

Immersion blender

Jars, all sizes with airtight lids

Juicer, handheld or automatic

Kitchen scale

Madeleine pan, standard (holds 12 cakes)

Microplane zester

Mortar and pestle

Oyster knife

Pastry brush

Pinking shears

Resealable, food-grade cellophane (cello) bags

Ruler

Squeeze bottles

Stand mixer

Thermometers, candy, chocolate

GIFT-WRAP BASICS

How It Started

The gift-wrap parts of a *Food Gift Love* pantry are always a work in progress and include all of the tools that help you contain, wrap, tie, mark, decorate, adorn, and transport your food gifts. The collecting may start with everyday activities, like a stop at the local grocery store that results in extra rubber bands or a butcher shop visit that leaves you with piles of extra string. For me, it began with the *New York Times*.

In the days when everyone used to get the daily newspaper tossed at their front door, I would devour the freshly delivered food section of Wednesday's *New York Times* and save every copy. My mother, ever ready to support any new-fangled ambition, would scope random coffee shops for my favorite food section. She'd hand them off to me, no questions asked, as if a secret currency between us. And when the pile finally got too large to handle, I started wrapping every sort of gift with food-filled newsprint.

From there, it grew. Paper needed tape to stick it in place. A simple knot of twine held it all together, and a swipe of a pencil addressed my recipient. Paper, pencil, tape, and twine: that's all it takes.

These four gift-wrap essentials—paper, pencil, tape, and twine—are probably hidden in different parts of your home today, just waiting to be placed in the same drawer or closet. They can be as simple or as extravagant as your means allow and, in my case, they really were quite simple at the start.

PAPER: Grab a sheet to wrap everything from a warm baguette to a tray of something delicious. It can be craft paper or white butcher paper, newsprint or parchment paper, waxy or chalkboard-style paper. I started with newsprint but now keep a bit of everything on hand.

PENCIL: I prefer writing with pencils—food gifting is an old-fashioned, enduring art, and I love how pencil swipes honor the past—but I use the term universally here to include all variety of pencils, pens, and markers. Eventually, I added in label makers, glitter pens, homemade stamps, and highlighters, but you don't really have to. Anything that helps you scribble a personal freehand note will do just fine.

TAPE: Plain creamy masking tape has dual purposes: it sticks paper together (*voila!*) and becomes an instant label. I found a few rolls of craft-colored masking tape at my local dollar store years ago, and it does the trick. All those new colorful washi tapes are extra lovely but are a bit costly, so I use them sparingly for special occasions.

TWINE: Everyday garden twine makes a pretty nice bow and white kitchen string is a perfect stand-in when spun around a jar or package a few extra times. Bakery twine can be colorful and festive, and such a nice way to fasten a label to a jar. I use the term twine to cover all forms, including string and ribbon.

My closet quickly expanded beyond the basics. Eventually, I moved beyond the printed word to tissue paper and printing labels, hangtags and yarn, stickers and leftover gift boxes, tape and twine, rubber bands and clothespins, jars, bottles, ribbons, hand-me-down fabric, markers, and I'd even stashed away the crinkly paper used to protect items shipped to me from online shops. A few shelves became a full closet, and without any sort of tactical agenda, no planning or forethought, only a rising passion for all things food, I had built my own *Food Gift Love* pantry—a space that now includes both preserved food and everything needed to make that food beautifully giftable because, if you keep it all together, you'll wrap and gift often.

Gift-Wrap Supplies

Today, my *Food Gift Love* pantry consists of the four food gift-wrapping essentials—paper, pencil, tape, and twine—and, by extension, most of the following:

PAPER (items to hold and wrap gifts)

Butcher and craft papers in brown, white, and black

Various newspapers and magazines

Parchment, wax paper, and cheesecloth

Strips of leftover paper

Tissue paper and gift wrap

Muffin and bread wrappers

Fabric scraps, napkins, and kitchen towels

Glassine bags, lunch bags, and food-grade cellophane bags

Boxes, spice tins, tea tins, and old mugs

Jars, bottles, jugs, and medicine bottles

Baskets, trays, old drawers, and wooden boxes

PENCILS (items to write labels and notes for gifts)

Classic pencils, colored pencils, and crayons

Glitter pens, fine-tip pens, and markers

Markers for glass

Water color brushes and paints

TAPE (items to seal and label gifts)

Masking tape in various colors

Washi tape

Mailing labels and label makers

Hang tags and stickers

Glue and glue sticks

TWINE (items to secure and decorate gifts)

Kitchen string and garden twine

Rubber bands and thin wire

Beads and garland of all sorts

Everyday, fancy, and vintage ribbon

Old postcards and travel images

Family photos and Polaroids

Wine corks and clothespins

Bits of nature: twigs, leaves, branches, and dried flowers/fruit

You may have one cardboard box, one drawer, or a few shelves in a closet available for your gift-wrap supplies, but when you have everything in one place, you'll actually consider using them. After putting it all together and trying some of the gift wrap in this cookbook, you'll be so impressed with your own creative talents that you'll want to keep every decorated food gift for yourself (but of course, you won't).

Gift-Wrap Styles

Every container or vessel—whether bag or jar—can become gift-worthy with very low effort and basic supplies. Here are three easy approaches to take your gift from simple to sweet or all the way to sophisticated.

	SIMPLE	SWEET	SOPHISTICATED
Description	Seal and label with tape.	Embellish with twine.	Add fun with a fancy technique or polish with decorative paper.
Alternatives	Gift tags, label embossers, and a simple marker can stand in for tape.	Ribbon or string can stand in for basic twine.	Fabric or kitchen linens can stand in for paper.
VESSELS			
Bag	Label (with date) on tape and stick on bag.	Wrap twine around top of labeled bag and tie in knot or bow.	Fold top of labeled bag over, punch hole and thread twine through hole; tie in a knot or bow.
Bottle	Label (with date) on tape and stick on bottle.	Wrap twine around neck of labeled bottle and tie in knot or bow.	Wrap labeled bottle in pretty paper either by: (a) placing bottle in center of paper and gathering sides up toward neck before tying twine around neck or (b) placing bottle on its side and rolling paper around it before tying twine around neck and taping bottom.
Box	Label (with date) on tape and stick on box.	Wrap twine around labeled box several times and tie in knot or bow.	Wrap labeled box in decorative paper before wrapping twine around box several times and tying in knot or bow.
Bowl or Dish	Seal bowl with plastic wrap or slip of paper and a rubber band; label (with date) on tape and stick on bowl.	Wrap twine around sealed, labeled bowl several times and tie in knot or bow.	Wrap sealed, labeled bowl in decorative paper before wrapping twine around bowl several times and tying in knot or bow.
Jar	(a) Label (with date) on tape and stick on jar, or (b) slide a rubber band around jar and slip paper label (with date) between rubber band and jar.	Wrap twine around labeled jar and tie in knot or bow.	Wrap labeled jar in decorative paper by placing jar on its side and rolling paper around it and taping top and bottom in place and then wrap twine around wrapped jar several times and tie in knot or bow.

Gift Labels

Labels for food gifts can be simple if the use is obvious like a tart or cookies—for example, you just eat those as is. But for food gifts that offer multiple uses or might be something new and different for your recipient, such as Infused Sea Salts, Simple Syrups, Ricotta Cheese, or Coffee Rub, be sure to add a brief note sharing what the gift is and how it might be used. For example, for Ricotta Cheese, I may add a note that says, "Spread on toast as is, mix with fresh fruit, or fold into homemade Tiramisu." If needed, add any notes on perishability such as how long it will keep and the best place to store it, like at room temperature or in the fridge.

How to Choose the Perfect Gift

How do I know what food gift to give? I like to share more universally loved and classic flavors with folks I don't know too well, reserving the more distinct and strong flavor combinations for those with whom I'm more familiar or who I know will most certainly appreciate them. Follow the easy flowchart on the next page for my suggestions.

DO I KNOW THE RECIPIENT?

no

IS IT A HAPPY OR SAD OCCASION?

HAPPY!

WHAT FLAVOR DO YOU WANT TO SHARE?

Boozy

SPIRITED: Strawberry Cordial (p.232)
or
Sparkling Elderflower Punch (p. 222)

Fruity

PRESERVED: Orange-Cinnamon Marmalade
(p. 194)

Salty

PANTRY: Infused Sea Salts (pgs. 90–93)

Savory

FRESH: Lemony Bean Dip (p. 42)
BAKED: Tomato Tart (p. 168)

Spicy

PANTRY: Brown Sugar Rub (p. 99)
CANDIED: Smoky Candied Popcorn (p. 120)

Sweet

CANDIED: Graham Cracker Toffee (p. 135)
or
Chocolate Truffles (p. 130)
BAKED: Apple Galette (p. 158)

Tart

PANTRY: Raspberry Vinegar (p. 111)
BAKED: Spring Pie (p. 163)

SAD

WHAT FLAVOR DO YOU WANT TO SHARE?

Boozy

SPIRITED: Irish Cream (p. 240)

Fruity

BAKED: Roasted Banana Bread (p. 148)

Salty

BAKED: Pizza Rolls (p. 172)

Savory

FRESH: Smoky Chicken Soup (p. 62)

Spicy

FRESH: Salt & Pepper Pita Chips (p. 45)
PANTRY: Mint Tea (p. 87)
and
Thyme Honey (p. 89)
SPIRITED: Ginger Simple Syrup (p. 214)

Sweet

CANDIED: Chocolate Hazelnut Spread (p. 136)
BAKED: Molasses Cookies (p. 155)

Tart

PRESERVED: Rhubarb Vanilla Jam (p. 188)

DO I KNOW THE RECIPIENT?

yes

IS IT A HAPPY OR SAD OCCASION?

HAPPY!

WHAT DO THEY LOVE?

Boozy
FRESH: Amaretto Tiramisu (p. 76)
SPIRITED: Margarita Mix (p. 236)

Fruity
CANDIED: Candied Blood Orange Rinds (p. 142)
PRESERVED: Quick Strawberry Jam (p. 185)

Salty
FRESH: Mixed Cocktail Nuts (p. 46)
PRESERVED: Preserved Lemons (p. 178)

Savory
FRESH: Arugula & Pistachio Pesto (p. 50)
BAKED: Savory Cheese-Plate Quick Bread (p. 171)

Spicy
PRESERVED: Candied Jalapeños (p. 206)

Sweet
PANTRY: Citrus Sugars (p. 94)
CANDIED: Chocolate-Dipped Everything (p. 126)
BAKED: Sweet & Salty Pantry Cookies (p. 152)

Tart
PANTRY: Balsamic Blackberry Glaze (p. 112)
PRESERVED: Sweet & Sour Cranberries (p. 181)

SAD

WHAT DO THEY LOVE (OR NEED)?

Boozy
SPIRITED: Limoncello (p. 227)

Fruity
FRESH: Meyer Lemon Curd (p. 70)
SPIRITED: Cider-Chai Syrup (p. 217)

Salty
FRESH: Salty Maple Butter (p. 66)

Savory
FRESH: Mozzarella, Basil & Quick Tomato Jam (p. 58)
BAKED: Homemade Granola, Your Way (p. 147)

Spicy
FRESH: Pico de Gallo (p. 41)
PANTRY: Cinnamon Sugar (p. 96)

Sweet
CANDIED: Salty Dark Caramel Sauce (p. 139)
BAKED: Brown Butter Madeleines (p. 151)
PRESERVED: Fig-Rosemary Jam (p. 192)
or
Pear-Pineapple-Ginger Jam (p. 190)

Tart
SPIRITED: Lemon-Rosemary Simple Syrup (p. 214)

how to ship food gifts

PERISHABLE ITEMS

Many of the food gifts in this cookbook are considered perishable, whether within a few days or a few weeks; prior to shipping, factor in how long your food gifts will last and mail them accordingly. Here are tips for shipping your food gifts safely.

LIGHTER ITEMS

Lighter items—like bags filled with spices or boxes filled with popcorn—need a little padding when shipped via mail. It's important to fill up the space in the box to hold the item in place and prevent jostling, which may damage your gift. Wrap lighter items with a single piece of bubble wrap before placing them in a larger box that's been lined with cushioned material like shredded newspaper or grocery store bags. Gently shake your box to see whether your gift is secure; add more padding if you feel things moving around. Tape your box closed with 2-inch-wide tape. Mark the outside of the box: "Fragile."

HEAVIER ITEMS

Heavier items—like sealed plastic containers filled with cookies or large boxes filled with granola—are best shipped via mail with two layers of padding. Wrap heavier items with several pieces of bubble wrap before placing them in a larger box that's been lined with several inches of cushioned material like shredded newspaper or grocery store bags. Gently shake your box to see whether your gift is secure; add more padding if you feel things moving around. Tape your box closed with 2-inch-wide tape. Mark the outside of the shipping container: "Fragile."

GLASS AND LIQUID ITEMS

Glass and liquid items—like jars of marmalade or bottles of syrup—should be sealed tightly. If you're shipping a glass jar or liquid-filled bottle that's not canned (preserved), add an extra layer of tape around the entire seal of the lid to hold it in place. Place the jar or bottle in a sealed plastic bag. Wrap these items with several pieces of bubble wrap before placing them in a larger box that's been lined with cushioned material like several inches of shredded newspaper or grocery store bags. Position the items so that they're upright, as you would place them on a table, and make sure there is ample padding between items. Gently shake your box to see whether your gifts are secure; add more padding if you feel things moving around. Don't forget to add extra padding material on top of the items before closing. Tape your box closed with 2-inch-wide tape. Mark the outside of the box: "Fragile" and "This side up," to indicate that the box should be handled with care.

Note: There are restrictions for shipping alcoholic beverages by United States Mail; check regulations before considering sending this kind of gift.

HEAT-SENSITIVE ITEMS

Some of the food gifts in this cookbook—like the chocolate gifts or dairy-intensive gifts—are heat-sensitive. Do not ship chocolate gifts during warm seasons or through warm climates without taking extra steps for preservation during shipping. For example, I do not ship chocolate gifts from May to October without adding ice packs to the containers, and I send by expedited (typically overnight) shipping. In addition, I always consider the climate through which my chocolate gift will travel. It may be cold in Boston and San Francisco but your gift will travel through the middle of the country, which may be in the middle of a heat wave. Also avoid shipping dairy-based food gifts like curd, cheese, and butter unless you can guarantee a perfectly chilled climate within the box for the entire shipping process.

10 tips to make you the quintessential food gifter

1. **KNOW YOUR RECIPIENT:** If you don't know your recipient's favorite foods and flavors, just ask—she or he will be flattered you did! The answer will help you choose the perfect recipe to impress and delight.

2. **MASTER A SIGNATURE FOOD GIFT:** You have an arsenal of more than 100 recipes within this cookbook. Make gifting easy by learning and mastering one of them. Memorize the recipe or make it in large batches, so you can give this personal gift year-round.

3. **EMBRACE IMPERFECTION:** Don't make it perfect, just make it. Food gifts that look homemade will tug at someone's heartstrings in a great way. Learn to love crooked bows (or tie knots), your own handwriting, and crinkled newspaper as gift wrap.

4. **PUT A LABEL ON IT:** Be sure to label food gifts that go into your pantry with the name and the date prepared (and, if you like, a date by which to gift it). You'll know exactly how long you have to share them.

5. **CHRISTMAS IS IN JULY:** If you can, make food gifts when the harvest is unstoppable during the summer. This requires a little planning, but it's especially great for infusing spirits and extracts and making preserves in time for the winter holidays.

6. **STORE THE GIFT AND WRAP TOGETHER:** Place your paper, pencil, tape, and twine in the same room as your *Food Gift Love* pantry. Just make space in a drawer or on a small shelf. If it's all side-by-side, you're more likely to make and wrap a food gift.

7. **RE-GIFTING GIFT WRAP IS A-OK:** Save old but clean gift wrap and reuse it for new gifts. Making use of old ribbon and paper multiplies your gift decor options and lengthens their lives before being recycled.

8. **YOUR TRASH IS A TREASURE:** Before tossing old jars, cups, drawers, or boxes, inspect them to see if they're gift-worthy. Clean and add them to your décor collection.

9. **SHOP YOUR PANTRY:** With a stocked food gift pantry, there's no need to hit up a shop for a gift. Review your pantry regularly to use up soon-to-expire foods in your daily meals and to gift things way in advance of expiration.

10. **HOST FOOD-GIFT-MAKING PARTIES:** Turn a holiday get-together into a marmalade-making session or chocolate-dipping feast. Attendees can contribute food and gift-wrap supplies. Share the expense, the work, and the bounty.

potluck gifts

When you prepare food for potlucks and get-togethers, you're gifting food. In fact, potlucks are my favorite form of *Food Gift Love* because everyone is sharing a bit of themselves with each other, hopefully along with some very good wine.

POTLUCK GIFT RECIPE LIST

Recipes perfectly suited to potlucks—either because they're made for a meal or are sized up for larger portions—can be found throughout this cookbook and, for quick access, they are all listed below, too.

Amaretto Tiramisu (page 76)

Cheesy Mushrooms (page 60)

Chocolate-Coconut Popcorn (page 119)

Cold-Brew Coffee (page 239)

Cucumber-Lime Pitcher (page 211)

Graham Cracker Toffee (page 135)

Grainy Mustard Dressing (page 55)

Irish Cream (page 240)

Jam-Swirled Marshmallows (page 140)

Kitchen-Sink Salad (page 56)

Lemony Bean Dip (page 42)

Margarita Mix (page 236)

Molasses Cookies (page 155)

Mozzarella, Basil & Quick Tomato Jam (page 58)

Nectarine-Almond Crisp (page 156)

Panna Cotta Cups (page 78) with Quick Strawberry Jam (page 185)

Peanut Butter Balls (page 132)

Petite Pavlovas (page 166)

Pico de Gallo (page 41)

Pizza Rolls (page 172)

Roasted Banana Bread (page 148)

Rompopo (page 243)

Salt & Pepper Pita Chips (page 45)

Smoky Candied Popcorn (page 120)

Smoky Chicken Soup (page 62)

Savory Cheese-Plate Quick Bread (page 171)

Sparkling Elderflower Punch (page 222)

Spring Mignonette (page 49)

Spring Pie (page 163)

Tomato Tart (page 168)

Vin d'Orange (page 224)

POTLUCK GO-TO DISHES

The following three bonus recipes are stylish, easy, and have pleased crowds for years.

Traveling Cheese Tray · Camembert & Calvados · French-Style Baguette Sandwiches

TRAVELING CHEESE TRAY

MAKES 10 TO 16 SERVINGS, AS AN APPETIZER
(2 TO 3 OUNCES PER PERSON)
PREPARATION TIME: 30 MINUTES

When I need a simple crowd pleaser for a potluck or get-together and I'm on the go, a Traveling Cheese Tray is the only thing that will do. Everything can be picked up on the way or some of the add-ons can be pulled from my *Food Gift Love* pantry as I run out the door to the market for the cheese and then on to the potluck. Be sure to pull a pretty paper bag, some newspaper, parchment paper, masking tape, and a pen from your stash to carry all of your goodies, and then assemble when you arrive.

To create the perfect Traveling Cheese Tray, pick one cheese from each of the following:

Fresh cheeses are ready-to-eat creamy cheeses that haven't been aged. They are typically fresh-tasting, mild, and milky like goat cheese (nonaged), mozzarella, or ricotta cheese.

Soft cheeses have white rinds and are typically creamy inside. They get creamier as they age and include Brie, feta, Camembert, and vacherin (a favorite).

Hard cheeses are firm, sharp, and aged. When you think hard cheese, think of Parmesan, Piave, Cheddar, and certain Goudas.

Blue cheeses are just that, creamy with streams of blue moldy veins. My favorite blues are from France (Roquefort), Italy (Gorgonzola), England (Stilton), and Ireland (Cashel Blue).

To add ideal accompaniments to your Traveling Cheese Tray, pick something from each of the following categories:

Sweet: All things salty and creamy can benefit and even taste better when saddled next to something sweet. Consider a range of sweets like honey, marmalade or jam, fresh fruit, or even chocolate.

Tart: A little something tart helps to balance the creaminess of all this rich cheese. I like to pick at least one tart item such as cornichons, pickled vegetables of any kind, marinated red bell peppers, or even caper berries.

Nutty: While nutty items may seem obvious, don't rule out the unexpected. This certainly includes all sorts of traditional shelled nuts like walnuts, almonds, and pecans, but I also think of pistachios, pine nuts, corn nuts, or edible seeds. The last two aren't really nuts, but they taste nutty.

INGREDIENTS:

- ½ pound fresh cheese (nonaged goat cheese, mozzarella, feta, or ricotta cheese)
- ½ pound soft cheese (Brie, Camembert, or vacherin)
- ½ pound hard cheese (Parmesan, Piave, Cheddar, or certain Goudas)
- ½ pound blue cheese (Roquefort, Gorgonzola, Stilton, or Cashel Blue)
- ¼ cup something sweet (honey, marmalade or jam, fresh fruit, or chocolate)
- ½ cup something tart (cornichons, pickled vegetables of any kind, marinated red bell peppers, or even caper berries)
- ½ cup something nutty (walnuts, almonds, pecans, pistachios, pine nuts, corn nuts, or edible seeds)
- 1 large fresh baguette

SPECIAL EQUIPMENT:

- 1 paper bag
- 1 piece newspaper, rolled or folded
- Parchment paper
- Small knives and spoons
- Sharp knife, for slicing baguette

1. Once you have all of your food ingredients, pile them into your large paper bag (you'll need it later) with your styling materials, and take, as is, to your potluck. The cheeses are best at room temperature, so only include ice packs if you don't plan to eat the cheese within a few hours or if it's a very hot day.

2. Upon arrival at the potluck, find a spot to set up your Traveling Cheese Tray. Tear your paper bag open along the edges so it will lay flat; place it on your surface. Unroll and place your newspaper on top of the bag, leaving some

of the paper bag exposed. You may need to fold some of the newspaper to make this work. Repeat this step with the parchment paper.

3. Unwrap all the cheeses and place them on the parchment paper, leaving a bit of room for the remaining ingredients. Write the names onto pieces of masking tape and affix the tape next to each cheese.

4. Open and place your sweet, tart, and nutty accompaniments on the parchment paper, in between each of the cheeses. Ask your host for some small knives to put next to each cheese—each cheese should have its own knife. Ask for a few spoons for the accompaniments. Place the spoons on the parchment or in the ingredients.

5. With a sharp knife provided by your host, slice the baguette into thin slices and scatter all around the tray. Serve immediately.

CAMEMBERT & CALVADOS

MAKES: 3 TO 4 SERVINGS, AS AN APPETIZER
PREPARATION TIME: 30 MINUTES

I learned about this gift from my dearest French friend, Lise. It's a traditional and spectacular combination of two great Normandy exports: Camembert cheese and Calvados (apple brandy). It is wonderful to gift to dinner parties because it basically makes itself: just a few minutes in the oven at your host's home, a splash of sweet liquor, and piles of bread make everyone happy.

As an alternative to Calvados, try a pear brandy or even a fruity white wine. I like to dredge baguette slices and endive leaves through the molten cheese, but any food dipper will do—consider celery, carrots, red bell peppers, or even raw zucchini sticks. Just make sure to use parchment paper and not wax paper; the wax will melt into the dish and make it inedible.

INGREDIENTS:

1 Camembert cheese in a round wood box

2 Belgian endive bunches

1 baguette, cut into 1-inch pieces

2 tablespoons Calvados (apple brandy)

1. Preheat the oven to 400°F. Remove the Camembert from the little round wood box it comes packaged in; retain the wood base but discard the lid. Slip in a square or round piece of parchment paper (not wax paper) cut to twice the size of the wood box. Place the Camembert on the parchment in the wood base. With a sharp knife, make 5 to 6 slits just in the top of the Camembert.

2. Place the wood box on a baking sheet in the oven. Bake about 12 minutes or until soft and gooey. (If you're not sure, insert a spoon into the cheese to check.)

3. Prepare the endive by rinsing well, trimming, and separating the leaves. Place the endive and baguette slices on a serving platter.

4. Remove the cheese from the oven and place it, still in its box, on your serving platter. Moments before serving, pour the Calvados onto the hot cheese. Slice just a few more slits into the top of the cheese to combine the booze. Enjoy by dipping bread slices and endive into the cheese.

GIFT WRAP

Brown paper bag

Twine

Parchment paper

Cheesecloth

Place the brandy in a brown paper bag. Shape the bag against the bottle, twisting the bag opening around the neck of the bottle. Tie the neck with a piece of twine. Fold a piece of parchment paper to half the width of a baguette. Roll the baguette in the paper. Tie around the center with a piece of twine. Cut a piece of cheesecloth to 3 times the width of the cheese. Place the cheese in the center and pull up all the sides of the cheesecloth. Twist the ends and tie with a piece of twine. Refrigerate the cheese until ready to gift. Gift as is or in a bag with recipe instructions.

FRENCH-STYLE BAGUETTE SANDWICHES

MAKES: 4 SERVINGS, AS AN APPETIZER
PREPARATION TIME: 15 MINUTES

When I lived in Paris, I would eat this sandwich once or twice per week. They're piled high in bakeries each morning, ready for the lunch crowd to make them disappear by midday. They're reliably good, almost everywhere I tried in Paris. And it will be so good for you, too; however, this recipe depends on the ingredients. Splurge on high-quality, salted, cultured butter that is richer and higher in fat. Splurge on an artisanally made salami. And, please, splurge on a real French-style baguette; bland grocery store loaves just won't do. Find a baguette with a crunchy exterior and a soft chewy center. If cornichons aren't your thing, any sour pickle will do well. You can also try Minty Pickles (page 186), which add a sweeter taste to the final sandwich.

For potlucks or parties, I serve several of these sandwiches sliced up into 2-inch pieces. You can decorate by skewering each piece with a toothpick and a pickled onion or an extra cornichon.

INGREDIENTS:

1 (8-inch) French-style baguette (about 2 inches wide)

2 tablespoons salted European-style (cultured) butter, softened

8 to 10 cornichons (small pickled gherkins), sliced in half lengthwise

5 to 6 thin slices artisan salami or ham

Pinch of fine sea salt

GIFT WRAP

Cloth napkins

Twine

Tags

Metal box or lunch box (optional)

Cut the sandwich in half lengthwise. Lay your napkin on a table with the long side in front of you. Fold the napkin, as needed, to match the length of a sandwich half. Place the sandwich on one end of the folded napkin, and roll up the sandwich until the entire napkin is wrapped around it. Wrap a piece of twine around the sandwich at least 3 times. Tie off into a knot and cut the extra string. Write the label on a tag and slip the tag under the twine.

Refrigerate until ready to gift. Deliver in a box (if using).

Slice the baguette in half horizontally. Spread the butter on both halves of the baguette. Place the cornichons at an angle on the baguette and layer the salami on one half. Sprinkle a pinch of salt over the salami. Top with the other baguette half. This is best enjoyed on the day it's made.

fresh gifts

Let's begin with food gifts prepared and gifted *à la minute* (pronounced ah la min-OOT). In a restaurant, this is a style of cooking where an item is prepared to order, rather than prepped and kept ready for service. In my world, this is the style of food gifting that's made, wrapped, gifted, and devoured almost immediately. It's one of the best kinds of *Food Gift Love*.

This chapter provides basic fresh foods for the day-to-day. Some of these recipes come together in mere moments, while others require a little patience, some reliance on your senses, or the just-right gifting occasion like a friend's dinner party, a work event, or a neighbor who needs a little TLC. In any case, you'll share the sort of instant gratification that makes her or his day, and yours, for sure.

◆

pico de gallo // lemony bean dip // salt &
pepper pita chips // mixed cocktail nuts // spring
mignonette // arugula & pistachio pesto // chard
& walnut pesto // grainy mustard dressing //
kitchen-sink salad // mozzarella, basil & quick
tomato jam // cheesy mushrooms // smoky chicken
soup // homemade butter // salty maple butter //
basil-feta butter // cinnamon-sugar butter // meyer
lemon curd // ricotta cheese // mascarpone cheese //
amaretto tiramisu // panna cotta cups

pico de gallo

MAKES: ABOUT 2 CUPS // PREPARATION TIME: 30 MINUTES

Pico de Gallo, also known as *salsa fresca*, is very serious business in my Latino family. It's produced for every family event, big or small, and shared as a food gift for game-day celebrations, graduation parties, fancy cocktail hours, or a regular Friday night. I often make two jars—one as a gift to the event and the other as a gift to the host's fridge for the next day. It's amazing the next day.

My family's version is loaded with red onions, two citrus juices, and a secret weapon: ketchup. You may gasp, but this really shouldn't surprise you. Ketchup is concentrated tomato that's been cooked down with vinegar, sweetener, and spices, so it plays very well against the fresh ingredients and binds everything together quite beautifully. I use an artisanal ketchup, but use whatever suits you, or omit it altogether. If red onions are too sharp for you, soak them in ice-cold water for 20 minutes and then drain them; soaking will remove a little of the pungent flavor.

Serve this alongside the Salt & Pepper Pita Chips (page 45) for a simple, healthy hors d'oeuvre.

INGREDIENTS:

1 cup finely diced red onions (about 2 medium onions)

1 cup finely diced tomatoes (about 2 medium tomatoes)

1 tablespoon finely diced jalapeño (seeds and ribs omitted; about ½ jalapeño)

2 scallions, green and white parts, finely diced

3 tablespoons cilantro, finely chopped

2 tablespoons fresh lime juice

2 teaspoons fresh lemon juice

2 tablespoons ketchup

½ teaspoon fine sea salt

¼ teaspoon freshly ground black pepper

1. In a medium bowl, place the onions, tomatoes, jalapeño, scallions, cilantro, citrus juices, ketchup, salt, and pepper. Stir to combine very well.

2. Refrigerate 1 to 2 hours to let flavors fully mesh or until ready to use. Store in the fridge up to 3 days.

GIFT WRAP

Glass jar with airtight lid

Stickers

Fill a glass jar with Pico de Gallo. Wipe the rim and seal. Write the label on a sticker and stick to the jar. Refrigerate until ready to gift.

lemony bean dip

MAKES: ABOUT 3 CUPS // PREPARATION TIME: 15 MINUTES

This is my go-to dip as a starter appetizer or gift to a casual supper when you don't want to try too hard but want something that tastes a whole lot better than grocery store fare. Packaged up with a bag of my Salt & Pepper Pita Chips (page 45), this Lemony Bean Dip is definitely the dish everyone will devour fast. Hovered over your dish, they won't be able to figure out exactly what makes it so good, and when you say, "it's the preserved lemon," you'll have everyone intrigued.

The preserved lemon is optional, but it's worth adding. My Preserved Lemons recipe (page 178) can be made in advance to have at the ready in your fridge, or you can buy a high-quality small-batch sort. If you omit it, add 1 extra tablespoon of lemon juice. Feel free to decrease the garlic, replace the thyme with rosemary or oregano, or use dried spices instead of fresh. This is a simple recipe that can be modified with great results, so make it yours.

INGREDIENTS:

- 1 (29-ounce) can white cannellini beans, rinsed and drained
- ¼ cup fresh lemon juice
- 3 garlic cloves, minced
- ¼ cup extra-virgin olive oil, plus extra for garnish
- 2 tablespoons thyme leaves, plus extra for garnish
- ½ teaspoon fine sea salt
- 2 tablespoons roughly chopped preserved lemon (optional)

1. In the bowl of a food processor, place the white beans, lemon juice, garlic, oil, thyme, salt, and preserved lemon (if using), and blend until smooth and thick. This recipe will also thicken up in the fridge.

2. When serving, garnish with extra thyme leaves and a little extra-virgin olive oil. Store in an airtight container in the fridge up to 1 week.

GIFT WRAP

Glass bowl or plastic container with airtight lid

Butcher paper

Ribbon

Tag

Sprig of thyme

Fill a bowl with Lemony Bean Dip. Wipe the rim and seal. Wrap the sealed bowl in butcher paper as you would a gift. Tie with a piece of ribbon. Write the label on a tag and slip it, along with the herb sprig, under the ribbon. Refrigerate until ready to gift.

salt & pepper pita chips

MAKES: UP TO 40 CHIPS // PREPARATION TIME: 20 MINUTES

Soft, pillowy pitas take on a new, crisp life here as the easiest chips ever for an instant snack, a reliable potluck contribution, or the base of a makeshift nacho-style dinner. The sea salt and black pepper combination is so tasty but just the start: add in other spices like ground cumin or fennel, or dried thyme or rosemary leaves, to amp up the flavor. For a sweet interpretation, sprinkle the chips with Cinnamon Sugar (page 96). Either way, make them the same day you plan to gift; they're best when fresh and crispy.

Use white or whole wheat pitas, and keep the two layers intact; the final chip needs to be solid enough to hold a heavy dip. If yours are larger than 8 inches in diameter, just add a touch more oil to evenly coat all the triangles.

INGREDIENTS:

4 large (8-inch) white pitas

2 tablespoons extra-virgin olive oil

¼ teaspoon fine sea salt, plus more to taste

¼ teaspoon freshly ground black pepper, plus more to taste

1. Preheat the oven to 325°F. Line 2 large baking sheets with parchment paper or silicone pan liners.

2. Slice each pita into 8 to 10 wedges. You can do this individually or by stacking some of the pitas and using a very sharp knife.

3. Place the pita wedges in a big bowl and drizzle with the olive oil. Toss the pita until well coated with olive oil and then arrange in a single layer on the baking sheets. Sprinkle the salt and pepper evenly over all the pita wedges.

4. Bake 10 to 15 minutes, rotating the pans and tossing the pita chips once or twice during baking. Remove from the oven when they're golden, crisp to the touch, and a little shiny from the oil. Let them cool slightly before serving, or cool to room temperature before packaging for a gift.

GIFT WRAP

Parchment paper

Basket

Ribbon

Tag

Cut a piece of parchment paper to line the basket. Pile the chips in the parchment-lined basket. Tie a length of ribbon around the basket handle. Write the label on a tag and slip into the basket.

mixed cocktail nuts

MAKES: ABOUT 5 CUPS // PREPARATION TIME: 30 MINUTES

You can't walk around Paris in the winter without inhaling the perfume from just-roasted chestnuts. They smell sweet and smoky and inspired my Mixed Cocktail Nuts recipe. The nutty blend is entirely up to you, but I highly recommend hazelnuts. Toasted and coated in butter, honey, herbs, and spices, hazelnuts have truly amazing flavor, especially when enjoyed with a glass of dry champagne. In fact, you could gift a row of these bags, all lined up in a container, with a bottle of bubbly or a six-pack of good beer.

Instead of fine sea salt, consider finishing this dish with my Lemon-Infused Sea Salt (page 92).

INGREDIENTS:

2 cups hazelnuts

2 tablespoons (1 ounce) unsalted butter

2 tablespoons mild-flavored honey

3 tablespoons finely chopped rosemary (about 4 small stems)

¼ teaspoon cayenne pepper

½ teaspoon smoky paprika

3 cups unsalted, shelled mixed nuts (Brazil nuts, pecans, walnuts, almonds, pine nuts)

1 teaspoon fine sea salt, plus more to taste

1. Preheat the oven to 350°F. Spread the hazelnuts on a baking sheet. Toast in the oven 10 minutes or until brown, remarkably fragrant, and the skins come off easily. Carefully pour the hazelnuts into a clean kitchen towel. Wrap them up in the towel completely, and shake and rub the hazelnuts until the skins break free from the meat. Set the nuts aside and discard the skins.

2. In a sauté pan over medium-low heat, melt the butter, honey, rosemary, cayenne pepper, paprika, and salt until the honey is very runny. Stir a few times until well combined.

3. To the baking sheet, add the skinned hazelnuts, mixed nuts, and melted butter mixture. Toss until evenly and well coated. Roast 10 to 12 minutes until their fragrant aroma fills the air around you and they have dried slightly, though they will still look a bit shiny. Toss a few times while roasting.

4. Let the nuts cool to room temperature, stirring occasionally to promote drying and to ensure that the nuts stay coated. Add salt, to taste, just before gifting or serving. Store in an airtight container at room temperature up to 2 weeks, though they taste their crunchiest during the first 4 to 5 days, so gift them the same day you make them.

GIFT WRAP

Resealable, food-grade cellophane bags

Washi tape

Tin (optional)

Fill the bags with nuts and seal. Write the label on tape (if needed), cut tape to fit and place on the bag.

Stack several bags in tin, if using, to gift.

handmade with love

spring mignonette

MAKES: ABOUT 2 CUPS // PREPARATION TIME: UP TO 2 HOURS (WITH MARINATING TIME)

Oysters are often served during the winter holidays, preferably with a stiff martini or champagne. I actually like to gift them beyond winter and well into spring or early summer when they can be shucked out on a patio and served with an icy beer or lively white wine. And when a potluck host assigns me an appetizer, I offer oysters and my shucking skills (or my husband's shucking skills because that's one of the reasons I married him).

I concentrate my efforts on the fresh mignonette; it's a condiment that is served alongside the oysters. Sometimes I go classic (shallots, black pepper, and red wine vinegar), but in the spring, I gift oysters with a new take on mignonette that's full of cucumber, rhubarb, and rice wine vinegar. During the summer months, I swap in melon for the rhubarb. Either way, a martini is optional, but a cold drink accompaniment is definitely required.

In a medium bowl, place all the ingredients and stir to combine very well. Refrigerate 2 hours to mesh flavors or until ready to use. The longer it marinates, the better. Store in the fridge up to 3 days.

GIFT WRAP

Jar with airtight lid

Sticker

Crushed ice

Metal or plastic basket

Small towel or shucking glove

Shucking knife

Pour Spring Mignonette into a jar and seal. Write the label on a sticker and adhere to the top of the lid. Refrigerate until ready to gift.

Oysters need to be kept chilled until consumed, so place them over ice in a metal or plastic basket, but don't submerge them in water. Add in the towel and knife. Gift with the jar of mignonette.

INGREDIENTS:

1 cup finely diced English-style (seedless) cucumber (about 5 ounces)

1 cup finely diced rhubarb (about two 8-inch stalks)

2 cups rice wine vinegar

3 tablespoons granulated sugar

½ teaspoon fine sea salt

½ teaspoon freshly ground black pepper

arugula & pistachio pesto

MAKES: ABOUT 2 CUPS // PREPARATION TIME: 30 MINUTES

Pesto is a sauce traditionally crafted with aromatic garden basil. But the word "pesto" is derived from an Italian word that literally means to pound or to crush. With that interpretation, we can "pound" anything into pesto—from soft garden herbs to dark leafy greens.

Arugula pesto may be my favorite, and my version, loaded with pistachios, forms the most delectable crust on grilled meats, spreads thickly on toasted bread for cocktail hour, mixes well with angel hair pasta, and makes the very best everyday food gift. Take a jar to a potluck-style barbecue with some lamb chops, a butterflied whole chicken, or an extra-large pile of mushrooms. Tell the grill master to brush a little pesto on just before grilling or, better yet, offer to do it yourself.

This arugula pesto is brighter than the basil variety and preserves the bite it's known for when blended up with olive oil, cheese, and nuts. To preserve the color longer, blanch the arugula for 5 seconds and then squeeze out excess water. As for nuts, I prefer pistachios in this pesto over the classic pine nuts or other nuts because they add a gentle sweetness. You don't need to roast them, but the sauce will be more fragrant after a brief toasting.

INGREDIENTS:

½ cup shelled pistachios, unsalted

2 cups tightly packed, well-rinsed arugula leaves and stems

1½ teaspoons finely chopped garlic (about 3 cloves)

¼ cup plus 1 tablespoon grated Parmesan cheese

1 tablespoon fresh lemon juice

⅛ teaspoon fine sea salt

⅛ teaspoon freshly ground black pepper

¾ cup extra-virgin olive oil, plus extra for storage

1. Preheat the oven to 350°F. Roast the pistachios on a baking sheet 10 minutes. Set aside to let cool.

2. In the bowl of a food processor, add the pistachios, arugula, garlic, Parmesan cheese, lemon juice, salt, pepper, and olive oil. Process about 10 to 12 seconds until the pesto is blended but still chunky.

3. Store in an airtight container in the fridge up to 3 days. Before sealing the container, add an extra tablespoon or two of olive oil on top of the pesto to create a thin layer that helps preserve the color.

GIFT WRAP

Glass jar with airtight lid

Tag with string

Fill a glass jar with pesto. Wipe the rim and seal. Write the label on a tag and tie it around the jar. Refrigerate until ready to gift.

chard & walnut pesto

MAKES: ABOUT 2 CUPS // PREPARATION TIME: 30 MINUTES

In this recipe, I blend Swiss chard and walnuts into a chunky pesto that looks like it came from a mortar and pestle, the traditional implements for pesto making. You may be familiar with the smooth-style pesto sold in markets, but try thicker pesto. The texture adds wondrous substance to everyday pasta and looks like a truly homemade food gift.

INGREDIENTS:

½ cup unsalted shelled walnuts, and chopped

3 cups Swiss chard leaves and stems, tightly packed, cleaned

1½ teaspoons finely chopped garlic (about 3 cloves)

¼ cup plus 1 tablespoon grated Parmesan cheese

1 tablespoon fresh lemon juice

⅛ teaspoon fine sea salt

⅛ teaspoon freshly ground black pepper

¾ cup extra-virgin olive oil, plus extra for storage

1. Preheat the oven to 350°F. Spread the walnuts on a baking sheet and roast 10 minutes. Set aside to let cool.

2. Chop the chard into 1-inch ribbons and stem pieces.

3. In the bowl of a food processor, add the walnuts, chard, garlic, Parmesan cheese, lemon juice, salt, pepper, and olive oil. Pulse in 5-second intervals (about 4 times) until the pesto is blended but still chunky.

4. Store the pesto in an airtight container in the fridge for up to 3 days. Before sealing the container, add an extra tablespoon or two of olive oil on top of the pesto to create a thin layer that helps preserve the color.

GIFT WRAP

Glass jar with airtight lid

Marker

Write the label directly on the lid of a glass jar. Fill the jar with pesto. Wipe the rim and seal. Refrigerate until ready to gift.

Swiss Chard
Walnut Pesto

grainy mustard dressing

MAKES: ABOUT 1 CUP // PREPARATION TIME: 10 MINUTES

Salad dressing is so simple and quick to make and infinitely better tasting than the store-bought sort. When you make your own, it's also easy to adapt to personal tastes—your own or those who will receive the gift.

I eat salads daily with a drizzle of good oil and a splash of something bright or a squeeze of something citrusy, and this recipe captures that simple flavor balance. It provides the perfect "tart" element for my Kitchen-Sink Salad (page 56)—and is more tart than the average recipe.

The quality of the dressing will depend entirely on the quality of the ingredients. Find a mild, grassy olive oil and a good maple syrup. If you like, replace the whole-grain mustard with one that suits your taste, like a milder honey mustard or a regular Dijon.

INGREDIENTS:

1 tablespoon whole-grain Dijon mustard

1 tablespoon maple syrup

½ cup extra-virgin olive oil

½ cup white wine vinegar

¼ teaspoon fine sea salt

⅛ teaspoon freshly ground black pepper

SPECIAL EQUIPMENT:

Glass jar with airtight lid

Place the mustard, maple syrup, olive oil, vinegar, salt, and pepper into a jar. Wipe the rim and seal. Shake 30 seconds to blend. Use immediately or refrigerate up to 1 week. Bring the dressing to room temperature and shake before using.

GIFT WRAP

Fabric

Glass jar with airtight lid

Rubber band

Trim a small square of fabric to fit over the opening of a jar. Pour the dressing into the jar. Wipe the rim and seal. Place the fabric over the top of the jar, and wrap a rubber band around it to keep it in place.

kitchen-sink salad

PREPARATION TIME: 30 TO 60 MINUTES

A well-balanced salad is a dish with which even chefs struggle. For restaurants, they strive to perfect the combination of mild, bitter, crunchy, sweet, rich, nutty, salty, and acidic elements. But in everyday life, precise proportions do not matter. For a potluck, a smorgasbord, or a pitch-in where everyone brings something, your gifted salad should be special but fairly effortless.

My Kitchen-Sink Salad can be pulled together from whatever is in your kitchen and a few extras from the market. The basic recipe requires a pile of **mild** greens and elements for five tastes—**bitter, crunchy, sweet, rich, nutty**—from your fridge or pantry, and then add in fine sea salt for the **salty** kick and lemon juice for the **acidic** edge. Let's talk about all these tastes:

Mild is meant to cover all types of mellow salad greens like butter lettuce, romaine lettuce, mâche, red-leaf lettuce, cabbage, mesclun, and Bibb lettuce. This is the base of your salad.

Bitter covers anything with a bite, like arugula, fennel, kale, mustard greens, watercress, frisée, red onions, Brussels sprouts, endive, escarole, and radishes.

Crunchy covers veggies that snap when you take a bite, like cucumber, cauliflower, broccoli, green beans, snap peas, and haricots verts (green string beans).

Sweet is something that is naturally a touch higher in sugar, like fresh tomatoes, apples, pears, blueberries, strawberries, grapes, cherries, figs, peaches, or mangoes, as well as dried fruit like apricots, figs, raisins, and currants.

Rich is meant to represent a slightly more indulgent, complex, or even buttery taste. When you add something rich to a salad, you're adding a little more luxury in the form of roasted corn, roasted smoky eggplant, boiled or roasted potatoes, avocado slices, spring peas, hard-boiled eggs, artichokes, mushrooms, or creamy cheeses.

Nutty is just that, anything that tastes like nuts. This includes cashews, pecans, hazelnuts, pine nuts, walnuts, peanuts, Brazil nuts, sunflower seeds, pumpkin seeds, sesame seeds, and even unsweetened granola clusters. These nuts are not meant to be the salty component—though it may be if you use, for example, salty roasted peanuts.

Salty can be as easy as fine sea salt and as complex as cooked bacon, feta or Parmesan cheese, capers, soy sauce, or cured black olives. And every salad does need a little sea salt; just make it a pinch if you add one of the ingredients above.

Acidic is all about lemon juice in my house, though sometimes I swap in balsamic vinegar, red wine vinegar, lime juice, or champagne vinegar.

Here are some possible combinations to inspire a Kitchen-Sink Salad as your next potluck gift:

- Butter lettuce, radicchio, green beans, blueberries, avocado, chopped hazelnuts, sea salt, lemon juice

- Romaine lettuce, kale, snap peas, tomatoes, hard-boiled egg, roasted almonds, sea salt, lemon juice

- Mâche (also known as field lettuce or lamb's lettuce), arugula, asparagus, strawberries, peas, granola, feta, lemon juice

- Napa cabbage, red onion, red bell peppers, carrots, edamame, peanuts, soy sauce, lime juice

- Mesclun mix, roasted Brussels sprouts, zucchini rounds, grape halves, roasted sweet potato cubes, pecans, sea salt, balsamic vinegar

- Boston Bibb lettuce, frisée, cucumber, green apple, corn kernels, pumpkin seeds, bacon, champagne vinegar

INGREDIENTS:

5 parts mild salad greens

1 part bitter

1 part crunchy

1 part sweet

1 part rich

1 handful of nutty

1 hefty sprinkle fine sea salt

1 hefty pinch freshly ground black pepper (optional)

1 heavy sprinkling acidic

1 heavy drizzle extra-virgin olive oil (optional)

1. Clean everything. Blanch (plunge into boiling water for a minute or two) any crunchy elements that you'd prefer to be a little softer, like asparagus, cauliflower, or broccoli. Prepare the bitter, crunchy, sweet, and rich elements by cutting them, as needed, into equal-size pieces. They should all be able to make their way onto a fork together.

2. Add the salad greens to a large bowl or platter. Add in the bitter, crunchy, sweet, and rich elements. Add in the nutty element, taking care to chop harder or larger types, like hazelnuts, walnuts, or big granola clusters, into smaller pieces. Sprinkle in the salt and pepper (if using) and cover. Mix the acidic element and olive oil (if using), in a sealable container. Transport all, covered.

3. Once you've presented the salad at your event, drizzle in the acidic element and olive oil (if using)—or my Grainy Mustard Dressing (page 55). Toss to combine very well. Taste and adjust seasoning. Serve immediately.

mozzarella, basil & quick tomato jam

MAKES: 4 TO 5 SERVINGS, AS AN APPETIZER // PREPARATION TIME: 15 MINUTES

This dish came together magically when my husband's Irish family came for a U.S. tour. When they visit, they end up traveling all over the States in a multi-week trip. He warned me, quite gently, that their distinct palates, especially on their first night abroad, may not crave milky cheese and sweet jam. I didn't listen and poured my Tomato Jam on top of fresh whole-milk mozzarella. They dug in and instantly relaxed. (I believe the wine helped, too.)

This salad is a play on a traditional Caprese salad that enables you to enjoy the combo of cheese, herbs, and tomatoes year-round with less than perfectly flavorful tomatoes. A big platter of this combination works wonders as is, but it can work as an appetizer course, salad course (atop a pile of small arugula leaves), or even as a savory meal finisher with whole-grain crackers. I am also resolute that this combo may make one of the best grilled cheese sandwiches ever, pleasing for a ladies lunch or a guys lunch or, really, any lunch. Gift the entire spread to your next event and assemble it on-site for the host.

The amount of sugar in the jam can be altered depending on the quality of your tomatoes: very sweet, juicy, in-season tomatoes require a bit less sugar. And if you're feeling adventurous, replace the lemon juice in the jam with balsamic vinegar, or add a pinch of crushed red pepper flakes or a little finely diced jalapeño to please spicy palates.

INGREDIENTS:

1 (³/₄-pound) ball whole-milk mozzarella (drained of liquid)

20 basil leaves, rinsed and dried

½ cup Quick Tomato Jam (recipe follows)

1 baguette, cut into ½-inch slices, for serving

1. Cut the mozzarella into ½-inch slices or 8 even wedges.

2. On a plate, arrange the cheese slices with slightly overlapping edges. Slip basil leaves between every slice. Pour jam on top of the cheese, and sprinkle with any remaining basil leaves.

3. Serve immediately with the baguette.

QUICK TOMATO JAM

MAKES: ABOUT 1 CUP
PREPARATION TIME: 30 MINUTES

INGREDIENTS:

2 cups (about 1½ dry pints) cherry or pear tomatoes

½ cup granulated sugar

1 tablespoon fresh lemon juice

1 tablespoon thinly sliced fresh basil

¼ teaspoon sea salt

⅛ teaspoon freshly ground black pepper

1. Slice the tomatoes in half. In a medium pot over medium-high heat, combine the tomatoes, sugar, and lemon juice. While the tomato mixture cooks, stir and crush it bit by bit.

2. Once the tomato mixture has reached the boiling stage, reduce the heat to medium and cook 10 minutes, stirring constantly to ensure that the mixture doesn't burn. Skim the foam that forms, if desired.

3. Once 10 minutes pass and the tomato mixture begins to stick to the bottom and side of the pan, remove from the heat and stir in the basil, salt, and pepper.

4. Let the mixture cool 2 to 3 minutes, then pour it in a glass jar. Alternatively, let it cool to room temperature before spooning into a plastic container.

GIFT WRAP

Glass jar with airtight lid

Ribbon

Basket

Before it cools, pour the jam into a jar. Wipe the rim and seal. Tie a bit of ribbon around the jar into a knot. Place the jar in a basket with a bunch of tied basil, a baguette, and a container of whole-milk mozzarella, still in its liquid.

cheesy mushrooms

MAKES: 20 TO 30 MUSHROOMS // PREPARATION TIME: 90 MINUTES

Over the years, I've made stuffed mushrooms all sorts of ways and, no doubt, adding cheese pleases everyone. In fact, adding three cheeses basically secures the title of "first dish devoured" at a potluck.

My Cheesy Mushrooms taste familiar but a little different, too. I love to replace the spinach with chard or kale. All bread crumbs work well—plain, seasoned, or panko, but if they're seasoned, omit the sea salt and oregano. Don't forget the drizzle of olive oil on every single mushroom—that helps achieve a golden color. Sometimes I add a little finely chopped jalapeño for an additional bite.

INGREDIENTS:

8 ounces frozen kale or spinach, thawed

1 tablespoon extra-virgin olive oil, plus more for drizzling

1/2 cup finely diced white onion (about 1/2 medium onion)

1 tablespoon finely diced garlic (about 3 small cloves)

1/8 teaspoon plus 1 teaspoon fine sea salt, separated

1/8 teaspoon freshly ground black pepper

1 1/2 pounds large (about 3 inches) stuffing button mushrooms

1 (8-ounce) package cream cheese, softened to room temperature

1/4 cup Parmesan cheese

1/4 cup plain bread crumbs

1/2 cup shredded mozzarella cheese

1 tablespoon dried oregano

1/2 teaspoon hot sauce

1/2 teaspoon lemon zest

1. Line a baking sheet with parchment paper and set aside.

2. Set the kale in a strainer over a deep bowl to drain. Squeeze as much water out of it as possible. Set aside.

3. Heat the olive oil in a skillet over medium heat. Add the onions, garlic, 1/8 teaspoon salt, and the pepper, and sauté until the onions are translucent, about 5 minutes. Set aside and let cool.

4. Rub the mushrooms with a dry towel to remove any dirt. Break the stems off the mushrooms to expose a well in the mushroom base. Use a knife or spoon to pick out any extra mushroom stem if necessary. Reserve the leftover mushroom stems for another use; here they would add too much filling and liquid to the stuffing.

5. In a large bowl, add the cream cheese, kale, onion mixture, Parmesan cheese, bread crumbs, mozzarella cheese, the remaining 1 teaspoon salt, the dried oregano, hot sauce, and lemon zest. Mix together until well combined.

6. Stuff each mushroom with 1 heaping tablespoon of the kale mixture; there should be a heaping mound, so add a little less or more as needed. Place each mushroom on the baking sheet. Place the baking sheet in the fridge (or even the freezer) for 10 minutes to chill the mixture. If taking to a potluck where you'll have an oven available, wrap and transport as is and bake at the potluck.

7. Preheat the oven to 375°F. Drizzle a few drops of olive oil on top of each mushroom. Bake 25 minutes or until the cheese has melted and the top has browned slightly. Let cool a few minutes; serve warm.

GIFT WRAP

2 matching, deep baking sheets

Parchment paper

String

Tape

Line a baking sheet with parchment paper. Place the Cheesy Mushrooms on the parchment-lined baking sheet. Reverse and lay the second baking sheet on top of the first. Tie with string, as you would a gift. Write the label on tape and affix to the top tray. To bake at your destination, remove the tape, string, and the top baking sheet before placing in the oven.

smoky chicken soup

MAKES: 6 TO 8 SERVINGS // PREPARATION TIME: 45 MINUTES

A big pot of warm soup actually makes a darling food gift for a sick friend, a family in need of TLC, or a group event. This version is smoky from the paprika but not really spicy, thanks to sweet corn and fresh cilantro; of course, you need to use sweet smoked paprika. Avoid spicy paprika because that would be too hot for many folks.

Homemade chicken stock will make a better home-made soup. I include my recipe to use for this soup as well as to freeze for future gifts or other cooking projects.

INGREDIENTS:

2 tablespoons extra-virgin olive oil

1 medium onion, sliced into thin half-moons

2 tablespoons Garlic Puree (recipe follows)

1/2 teaspoon chipotle pepper flakes

1 1/2 tablespoons sweet smoked paprika

1 bay leaf

7 cups chicken stock, store-bought or homemade (recipe follows)

1 1/2 cups corn kernels, fresh (trimmed from 2 or 3 cobs) or frozen

3 cups shredded cooked chicken

1 cup thinly sliced kale or spinach

1 teaspoon fine sea salt, plus more for serving

1/2 teaspoon freshly ground black pepper, plus more for serving

4 tablespoons finely diced cilantro, for garnish

1. Heat the oil in a large soup pot over medium-high heat. Add the onion, garlic puree, pepper flakes, paprika, and bay leaf and sauté until the onion is translucent.

2. Add the stock, corn, chicken, kale, salt, and pepper and bring to a boil. Reduce the heat to low and simmer and cook 20 minutes or until all the flavors combine into a rich, flavorful soup. Remove the bay leaf.

3. If serving immediately, add in the cilantro and check for seasoning, adding additional salt or pepper as needed. If taking to a potluck, reserve the cilantro and add just before serving.

◆

GARLIC PUREE

MAKES: ABOUT ½ CUP
PREPARATION TIME: 10 MINUTES

Preparing garlic puree in advance makes all your weeknight meals—and this Smoky Chicken Soup—much more of a snap when assembling.

INGREDIENTS:

10 garlic cloves, peeled

½ cup extra-virgin olive oil

Place garlic and olive oil in the bowl of a food processor. Blend about 30 seconds or until a thick puree forms. Store in an airtight container in the fridge up to 1 week.

◆

HOMEMADE CHICKEN STOCK

MAKES: ABOUT 2 QUARTS // PREPARATION TIME: UP TO 3 HOURS 30 MINUTES

This recipe is a weekly staple, easily made just after a dinner of roast chicken. Whether you roasted the chicken yourself or purchased a rotisserie-style chicken from the local market, homemade chicken stock is still fantastic and eases the assembly of most soups.

INGREDIENTS:

1 (4-pound) roasted chicken carcass

3 medium carrots

2 medium celery stalks

1 medium onion

1 handful (2 ounces) mixed herbs, stems and leaves

6 to 10 garlic cloves, peeled

1 (2-inch) knob of ginger, sliced in half

1 tablespoon fine sea salt

1 tablespoon freshly ground black pepper

6 quarts water

1. Pull any extra meat off of the chicken carcass, and reserve the meat for another use. Place the carcass in a very large soup pot.

2. Chop the carrots and celery into 2-inch pieces. Cut the onion, unpeeled, into 8 large wedges. Add the carrots, celery, onions, herbs, garlic, ginger, salt, and pepper to the soup pot. Add the water.

3. Bring the water to a boil over medium-high heat. Reduce the heat to medium and simmer 3 hours. Strain the stock into a new pot or bowl, and discard the solids. Let cool to room temperature. If you'd like, skim off any fat that collects at the top of the stock. Store in an airtight container in the fridge up to 1 week or freeze up to 3 months.

GIFT WRAP

Soup pot with lid

Ribbon

Ladle (optional)

Bowls (optional)

Spoons (optional)

Tray (optional)

When the soup pot is cool enough to handle, thread a long piece of ribbon through each pot handle. Bring both ends up over the pot and thread through the pot's lid handle. Thread it through one more time and tie off in a tight knot. Trim excess ribbon. Slide a ladle (if using) through the lid handle and gift. Add bowls and spoons on a tray (if using).

homemade butter

MAKES: 1 STICK, OR ABOUT 4 OUNCES // PREPARATION TIME: 30 MINUTES

Hand-churned butter is a glorious thing but time intensive. Instead, I make a food processor butter that will out-taste any grocery store version. It will also dazzle the person to whom it's gifted. I suggest that you gift it to someone who's just moved into a new home; those first few batches of morning toast in her or his new place are so special—and even more so with homemade butter. (See also three ways to flavor homemade butter, pages 66–69).

The very best butter flavor will develop from fresh, organic heavy cream from a local farm, but a grocery-store version will work, too. This recipe should be made in a food processor. A very powerful blender will produce too much heat and may not curd up. A stand mixer will eventually get you to curds but will probably take about double the time. If you do use a stand mixer, start with the whisk attachment until you get something that looks like over-whipped cream, and then graduate to the paddle attachment to form curds.

Remember to save the buttermilk that forms from both extracts. It's exactly like store-bought buttermilk, only homemade, and makes delicious pancakes. The cheesecloth itself is also reusable. Wash it by hand in very hot water and hang to dry.

INGREDIENTS:

1 pint heavy cream

½ cup cold water

⅛ teaspoon fine sea salt, plus more to taste

SPECIAL EQUIPMENT:

Cheesecloth

1. Line a fine-mesh strainer with 4 layers of cheesecloth and place it over a deep bowl. Set aside.

2. Pour the cream into the bowl of a food processor. Blend 4 to 5 minutes until the butter separates from the liquid (the buttermilk). When most of the butter has separated from the buttermilk and formed tiny curd-like bits, turn off the food processor. The process will go something like this:

   After 1 minute, the cream starts to become whipped cream.
   After 1½ minutes, the whipped cream starts to separate from the liquid.
   After 2 minutes, the mixture takes on a slightly pale yellow hue.
   After 4½ minutes, check it and feel the consistency. It should feel like soft butter.

3. With a rubber spatula, scoop the entire contents of the food processor into the cheesecloth. (If it leaks through the cheesecloth then it's likely not yet separated enough—return it to the food processor and keep blending.) Press down on the butter to help push out all the remaining buttermilk. To further help it along, pull up the sides of the cheesecloth to fully enclose the butter. Squeeze and press on the cheesecloth to push out any remaining buttermilk.

4. Clean out the bowl of your food processor completely. Remove the butter from the cheesecloth and return it to the food processor. Add the cold water. Turn the food processor on for 30 seconds to clean the butter. This helps to wash the butter and remove extra buttermilk.

5. Return the butter to the cheesecloth in the sieve. Squeeze out any remaining buttermilk. Place the butter in a bowl. Using a rubber spatula, mix it with the sea salt. You've just made butter.

6. Store the butter well wrapped in plastic wrap and sealed in an airtight container in the fridge up to 1 week or in the freezer up to 3 months. Store the buttermilk separately and use within 3 days.

salty maple butter

MAKES: ½ CUP // PREPARATION TIME: 5 MINUTES

My Salty Maple Butter is delicious in the most obvious application—atop a pile of puffy pancakes. But it's also wonderful on freshly popped popcorn, morning toast or afternoon scone, or even on grilled carrots.

If you're using homemade butter that's already salted, taste the final product before adding any extra salt. If you're not using homemade butter, a cultured butter would best suit this recipe.

INGREDIENTS:

½ cup Homemade Butter (page 64) or 1 stick (4 ounces) store-bought unsalted butter, room temperature

2 teaspoons light or dark maple syrup

¼ teaspoon fine sea salt

SPECIAL EQUIPMENT:

1 half-pint jar with airtight lid

In a small bowl, mix the butter, maple syrup, and salt together with a flexible rubber spatula or fork until well combined. Scoop and press the butter into a clean jar, then run a knife around the inside edge of the jar to remove air pockets and make it fit. Seal and store in the fridge up to 1 week or in the freezer up to 3 months.

GIFT WRAP

Teacup

Plastic wrap

Rubber band

Rolls (optional)

Butter knife (optional)

Fill a teacup with butter. Wipe the rim and seal with plastic wrap and a rubber band. Gift with rolls and a butter knife (if using).

basil-feta butter

MAKES: ½ CUP // PREPARATION TIME: 10 MINUTES

My Basil-Feta Butter is amazing slathered over just-grilled corn or dabbed on ripe tomato halves before a quick roast in the oven. The basil can be replaced with fresh oregano, savory, or sage. If you use oregano, add a little lemon zest to create a Greek-inspired butter.

   If you're using homemade butter that's already salted, taste the final product before adding any extra salt. If you're not using homemade butter, a cultured butter would best suit this recipe.

INGREDIENTS:

½ cup Homemade Butter (page 64) or 1 stick (4 ounces) store-bought unsalted butter, room temperature

1 tablespoon finely chopped basil leaves

3 tablespoons crumbled feta cheese

⅛ teaspoon fine sea salt

In a small bowl, mix the butter, basil, feta cheese, and salt together with a flexible rubber spatula or fork until well combined. Store the butter well wrapped in plastic wrap and then in an airtight container in the fridge up to 1 week or in the freezer up to 3 months.

GIFT WRAP

Parchment paper

Twine

Tape

Scoop the butter onto the center of a 12-inch square of parchment paper. Fold the paper in half and mold the butter into a 1-inch log. Roll the extra paper around the log. Tie each end off with twine or twist the paper until taut. Write the label on a piece of tape and stick to the butter log.

cinnamon-sugar butter

MAKES: ½ CUP // PREPARATION TIME: 10 MINUTES

In college, my friend Dawn introduced me to buttered toast topped with cinnamon sugar. The fact that I lived 18 years before sampling this culinary phenomenon is shocking, indeed. To thank her for the genius education on the most comforting late night meal on earth, I make her some Cinnamon-Sugar Butter that she can tuck in the back of her fridge when she's up late or just wants to remember the good old days. This butter is of course great on toast, but don't let that restrain you.

If you're using homemade butter that's already salted, taste the final product before adding any extra salt. If you're not using homemade butter, a cultured butter would best suit this recipe.

INGREDIENTS:

½ cup Homemade Butter (page 64) or 1 stick (4 ounces) store-bought unsalted butter, room temperature

3 tablespoons Cinnamon Sugar (page 96)

¼ teaspoon fine sea salt

In a small bowl, mix the butter, cinnamon sugar, and salt together with a flexible rubber spatula or fork until well combined. Store the butter well-wrapped in plastic wrap and sealed in an airtight container in the fridge up to 1 week or in the freezer up to 3 months.

GIFT WRAP

Small baking tin
Wax paper
Pinking shears (optional)
Tag
String

Line a small baking tin with wax paper that's been cut with pinking shears (if using). Press the room-temperature butter mixture into the tin and fold up the extra wax paper to cover. Write the label on a tag. Thread string through the tag and attach it to the tin by wrapping the string around the tin several times.

meyer lemon curd

MAKES: ABOUT 2 CUPS // PREPARATION TIME: 20 MINUTES

The rich texture and bright flavor of lemon curd always puts me in a sunny disposition. I love to make it for gifts to share my good cheer; otherwise, there's too much temptation to eat the whole lot.

Important to my recipe is a full cup of Meyer lemon juice but no zest. I like to achieve the smoothest texture and reserve the precious zest for another recipe, like my Infused Sea Salts (page 90). You can use traditional Eureka lemons, but the flavor will be slightly different.

Achieving the ideal set or texture of the curd is dependent on several factors. If your curd is a little loose, give it some time to set up in the fridge. If it stays loose, just embrace it. It won't change the fact that every last spoonful is lovely.

INGREDIENTS:

1 cup (2 sticks) unsalted butter, cut into tablespoon-size pieces

1¼ cups granulated sugar

¼ teaspoon fine sea salt

1 cup Meyer lemon juice or Eureka lemon juice (3 to 5 lemons)

4 large egg yolks, whites reserved for another use

SPECIAL EQUIPMENT:

Double boiler

Candy thermometer

Glass jar with airtight lid

1. Prepare an ice-water bath: Fill a large bowl halfway with water and plenty of ice. Set aside.

2. In a double boiler over medium heat, place a bit of water in the bottom pot—making sure the water doesn't touch the underside of the top pot. Assemble the double boiler. (If you do not have a double boiler, place a metal or glass bowl on top of a medium pot.)

3. Add the butter, sugar, and salt to the top pot. Whisk until the sugar dissolves.

4. Keep whisking while adding the lemon juice.

5. Add the egg yolks, one at a time, whisking after each addition.

6. Whisk constantly and continue to cook 10 to 15 minutes or until the temperature reaches just above 170°F. Remove from the heat when the curd gets thicker and coats the back of a spoon; it will continue to thicken when refrigerated.

7. With a kitchen towel, carefully remove the top pot from the heat and place it into the ice-water bath to bring the temperature down. If any egg yolks have clumped up in the curd, strain it into jar. Store the curd in an airtight container in the fridge until ready to use.

GIFT WRAP

Glass jar

Plastic wrap

Rubber band

Tag

Twine

Fill a jar with curd. Wipe the rim and seal with plastic wrap and a rubber band. Write the label on a tag. Wrap twine around the jar, slipping it through the tag before tying the twine into a knot.

ricotta cheese

MAKES: ABOUT 2 CUPS // PREPARATION TIME: 30 MINUTES ACTIVE TIME
(UP TO 1 HOUR 30 MINUTES TOTAL TIME)

Some say homemade ricotta cheese is making a comeback; every city has at least one cheese maker reviving a classic recipe. I say making ricotta cheese has always been a staple in my family, for both sweet and savory applications. It comes to life in under an hour with stunning results. It's a peaceful, Zen-like, early morning activity before the rest of the house awakes.

Fans of sweet flavors can serve homemade ricotta as a dessert, drizzled with honey or maple syrup or underneath a dollop of your favorite jam in tiny glass cups. Those who favor savory flavors can chop fresh, soft herbs—like basil, oregano, and chives—and stir them into the ricotta. Drop spoonfuls on toasted bread slices and sprinkle with a bit of Lemon Infused Sea Salt (page 92) or diced Preserved Lemons (page 178).

Please don't discard the whey. It's packed with good protein and low in fat. Store it in the fridge up to 1 month. Add to smooth out fruit smoothies, flavor pasta water, or simply to nourish your potted plants. The cheesecloth itself is also reusable. Wash it by hand in very hot water and hang to dry.

INGREDIENTS:

8 cups whole milk

1 teaspoon fine sea salt

⅓ cup fresh lemon juice (2 lemons)

SPECIAL EQUIPMENT:

Cheesecloth

Candy thermometer

1. Line a large sieve or fine-mesh strainer with 4 layers of cheesecloth. Set it over a deep bowl. (If needed, use a little masking tape to secure the sieve to the bowl so it doesn't fall in.) Set aside.

2. Add the milk to a large (at least 8-inch) stainless steel, heavy-bottom pot set over medium heat. Bring to a low simmer until tiny bubbles form around the outside edges of the milk, or until the milk reaches about 180°F on a candy thermometer (about 25 minutes). Stir occasionally with a rubber spatula to prevent scorching. Remove from the heat.

3. Add the salt and lemon juice. Stir to combine. Let the milk sit 10 minutes to allow the curds to form.

4. Pour the curd-filled mixture into the cheesecloth-lined sieve and allow it to drain. Let drain 30 minutes for a softer ricotta cheese and 60 minutes or more for a firmer ricotta cheese. Use or gift immediately, or store in an airtight container in the fridge up to 1 week.

GIFT WRAP

Straight-sided container

Plastic wrap

Tag

Twine

Fill the container with cheese. Wipe the rim and seal it with plastic wrap. Write the label on a tag, thread with twine, and wrap the twine around the lip of the container.

mascarpone cheese

MAKES: ABOUT 1 CUP // PREPARATION TIME: 60 MINUTES ACTIVE TIME
(UP TO 8 HOURS TOTAL TIME)

Mascarpone cheese is an Italian-style cream cheese that is best known for its use in tiramisu (see my Amaretto Tiramisu on page 76). It's also great for spreading on toast with honey, enriching baked pasta dishes, boosting single-vegetable soups, and enhancing almost everything. Fruit also loves mascarpone cheese. When bringing this cheese to a dinner party, set up an impressive dessert platter by bringing along and layering freshly washed strawberries and freshly sliced peaches on a serving plate with a big bowl of mascarpone cheese that's been whipped with lemon zest and sugar. Everyone will love it.

Although a similar process to making fresh ricotta, making mascarpone requires a little advanced planning and achieving a higher temperature. If you don't own a candy thermometer, get one for this recipe. You'll also use it again in the "Candied Gifts" and "Preserved Gifts" chapters. The cheesecloth itself is also reusable. Wash it by hand in very hot water and hang to dry.

INGREDIENTS:

2 cups (not ultra-pasteurized) heavy cream

1 tablespoon fresh lemon juice

Fine sea salt, for serving

SPECIAL EQUIPMENT:

Cheesecloth

Candy thermometer

1. Line a large sieve or fine-mesh strainer with 4 layers of cheesecloth and set over a deep bowl. Set aside.

2. Add the heavy cream to a large (at least 8-inch) stainless steel, heavy-bottom pot set over medium heat. Bring to a low simmer until tiny bubbles start to pop up all over the surface of the cream or until the cream reaches about 190°F on a candy thermometer (about 30 minutes). It will look like a low rolling boil. Stir constantly with a rubber spatula to prevent scorching.

3. Once the cream reaches 190°F, add the lemon juice. Stir and cook about 10 minutes, aiming to keep the cream's temperature at 190°F throughout by raising and lowering the temperature (removing it from the heat for a few minutes, as needed). Test the cream mixture texture with a wooden spoon. When the cream coats the back of the spoon and retains the line made by a finger swipe, stop cooking and remove the pot from the heat. Let the cream mixture cool 30 minutes—it will continue to thicken as it cools.

4. Pour the cream mixture into the cheesecloth and cover with a bit of plastic wrap placed right up against the mixture. Place in the fridge and allow it to drain, chilled, 8 hours or overnight. The longer it sits, the firmer your mascarpone cheese. The liquid that drains from the cheese is whey and can be reserved for another use. Once it has adequately drained, pull the cheese from the cheesecloth with a rubber spatula and place in an airtight container. Use or gift immediately, or store in an airtight container in the fridge up to 1 week. If using as is, add a little salt just before serving. If using in a recipe, like my Amaretto Tiramisu (page 76), omit the salt.

GIFT WRAP

Bowl

Plastic wrap

Rubber band

Tag

Ribbon

Vintage knife (optional)

Fill a bowl with cheese. Wipe the rim and seal with plastic wrap and a rubber band. Write the label on a tag. Wrap the ribbon around the bowl as you would a gift. Slip the tag on the end of the ribbon, tie in a knot, and clip any excess ribbon. If you'd like, slip a vintage knife under the ribbon.

Mascarpone
Cheese

amaretto tiramisu

MAKES: ABOUT 15 TO 18 SERVINGS // PREPARATION TIME: 30 MINUTES ACTIVE TIME
(UP TO 4 HOURS TOTAL TIME)

Tiramisu is a celebration. My version is cakey, creamy, boozy, and laden with coffee; basically, everything dessert should be. You may decide to omit the Amaretto, especially if someone has a nut allergy. Without it, the Amaretto Tiramisu won't exactly be Amaretto Tiramisu, but it will still be pretty great. Instead of the liqueur, use 3 tablespoons of vanilla extract in the cream and 2 cups of espresso for the ladyfingers.

Ladyfingers are typically soft, sponge-like cakes, but they are also made into a crisp-style cookie. For this recipe, I recommend the crisp-style ladyfingers that are about 4 inches long by 1 inch wide. You can make your own, but there's bound to be an Italian bakery in your city that has delicious fresh cookies you can use. They are also available at many grocery stores, and my local Italian grocer sells packages filled with twenty cookies. Two packages fill up the tray perfectly, but you may want to get three packages in case your baking dish is larger.

Always ask the host, in advance, if you may use fridge space to store your food gift until dessert hour.

INGREDIENTS:

6 large egg yolks, whites reserved for another use

¼ cup granulated sugar

3 tablespoons plus ½ cup Amaretto, separated

1 tablespoon vanilla extract

1 pound mascarpone cheese

¼ teaspoon fine sea salt

1½ cups espresso or strong coffee, cooled to room temperature

40 ladyfingers

1 tablespoon cocoa powder, for garnish

1 teaspoon ground cinnamon, for garnish

SPECIAL EQUIPMENT:

13x9-inch glass baking dish

Stand mixer (or a whisk)

1. Place the egg yolks and sugar in the bowl of a stand mixer with the whisk attachment. Whisk about 4 minutes on medium-high speed until well combined, thick, and pale yellow in color.

2. Add the 3 tablespoons Amaretto and the vanilla extract to the mixer. Whisk on low 1 minute until combined.

3. Add the mascarpone cheese and salt to the mixer. Whisk on low speed 2 minutes until loosened, then slowly increase the speed to medium. Whisk 4 minutes longer to finish combining and add some air to the mixture. Stop the mixer, scrape down the side of the bowl, and whisk again to ensure that everything is well-blended. Set aside.

4. In a shallow bowl, combine the remaining ½ cup Amaretto and the espresso. Dip each of 20 ladyfingers into the espresso mixture, turning once to wet both sides, and arrange in the bottom of the baking dish in a single layer of about 20 ladyfingers. You may need to break up the cookies to fill up the layer. Pour half of your mascarpone mixture over the first layer of ladyfingers. Spread to create an even, smooth layer of mascarpone.

5. Dip the remaining 20 ladyfingers into the espresso mixture, turning them once to wet both sides, and arrange them in a single layer on top of the mascarpone layer. I end up using all of the Amaretto-espresso mixture; so make sure you get enough liquid on the cookies. Break the cookies up to fill the entire dish in 1 layer.

6. Pour the remaining half of the mascarpone mixture over the second layer of ladyfingers. Spread to create an even, smooth layer. Cover with plastic wrap and refrigerate at least 4 hours but ideally overnight.

7. When ready to serve, remove the plastic wrap from the tiramisu. Combine the cocoa powder and cinnamon and sift over the top. Slice into cake-size rectangles with a knife or even your spatula, and serve on individual plates. If you'd like a more rustic serving, spoon the tiramisu out onto each plate. Serve very soon after it's ready, but it will keep in the fridge tightly wrapped 1 to 2 days (though it will get boozier as it sits).

GIFT WRAP

Parchment paper
Clear tape
Ribbon

Cut a piece of parchment paper to three times the width of your baking dish. Trim the width of the paper, as needed, to match the length of your baking dish. Place the parchment flat on a table and arrange the baking dish in the center. Fold up both flaps of parchment over the baking dish, and place a few small pieces of tape to stick them together. Cut a large length of ribbon and lay it flat on a table. Place the wrapped baking dish in the center of the ribbon. Fold up the ribbon and tie off in a bow. Trim the ribbon, if necessary.

panna cotta cups

MAKES: 6 (½-CUP) DESSERTS // PREPARATION TIME: 15 MINUTES ACTIVE TIME
(UP TO 12 HOURS TOTAL TIME)

This recipe is the embodiment of *Food Gift Love*. It's one of the first desserts I made for a big potluck, and when the crowd loved it, I felt like a superhero. I now cart dozens of panna cotta jars, along with a trio of homemade jams, to parties, encouraging folks to create their own dessert. I typically make this gift about 8 hours before I need it or in the morning for gifting that evening.

The Greek yogurt tastes healthy but, more importantly, provides a pleasant tang that blends with heavy cream to make for a rich cup. The sweetness, however, is muted purposefully because the homemade Quick Strawberry Jam is sweet enough. If you plan to serve this without jam, increase the sugar in the panna cotta just a bit. I prefer panna cotta that is thick but less bouncy and gelatinous. If you prefer a firmer set, increase the powdered gelatin to 2 teaspoons.

INGREDIENTS:

2 tablespoons lemon juice

2 tablespoons water

1 teaspoon powdered gelatin

½ cup granulated sugar

¾ cup plus 1 cup heavy cream, separated

1 teaspoon vanilla extract

1 teaspoon lemon zest

1 cup plain Greek-style yogurt

1¼ cups Quick Strawberry Jam (page 185)

SPECIAL EQUIPMENT:

6 (½-cup) glasses or jars

1. Place the lemon juice and water in a small bowl. Sprinkle the powdered gelatin on top and let sit 15 minutes.

2. In a medium pot over medium-low heat, combine the sugar, the ¾ cup cream, and the vanilla extract. Bring to a very low simmer (do not boil) just until the sugar dissolves. Swirl the pot a few times to help it along.

3. Meanwhile, in a separate large mixing bowl or extra-large measuring cup, whisk the remaining 1 cup cream, the lemon zest, and Greek yogurt until smooth and combined.

4. When the warm mixture has completely dissolved, remove from the heat and whisk in the lemon juice–water-gelatin mixture until combined. Slowly pour the warm mixture in a steady stream into the cream–lemon zest–Greek yogurt mixture, whisking continually until combined and well blended.

5. Arrange 6 glasses on a small tray, pan, or large plate, and in advance prepare a spot in the fridge that fits the tray. Pour the panna cotta mixture evenly into the 6 glasses. Place the tray in the fridge and let set at least 6 hours or up to 12 hours. If you plan to keep the panna cotta in the fridge 12-plus hours, then cover each glass with a small piece of plastic wrap—this prevents the panna cotta from absorbing any fridge odors.

6. Remove the plastic wrap and serve with a dollop of strawberry jam.

7. To gift, use clean glass jars and cover with the lids or plastic wrap during travel time. To serve, let recipients top their panna cotta with spoonfuls of strawberry jam.

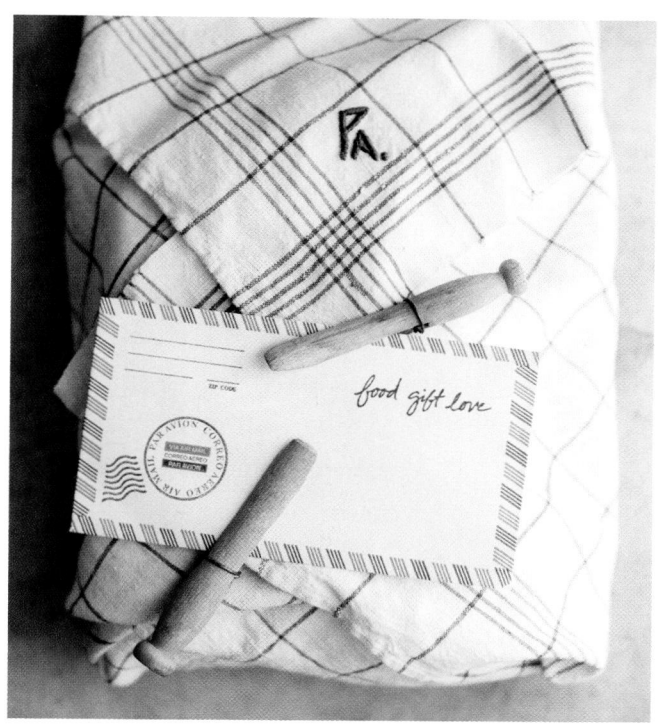

GIFT WRAP

Tray
Kitchen towel
Clothespins
Envelope (or tag)

Place the covered jars, including the jam, on a small tray. Spread out an extra-large kitchen towel that will completely cover the tray on a clean surface, and place the tray in the center. Fold up each side of the towel. Secure the towel in place, loosely, with clothespins. Write the label on an envelope and attach it with the clothespins.

pantry gifts

Your pantry can be an easy source of *Food Gift Love*. It might already be stocked with essentials to pull together a favorite dinner or a batch of prize cookies, but many near-effortless food gifts like flavored seasonings, herbs, extracts, and dressings can be made in advance and stored. The avid home cook or baker in your life will most definitely dig these unique gifts, the sort they may ogle in the specialty food shop but rarely buy for themselves.

This chapter provides simple recipes for foundation ingredients that are always in my kitchen. On a regular basis, I use, gift, and replenish every single one. When I need a gift in a rush, I reach into my pantry to pull a jar from my stash or quickly fill a gift bottle from a larger batch in storage—and you can, too. Just add a length of ribbon and a little note with winning uses for these prime pantry possessions.

◆

sage jars

MAKES: 3 OR 4 (2-OUNCE) JARS // PREPARATION TIME: 30 MINUTES ACTIVE TIME
(UP TO 4 WEEKS TOTAL TIME)

I tend a large garden behind my home and grow all sorts of perennial herbs. Sage is a hardy herb that just keeps on giving—the more I grow, the more I preserve, the more I cook with and gift it, the more I want to grow. One small pot became a 2-foot pot, and now I dedicate a 4-foot by 4-foot bed to sage. In sharp contrast to soft leaf herbs like basil or parsley that don't stand up to cold temperatures, sage is one of the last herbs to die off before winter. In fact, when my travel schedule keeps me away, it even dries on the stem. (Save the stems to add flavor to a smoker to smoke meat or the holiday turkey; or try them as makeshift skewers to seal gift bags; more on that later.)

Sage is an often-underestimated seasoning that can make so many foods come alive with toasty flavor. Sweet potatoes and white potatoes—roasted or baked—are wonderful sprinkled with sage. Poultry and pork get quickly rubbed with dried sage just before a quick pan-fry. And browned butter with sage is an easy dressing for pasta, raviolis, butternut squash chunks, or even sweet potato gnocchi. Every autumn, feel the love for sage by drying them bunches at a time and then giving some away all year long.

INGREDIENTS:

2 bunches (about 2 ounces each) sage

SPECIAL EQUIPMENT:

3 or 4 (2-ounce) jars (glass or other style) with airtight lids

1. Scout out a place in your kitchen to hang sage bunches. Look for a spot that permits the herbs to hang freely with air circulating around them and that won't be in the way of tall (or short) people standing upright. I prefer to use a chandelier, but a window latch or even an exposed shelf will work.

2. Split each bunch of sage in half to form 4 small bunches. For each bunch, tie one end of kitchen string tightly around the stem end. Make a double knot. Cut the long end of the string to a 12-inch length. Repeat for the remaining bunches.

3. Tie the long end of the string (attached to each bunch) to your drying spot. Let dry 3 to 4 weeks until crisp and brittle to the touch.

4. Once dried, carefully untie or remove the string. Over a piece of parchment paper, pull the leaves off of the stems and save the stems for another use. Pile all the dried sage leaves in the center of the parchment paper and, with your fingers, break up the leaves into smaller bits. The air around you will begin to become aromatic.

5. Fill clean and dry jars with all of your herbs and seal. Store in an airtight container up to 1 year.

GIFT WRAP

Jars (glass or other style) with airtight lids

Wire

Masking tape

Fill a jar with sage and seal. Cut a longer bit of wire and a longer bit of tape. Fold the tape over a section of the wire, matching up one end of the tape to the other perfectly. Trim the end to create a little flag. Write the label on the tape, vertically. Tie the wire around the jar, twisting to create a tight hold. Trim any excess wire and turn the tips in to prevent scraping.

herbes de provence jars

MAKES: 3 OR 4 (2-OUNCE) JARS // PREPARATION TIME: 30 MINUTES ACTIVE TIME
(UP TO 4 WEEKS TOTAL TIME)

When I returned from my first long trip to Paris, I brought souvenirs for all my friends and family. In fact, I began making these mementos weeks earlier by drying bunches of fresh herbs from the organic outdoor market at Boulevard Raspail. I hung the herbs around my temporary Paris flat and, once dried, pulled the leaves into plastic bags for the journey home.

The following is my recipe for Herbes de Provence, a medley of herbs typically grown, dried, and used in dishes all over the south of France. The collection varies by region; some swap in lavender or fennel or even savory and rosemary. My favorite assortment follows and, mixed with a little coarse sea salt, it makes a fragrant and savory Infused Sea Salt (page 90).

INGREDIENTS:

1 bunch (1 to 2 ounces) sage

1 bunch (1 to 2 ounces) thyme

1 bunch (1 to 2 ounces) marjoram

1 bunch (1 to 2 ounces) oregano

SPECIAL EQUIPMENT:

3 or 4 (2-ounce) jars (glass or other) with airtight lids

1. Scout out a place in your kitchen to hang herb bunches. Look for a spot that permits the herbs to hang freely with air circulating around them and that won't be in the way of tall (or short) people standing upright. I prefer to use a chandelier, but a window latch or even an exposed shelf will work.

2. Split each herb bunch in half to form 8 small bunches. Tie one end of kitchen string tightly around the stem end of an herb bunch. Make a double knot. Cut the long end of the string to a 12-inch length. Repeat for the remaining bunches.

3. Tie the long end of the string (attached to each bunch) to your drying spot. Let dry 3 to 4 weeks until crisp and brittle to the touch.

4. Once dried, carefully untie or remove the string. Over a piece of parchment paper, pull the leaves off of the stems and save the stems for another use. Pile all the dried herb leaves in the center of the parchment paper and, with your fingers, break up the leaves into smaller bits, mixing the different herbs together. The air around you will begin to become aromatic.

5. Fill clean and dry jars with all of your herbs and seal. Store in an airtight container up to 1 year.

GIFT WRAP

Fabric stamp

Small drawstring muslin bag

Resealable, food-grade cellophane bags (optional)

Stamp a design of your choosing on the muslin bag. Give it a few moments to dry, and then fill with the herbs. To preserve the flavor even longer, place the herbs into a small plastic bag before sliding into the muslin bag. Pull strings to close the bag.

mint tea

MAKES: 3 OR 4 (2-OUNCE) JARS // PREPARATION TIME: 30 MINUTES ACTIVE TIME
(UP TO 4 WEEKS TOTAL TIME)

Although mint has a tendency to spread fast, it doesn't take over my garden each summer. I learned early on that mint is best grown in a pot, bound by its sides. Still, its weed-like abundance fuels my cooking and gifting inspiration at the end of each season. I cut it down and dry it for Mint Tea (for me and friends). It's wonderful all winter long in brew pots spiked with honey and lemon. Add 2 tablespoons of loose leaves to a pot of boiling water or just a heaping teaspoon to a single mug.

Mint comes in all different varieties from the most recognizable, like peppermint and spearmint, to more unique and fruity varieties like chocolate mint, apple mint, or even pineapple mint. The standard types are great in sweet and savory dishes—add a small handful to brighten your next pesto; the chocolate mint takes brownies to a whole other level; and, the fruitier varieties are just right in tea, in drink syrups, and tossed into salads. I grow several varieties and accent my kitchen with strung-up bouquets during the fall harvest. Store-bought mint bunches vary in size and weight, so just go with your gut here. You may need a few extra jars for weighty bunches, but that would be a nice surprise. If you don't have enough small jars, just put the extra dried leaves in a large jar in your pantry and portion it out as the gifting requires.

INGREDIENTS:

2 bunches (2 to 3 ounces each) mint, organic

SPECIAL EQUIPMENT:

3 to 4 (2-ounce) jars (glass or other) with airtight lids

1. Scout out a place in your kitchen to hang bunches of mint. Look for a spot that permits the herbs to hang freely with air circulating all around them and that won't be in the way of tall (or short) people standing upright. I prefer to use a chandelier, but a window latch or even an exposed shelf will work.

2. Split each bunch of mint into 2 small bunches to form 4 small bunches. Tie one end of kitchen string tightly around the stem end of a bunch of mint. Make a double knot. Cut the long end of the string to a 12-inch length. Repeat for the remaining bunches.

3. Tie the long end of the string (attached to each bunch) to your drying spot. Let dry 3 to 4 weeks until crisp and brittle to the touch.

4. Once dried, carefully untie or remove the string. Over a piece of parchment paper, pull the leaves off of the stems and save the stems for another use. Pile all the dried mint leaves in the center of the parchment paper and leave them whole.

5. Fill clean and dry jars with all of your mint and seal. Store in an airtight container up to 1 year.

GIFT WRAP

Jars (glass or other) with airtight lids

Washi tape

Fill jars with mint and seal. Cut a length of tape longer than the height and depth of each jar. Write the label on the end of the tape, vertically. Stick one end of the tape to the side of the jar, then wrap it around and over the top then down to the opposite side of the jar. Tuck it into the nooks of the jar. Trim the ends.

how to dry herbs

Choose Your Method There are two ways to dry herbs. Air-drying works best for herbs that hold less moisture, like thyme, sage, oregano, and lavender. In this cookbook, I feature mostly low-moisture, woody-stemmed herbs; they hold their shape well and dry rather quickly. Herbs with more moisture, like basil, parsley, and chives, are most easily dried in a dehydrator or a very low oven. If you don't have a dehydrator, you may still air-dry these types of herbs—it will just take a little longer to remove all that extra moisture.

Clean Your Herbs Before drying, herbs should be rinsed well and patted dry with a clean towel to remove as much moisture as possible. Make sure to inspect your stems and remove wilted leaves, insects, or any undesired (spotted, damaged) leaves.

Dry Your Herbs Gather a few stems into a small bunch and tie with kitchen string or a rubber band (in this case, affix a bit of string to hang). The smaller your bunch, the quicker they will dry.

Scout out a spot in your kitchen to hang the herbs upside down freely such that air circulates around them and they won't be in the way of people standing upright or passing by. You can attach to a chandelier, window latch, or exposed shelf. If you have a drafty or dusty kitchen, place the bunch in a paper bag and secure the end of the bag closed with a rubber band, taking care not to crush the herbs. Poke a few holes in the bag and hang.

Your herbs will be dried within 3 to 4 weeks. You'll know the herbs are dry when they crumble between your fingers.

Sort Your Herbs Place a clean piece of parchment paper on a table or on a large baking sheet. Carefully strip the leaves from the stems onto the parchment paper. If the leaves are larger, like with mint or sage, you may break them up into smaller bits. Reserve the stems for gift wrap or adding flavor to something you cook in a wood smoker. When you've stripped all the leaves, gather the ends of the parchment paper into a funnel-like shape and let the herbs slide into your storage container.

Store Your Herbs Herbs can be stored in any airtight container for long-term storage—like canning jars or freezer bags. Label and date the herbs, and use them within 1 year.

thyme honey

MAKES: 1 CUP // PREPARATION TIME: 20 MINUTES

My pantry is packed with dried herbs and many varieties of honey, both local and from as far away as Hawaii, Greece, and Italy, so it's no surprise that one day they met in the form of an infused honey. An infused honey preserves the herb flavor and combines the healthful properties of both the honey and the herbs. I grow and dry piles of lemon balm each harvest specifically to add its flavor and throat-soothing properties to my favorite local honey. I also love to infuse thyme into honey; it makes for a beautiful flavor to drizzle over a hard or runny cheese.

You can use your favorite local honey, just use a lightly flavored style. A deeply flavored honey, like a chestnut honey, may stifle the herb flavor. For flavoring, feel free to use any herb. My favorites to steep in honey are thyme, lemon balm, sage, oregano, mint, and lavender. You can also add some citrus zest to make an even more complex honey.

INGREDIENTS:

4 tablespoons dried thyme leaves, home-dried (opposite) or store-bought

1 cup light-flavored honey

SPECIAL EQUIPMENT:

Double boiler

Candy thermometer

4 (2-ounce) jars with airtight lids, sterilized

1. In a double boiler set over medium heat, place a bit of water in the bottom pot—making sure the water doesn't touch the underside of the top pot. Assemble the double boiler. (If you do not have a double boiler, place a metal or glass bowl on top of a medium pot.)

2. Crush the thyme leaves between your fingers. Place the thyme and honey in the top of the double boiler. Heat until just shy of 180°F, about 10 to 12 minutes—this will loosen it up without cooking it. Remove from the heat and let sit at room temperature 30 minutes.

3. Strain the honey through a sieve into a bowl to remove the herbs, pushing on the herbs with a spatula to extract all the honey; discard the herbs. Pour the honey into jars and store at room temperature up to 6 months.

GIFT WRAP

Glass jar with airtight lids

New kitchen towel

String

Tag

Safety pin

Fill a jar with honey. Wipe the rim and seal. Wrap it with a large kitchen towel, gathering all the ends up and tying them into place with string. Write the label on a tag, and thread the safety pin through the tag and towel. Secure in place.

infused sea salts

Many years ago, I spent a few days in Venice. Jet-lagged and bleary, I stumbled off the Venice Santa Lucia train and onto a water taxi with throngs of other travelers. Along with a native chef friend, I was swiftly deposited at the Rialto Market, a series of stalls rich with seafood that looked both familiar and strange and mountains of fresh fruits and vegetables. I like to call it Italian heaven.

We made our way through the market and sat down at a tiny table along the canal. As if knowing I was in no shape to make any decisions, my friend Davide ordered two Proseccos, a dry sparkling wine from the region, and two salads that were loaded with fresh produce from the nearby vendors. This salad was a thing of glory, filled with the first crop of paper-thin sliced fennel, sweet orange segments, and briny black olives. It was lightly dressed with a bit of olive oil and sea salt, and not much else. Heaven, indeed.

From that short trip, I returned with an extensive collection of food gifts but also the determination to preserve the memory of that salad. I created a coarse sea salt infused with dried fennel seeds and orange zest. Mixed with a bit of Italian olive oil, my Orange-Fennel Sea Salt dresses vegetables and takes me back to that moment along the canal. Even if you've never been to Venice, this blend will be a simple, special way to imagine that you're there.

Infused sea salts are the easiest food gifts. First, they don't really require cooking, unless the ingredient needs fast drying, which makes them ideal crafts during travel. They're versatile, emerging quite beautifully from elevated ingredients, like saffron, and also from everyday ingredients, like dried herbs from a jar. Their measurements are also forgiving because there are no hard rules to proportions: if you like more flavoring, add more flavoring!

The sea salt choice is up to you; however, consider whether you're making a salt to cook with, to bake with, or to finish a dish. If you intend for someone to sprinkle the sea salt on a freshly grilled steak or even my Chocolate Truffles (page 130), go with a flakey sea salt. If you plan to salt a roast chicken, then a medium-style coarse sea salt works well. And if the gift is for a baker, use a fine sea salt, or even grind up the end result so it will dissolve more easily during baking. I use various techniques to conjure my sea salt concoctions, from drying citrus in the oven to mashing flavor directly into salt grains with a mortar and pestle. Take all my recipes as guides to create your own signature blends.

Regardless of the infusion you choose to make, you can gift them all the same way. Fill a jar with the sea salt, wipe the rim, and seal. Write the label on the inside of a small sea shell (one with a natural hole) or on a tag. Thread a piece of string through the shell or tag hole and tie around the jar. Trim any excess string.

◆

LEMON SEA SALT

MAKES: 1 CUP

PREPARATION TIME: 20 MINUTES

INGREDIENTS:

2 large lemons

1 cup coarse or fine sea salt

SPECIAL EQUIPMENT:

Microplane zester

1. Preheat the oven to 150°F (or the next lowest possible temperature; some ovens only go down to 170°F). Wash and dry the lemons.

2. Line a large baking sheet with parchment paper. Over the lined baking sheet and with a zester, remove the top layer of the skin of each lemon, taking care to avoid any white pith. Measure the zest into tablespoon-size portions as you work. Once you've collected 2 tablespoons of zest, lightly move your fingers (or a fork) across the top of the zest to spread it evenly across the lined baking sheet. Bake 10 minutes or until the zest is fragrant and dry but not browned. (Don't expect the aroma alone to signify your zest is ready; it should be crispy and dry to the touch.) Remove the zest from the oven and let cool 2 to 3 minutes.

3. In a small bowl, add the zest and salt. Stir with a fork (or clean fingers) until well combined and the salt is very fragrant. Store in an airtight container up to 6 months.

◆

ORANGE-FENNEL SEA SALT

MAKES: 1 CUP

PREPARATION TIME: 20 MINUTES

INGREDIENTS:

2 large oranges

1 tablespoon fennel seeds

1 cup coarse sea salt

SPECIAL EQUIPMENT:

Microplane zester

1. Preheat the oven to 150°F (or the next lowest possible temperature; some ovens only go down to 170°F). Wash and dry the oranges.

2. Line a large baking sheet with parchment paper. Over the lined baking sheet and with a zester, remove the top layer of the skin of each orange, taking care to avoid any white pith. Measure the zest into tablespoon-size portions as you work. Once you've collected 2 tablespoons of zest, lightly move your fingers (or a fork) across the top of the zest to spread it evenly across the lined baking sheet. Bake 10 minutes or until the zest is fragrant and dry but not browned. (Don't expect the aroma alone to signify your zest is ready; it should be crispy and dry to the touch.) Remove the zest from the oven and let cool 2 to 3 minutes.

3. In a small bowl, add the zest, fennel seeds, and salt. Stir with a fork (or clean fingers) until well combined and the salt is very fragrant. Store in an airtight container up to 6 months.

HERBY SEA SALT

MAKES: 1 CUP
PREPARATION TIME: 10 MINUTES

___

INGREDIENTS:

1 tablespoon of your
favorite dried herb,
freshly dried (if
possible)

1 cup coarse sea salt

SPECIAL EQUIPMENT:

Mortar and pestle

1. With a sharp kitchen knife, chop the dried herbs into tiny bits no more than ⅛ inch long, though there's no need to be too precise.

2. In a mortar, add the chopped dried herbs and the sea salt. Using the pestle, grind the herbs into the sea salt until the salt takes on the perfume from your favorite herb. Store in an airtight container up to 6 months.

VANILLA SEA SALT

MAKES: 1 CUP
PREPARATION TIME: 10 MINUTES

___

INGREDIENTS:

1 vanilla bean, split
lengthwise

1 cup coarse or fine sea
salt

SPECIAL EQUIPMENT:

Mortar and pestle

1. Using the back of a knife, strip the seeds from each side of the vanilla bean.

2. In a mortar, add the vanilla bean seeds and the salt. Using the pestle, grind the seeds into the salt until the salt takes on the perfume of the vanilla and the beans are well dispersed. Slice the vanilla bean halves in half again and place the pieces in the sea salt to add extra vanilla flavor, or reserve them for your Vanilla Extract (page 101). Store in an airtight container up to 6 months.

SAFFRON SEA SALT

MAKES: 1 CUP
PREPARATION TIME: 10 MINUTES

___

INGREDIENTS:

1 tablespoon saffron
threads

1 cup coarse sea salt

SPECIAL EQUIPMENT:

Mortar and pestle

1. With a sharp knife, chop the saffron threads into tiny thread bits about ⅛ inch long, though there's no need to be too precise.

2. In a mortar, add the chopped saffron and the salt. Using the pestle, grind the saffron into the sea salt until the salt takes on a beautiful orange-like hue with flecks of red threads. Store in an airtight container up to 6 months.

citrus sugars

MAKES: 2 CUPS // PREPARATION TIME: 25 MINUTES

You may juice citrus regularly but perhaps don't realize what you're missing: all the flavor from the peel. Citrus zest brightens so many recipes, but if you have citrus sugar in your pantry, you've got a wonderfully fragrant gift. Keep it tucked away for sprinkling on cookies; rimming the glass of a tart cocktail, such as my Margarita Mix (page 236); or gifting to your favorite baker or mixologist who will delight in the flavors of preserved sunshine.

This recipe is for a lemon-lime version, but follow the fruit on your counter. I've used many combinations of orange, lemon, lime, and grapefruit to great results. (It's also easy enough to vary with other flavorings: I keep both lavender sugar and rose sugar on hand.) As a general rule of thumb, mix 2 tablespoons dried zest or culinary grade flowers to 1 cup granulated sugar, but this is a very forgiving recipe, so have fun with it. The flavorings are so pretty as is, but if you're using the floral sugars for baking, crush them in a grinder so the flavor blends into your batter well without big textural bits. If you don't choose organic fruit, just make sure to scrub the peel well before zesting.

INGREDIENTS:

2 large lemons

3 medium limes

2 cups granulated sugar

SPECIAL EQUIPMENT:

Microplane zester

1. Preheat the oven to 150°F (or the lowest possible temperature; some ovens only go down to 170°F). Wash and dry the citrus fruit.

2. Line a large baking sheet with parchment paper. Over the lined baking sheet and with a zester, remove the top layer of the skin of each citrus fruit, taking care to avoid any white pith. Measure the zest into tablespoon-size portions as you work. Once you've collected 2 tablespoons of lemon zest and 2 tablespoons of lime zest, lightly move your fingers (or a fork) across the top of the zest to spread it evenly across the lined baking sheet. Bake 10 minutes or until the zest is fragrant and dry but not browned. (Don't expect the aroma alone to signify your zest is ready; it should be crispy and dry to the touch.) Remove the zest from the oven and let cool 2 to 3 minutes.

3. In a small bowl, stir together the sugar and the zest with a fork 2 to 3 minutes until well combined and the sugar—and the air around it—is sweetly perfumed. Store in an airtight container up to 6 months.

GIFT WRAP

Glass jar (glass or other style) with airtight lid

Vintage ribbon

Typewriter (optional)

Tag

Fill a jar with the citrus sugar. Wipe the rim and seal. Cut a piece of ribbon and wrap it around the lid of the sealed jar a few times. Tie it in a knot and trim the ends. Type (if using a typewriter) the label on a tag and slide it between ribbon and jar.

cinnamon sugar

MAKES: 1 CUP // PREPARATION TIME: 5 MINUTES

Cinnamon Sugar is a sweet food gift that feels familiar and brand-new at the same time. Just one sprinkle triggers memories of apple picking or swirly coffee drinks. I prefer a super-fragrant Cinnamon Sugar, so a hearty one-eighth of the mixture is spice here; you can decide your own perfect ratio. Loaded with flavor, this gift is made for morning coffee and toast, breakfast smoothies, fresh cider, and just-baked sugar cookies.

INGREDIENTS:

1 cup granulated sugar

2 tablespoons ground
   cinnamon

SPECIAL EQUIPMENT:

1 pint jar with airtight lid

Add the sugar and cinnamon to a jar. Seal the jar and shake, shake, shake until well distributed and the cinnamon sugar becomes the color of light brown sugar. Store in an airtight container up to 1 year.

GIFT WRAP

Vintage sugar
container

Ribbon

Cinnamon sticks

Fill a clean vintage container with the sugar. Wipe the rim and seal. Wrap a length of ribbon around the rim of the container. Before tying off in a knot, slip a 2-inch piece of cinnamon stick into the knot.

coffee rub

MAKES: ABOUT ½ CUP // PREPARATION TIME: 10 MINUTES

Every summer, I host an all-day barbecue bash that seems to begin in the morning and end the next day. I don't plan for it to be a 24-hour party, but folks come by to share a beer to cool us down while we're cooking . . . and then stick around. Some seem to linger into the wee hours to take a final pass at the spread before it's put away. Several days before the big meal, I mix up a batch of this rub for all the various meats that will grace the grill or the smoker.

This is my standby meat recipe. It plays beautifully as a "Cowboy Rub," a mixture made especially to put on a bone-in rib-eye steak (where a cleaned part of the bone is used as a handle by a cowboy). For that use, I like to grind the rub into a very fine powder. Grinding helps to better distribute the flavor across the surface of the meat.

Six great uses for this Coffee Rub include: (1) press into a rib-eye steak 1 to 2 hours prior to cooking, (2) press into pork ribs up to 24 hours before smoking or grilling, (3) press into a pork shoulder about 12 to 24 hours before cooking, (4) add a few tablespoons to a slow cooker with a pork shoulder and vegetable stock, (5) rub all over chicken wings a few hours before roasting in the oven, and (6) make a paste with this rub and extra-virgin olive oil to drizzle over cleaned mushrooms before grilling.

When I get an invitation to a barbecue, I gift this Coffee Rub. Sometimes I even gift it with a few steaks or chicken wings or even a pile of big portobello mushrooms.

INGREDIENTS:

- 2 tablespoons sea salt
- 2 tablespoons ground coffee
- 1 tablespoon sweet (not spicy) paprika
- 1 tablespoon dark brown sugar, loosely packed
- 1 tablespoon chili powder
- 1 tablespoon dried oregano
- 1 teaspoon freshly ground black pepper
- 1 teaspoon ground cumin
- 1 tablespoon garlic powder (optional)

1. In a small bowl, add the salt, coffee, paprika, sugar, chili powder, oregano, pepper, cumin, and garlic powder (if using). Whisk to combine, and then use your clean hands to mash the spices further into the soft brown sugar. The resulting rub will be the color of dark clay with flecks of brown and red.

2. You can further intensify the flavor by grinding the rub into a fine powder using a spice grinder or food processor, but that's optional.

3. Store in an airtight container at room temperature up to 6 months or up to 1 year in the freezer.

GIFT WRAP

Small tins with lids

Tape

Fill a tin with the rub and seal. Write the label on a bit of tape. Stick the tape to the tin.

brown sugar rub

MAKES: ABOUT 1 CUP // PREPARATION TIME: 10 MINUTES

A rub is a dry mixture of herbs, salt, and spices added before cooking for a coating of intense flavor that seeps into your foods and is your secret weapon for amazingly flavorful meat (or veggies).

Once you cook with this rub, you will understand how amazing it is as a gift to an interested home cook. Rub it on a chicken breast or all over a pork loin. Sprinkle it over carrots before roasting. And slow-roasted ribs or chicken wings just love this rub—the slow cooking pulls out all the right sweet notes. Although there are savory flavorings in the Brown Sugar Rub, it is sweeter than the Coffee Rub (page 97), so choose the right recipe for you or your gift recipient.

INGREDIENTS:

½ cup light brown sugar, loosely packed

3 tablespoons fine sea salt

1 tablespoon dry mustard powder

1 tablespoon ground ginger

1 tablespoon sweet (not spicy) paprika

1 tablespoon garlic powder

1 tablespoon chili powder

1 tablespoon dried sage

1. In a small bowl, add the brown sugar, salt, mustard powder, ginger, paprika, garlic powder, chili powder, and dried sage. Whisk to combine, and then use your clean hands to mash the spices into the brown sugar. The resulting rub will be the color of creamy coffee with a hint of red.

2. You may further intensify the flavor by grinding the rub into a fine powder using a spice grinder or food processor, but this is optional.

3. Store in an airtight container at room temperature up to 6 months or up to 1 year in the freezer.

GIFT WRAP

Jar (glass or other style) with airtight lid

Tape

Fill a jar with the rub. Wipe the rim and seal. Write the label on a bit of tape. Stick the tape to the side of the jar. (Add a little extra tape to secure the lid of the jar, if needed.)

homemade extracts

I have about ten amazing bakers in my immediate circle of friends. They share the delights of their kitchens with me regularly, at dinner parties, at the holidays, or just because. I thank them in kind with baked goods, naturally, as well as these extracts to fuel their baking adventures.

These extracts are not sweetened. They are just the pure flavors extracted into vodka, a natural food and flavor preserver. When you apply very high heat to the extract for an extended period of time (for example, when you bake a cake), the alcohol evaporates and leaves only flavor essence.

GIFT WRAP

Medicine-style bottles, sterilized

Handheld tape embosser

Fill bottles with the extract and seal. Type the label on tape with a handheld tape embosser and stick onto the bottle.

VANILLA EXTRACT

MAKES: 2 CUPS
PREPARATION TIME: 10 MINUTES ACTIVE TIME
(UP TO 2 WEEKS TOTAL TIME)

INGREDIENTS:

2 cups vodka

6 vanilla beans, split lengthwise

Extra vanilla beans, for garnish (optional)

SPECIAL EQUIPMENT:

1 large glass jar with airtight lid, sterilized

4 (4-ounce) or 8 (2-ounce) medicine-style bottles, sterilized

Narrow-mouth funnel

1. Add the vodka and vanilla beans to the jar and seal. Shake a few times to distribute the beans. Write the name and date on a piece of tape and adhere to the jar—this will remind you when to check the infusion. Place the jar in a dark spot in your kitchen, shaking every couple of days to distribute the vanilla bean flavor. After 2 weeks, the extract can be bottled in a new large sterilized jar or bottle, garnished with a vanilla bean (if using), and presented as a gift. However, the extract gets better the longer it sits. You can keep the extract in your pantry and portion it out into new sterilized bottles as the gifting occasion requires.

2. Store at room temperature up to 1 year. Once you use up half of the extract, add another cup of vodka and 2 to 3 extra vanilla beans to keep the extract going, and repeat the above steps for infusing.

CINNAMON EXTRACT

MAKES: 2 CUPS
PREPARATION TIME: 10 MINUTES ACTIVE TIME
(UP TO 2 WEEKS TOTAL TIME)

INGREDIENTS:

2 cups vodka

6 (4-inch) cinnamon sticks

Extra cinnamon sticks, for garnish (optional)

SPECIAL EQUIPMENT:

1 large glass jar with airtight lid, sterilized

4 (4-ounce) or 8 (2-ounce) medicine-style bottles, sterilized

Narrow-mouth funnel

1. Add the vodka and cinnamon sticks to a large jar and seal. Shake a few times. Write the name and date on a piece of tape and adhere to the jar—this will remind you when to check the infusion. Place the jar in a dark spot in your kitchen, shaking every couple of days to distribute the cinnamon flavor. After 2 weeks, the extract can be bottled in a new sterilized jar or bottle, garnished with a cinnamon stick (if using), and presented as a gift. However, the extract gets better the longer it sits. You can keep the extract in your pantry and portion it out into new sterilized bottles as the gifting occasion requires.

2. Store at room temperature up to 1 year. Once you use up half of the extract, add another cup of vodka and 2 to 3 extra cinnamon sticks to keep the extract going, and repeat the above steps for infusing.

COFFEE EXTRACT

MAKES: 2 CUPS

PREPARATION TIME: 10 MINUTES ACTIVE TIME
(UP TO 5 DAYS TOTAL TIME)

INGREDIENTS:

2 cups vodka

½ cup coffee beans, coarsely ground

Extra whole coffee beans, for garnish (optional)

SPECIAL EQUIPMENT:

1 large glass jar with airtight lid, sterilized

Sieve lined with cheesecloth or coffee filter

4 (4-ounce) or 8 (2-ounce) medicine-style bottles, sterilized

1. Add the vodka and ground coffee to a large jar and seal. Shake a few times to distribute the coffee. Write the name and date on a piece of tape and adhere to the jar—this will remind you when to check the infusion. Place the jar in a dark spot in your kitchen, shaking every couple of days to distribute the coffee flavor. After 5 days, strain the extract through cheesecloth or a coffee filter to remove and discard the coffee grounds. The extract can be placed in a new sterilized jar or bottle, garnished with a few whole coffee beans (if using), and presented as a gift. However, it gets better the longer it sits. You can keep the extract in your pantry and portion it out into new sterilized bottles as the gifting occasion requires.

2. Store at room temperature up to 1 year. Once you use up half of the extract, add another cup of vodka and 4 tablespoons ground coffee to keep the extract going, and repeat the above steps for infusing.

ALMOND EXTRACT

MAKES: 2 CUPS

PREPARATION TIME: 10 MINUTES ACTIVE TIME
(UP TO 8 WEEKS TOTAL TIME)

INGREDIENTS:

2 cups vodka

1 cup sliced and peeled raw or blanched almonds

Extra peeled almonds, for garnish (optional)

SPECIAL EQUIPMENT:

1 large glass jar with airtight lid, sterilized

Sieve lined with cheesecloth

Coffee filter

4 (4-ounce) or 8 (2-ounce) medicine-style bottles, sterilized

Narrow-mouth funnel

1. Add the vodka and almonds to a large jar and seal. Shake a few times to distribute the almonds. Write the name and date on a piece of tape and adhere to the jar—this will remind you when to check the infusion. Place the jar in a dark spot in your kitchen, shaking every couple of days to distribute the almond flavor. After 4 weeks, strain the extract through cheesecloth to remove and discard the almonds. (If you have the time, wait 8 weeks for optimal flavor because the extract gets better the longer it sits.) Strain it again through a coffee filter to remove any extra particles.

2. The extract can be bottled in new sterilized jars or bottles, garnished with 2 to 3 skinned almonds (if using) per jar, and presented as a gift. Alternatively, you can keep the large jar of extract in your pantry and portion it out into new sterilized bottles as the gifting occasion requires.

3. Store at room temperature up to 1 year. Once you use up half of the extract, add another cup of vodka and ½ cup almonds to keep the extract going, and repeat the above steps for infusing.

HAZELNUT EXTRACT

MAKES: 2 CUPS

PREPARATION TIME: 10 MINUTES ACTIVE TIME
(UP TO 6 WEEKS TOTAL TIME)

INGREDIENTS:

1 cup hazelnuts

2 cups vodka

SPECIAL EQUIPMENT:

1 large glass jar with
airtight lid, sterilized

Sieve lined with
cheesecloth

Coffee filter

4 (4-ounce) or 8 (2-ounce)
medicine-style bottles,
sterilized

Narrow-mouth funnel

1. Preheat the oven to 350°F. Spread the hazelnuts in a single layer on a cookie sheet. Roast 10 minutes or until the skins begin to pull away from the nuts and the kitchen smells fragrant. Remove the cookie sheet from the oven and let cool 10 minutes. Rub the skins off of the hazelnuts with a kitchen towel until they're mostly removed. Discard the skins.

2. With a sharp knife or in the bowl of a food processor, chop half the hazelnuts. Add the vodka and all the hazelnuts to a large jar and seal. Shake a few times to distribute the hazelnuts. Write the name and date on a piece of tape and adhere to the jar—this will remind you when to check the infusion. Place the jar in a dark spot in your kitchen, shaking every couple of days to distribute the hazelnut flavor. After 3 weeks, strain through cheesecloth to remove and discard the hazelnuts. (If you have the time, wait 4 to 6 weeks for optimal flavor because the extract gets better the longer it sits.) Strain 2 more times through a coffee filter to remove any extra particles.

3. The extract can be bottled in new sterilized jars or bottles, garnished with 2 to 3 skinned hazelnuts, and presented as a gift. Alternatively, you can keep the large jar of extract in your pantry and portion it out into new sterilized bottles as the gifting occasion requires.

4. Store at room temperature up to 1 year. Once you use up half of the extract, add another cup of vodka and ½ cup roasted, shelled, and hand-chopped hazelnuts to keep the extract going, and repeat the above steps for infusing.

COCONUT EXTRACT

MAKES: 2 CUPS

PREPARATION TIME: 90 MINUTES ACTIVE TIME
(UP TO 6 WEEKS TOTAL TIME)

Opening a fresh coconut is the sort of DIY activity that requires patience, a sturdy cutting board that you won't mind getting a bit damaged, and a serious hammer. Once the extract is made, you'll be able to gift pretty vials of it and share your wisdom on how to open a fresh coconut. If you can't find a fresh white coconut, a brown version will do. For a time- and labor-saving option, some health food stores sell fresh pieces of coconut ready for you to grate. With extra coconut juice or pieces, you can make homemade coconut milk or toasted coconut for baking or add it into smoothies, or you can prepare an extra batch of extract for your *Food Gift Love* pantry.

INGREDIENTS:

1 small fresh white coconut

2 cups vodka

SPECIAL EQUIPMENT:

Hammer

Butter knife or oyster
shucking knife

Food processor or grater

1 large jar with airtight lid,
sterilized

Sieve lined with
cheesecloth

Coffee filter

4 (4-ounce) or 8 (2-ounce)
medicine-style bottles,
sterilized

Narrow-mouth funnel

1. Preheat the oven to 350°F. Hold the coconut with the eyes up on a large sturdy cutting board. Stick a sharp knife into each of the eyes to locate the weaker eye—where the knife goes in very easily. Stick your knife into that eye and puncture it completely. Drain the coconut water out of the eye into a glass and store for another use (like your morning smoothie).

2. Once all the water is drained, crack the coconut open slightly by hammering over the weak eye on top of the cutting board. Sometimes it's easiest to do this with the back of the hammer. Once the coconut is cracked, open

it up further—into 2 or 3 pieces—with your hands or the hammer.

3. Place the coconut pieces on a baking sheet and bake 20 minutes. This will dry the coconut a bit, helping to separate the meat from the shell. Remove from the oven and let it cool.

4. Once cool enough to handle, insert a butter knife between the meat and the shell. Pull all the shell away from the meat and discard the shell.

5. With a vegetable peeler, peel off the outer, slightly brown, layer around the coconut meat. Discard the outer layer. Slice the coconut into smaller pieces, and grate it into slaw-like pieces. I find it easiest to do this with a food processor.

6. Add the vodka and 1 cup of the shredded coconut to a large jar—reserve the remaining coconut meat for other uses. Seal the jar and shake a few times to distribute the coconut. Write the name and date on a piece of tape and adhere to the jar—this will remind you when to check the extract. Place the jar in a dark spot in your kitchen, shaking every couple of days to distribute the coconut flavor and keep it entirely immersed in the vodka. After 6 weeks, strain the extract through the cheesecloth to remove and discard the coconut. You can strain it again through a coffee filter to remove all the little particles.

7. The extract can be bottled in new sterilized jars or bottles, garnished with a fresh piece of coconut, and presented as a gift. However, the extract gets better the longer it sits. You can keep the extract in your pantry and portion it out into new sterilized bottles as the gifting occasion requires.

8. Store at room temperature up to 1 year. Once you use up half of the extract, add another cup of vodka and ½ cup grated coconut to keep the extract going, and repeat the above steps for infusing.

how to use infused extracts

Homemade extracts take just a few minutes to assemble, and the infusion time for each extract varies from a few days to a few weeks, primarily unattended. For your patience, you and your gift recipients are rewarded with cookies, cakes, and other desserts that improve in flavor and complexity from just a teaspoon or two.

Try or suggest some of these uses for the extracts:

- Vanilla extract in homemade whipped cream
- Cinnamon extract in cocoa baked goods or even in holiday eggnog
- Coffee extract in chocolate brownies
- Almond extract in lighter desserts, especially Petite Pavlovas (page 166) and Brown Butter Madeleines (page 151)
- Hazelnut extract in nutty cookies and Chocolate Hazelnut Spread (page 136)
- Coconut extract . . . in anything, but in frosting, it's pure joy

infused finishing oils

Like homemade extracts, infused oils capture the essence of herbs and citrus for finishing your favorite dishes. They're perfect to highlight a flavor already in the dish or to add a new one to deliver a more complex flavor accent. While you can infuse almost anything into oil, I have found that citrus zest, in this case Lemon Oil, and woodsy herbs, like Marjoram Oil, tend to strike the right flavor notes and have the most uses. I also like to mix soft herbs with woodsy herbs in my infusion, and that's how I fell for the Basil, Sage, and Mint Oil.

I drizzle Lemon Oil over lemon-roasted chicken or stream it into my salad dressing. Marjoram Oil offers a woodsy note to grilled vegetables, and my Basil, Sage, and Mint Oil is wonderful on just about everything from freshly made Ricotta Cheese (page 73) to linguine or a roast leg of lamb. Try them yourself, and then you can recount all the great ways to use these oils when you wrap and gift bottles for fellow cooks.

LEMON OIL

MAKES: 1 CUP

PREPARATION TIME: 30 MINUTES

INGREDIENTS:

1 cup extra-virgin olive oil

Zest of 1 large lemon
(about 1 tablespoon)

SPECIAL EQUIPMENT:

1 half-pint jar with airtight
lid, sterilized

1. Add the olive oil and lemon zest to a heavy-bottom saucepan over low heat. Bring just to a low simmer, when tiny bubbles begin to appear around the edge of the pot. Let simmer for just 1 minute and then remove from the heat.

2. Let the zest sit in the warm oil 10 minutes. Strain the zest out of the oil and discard, and let the oil cool to room temperature before bottling. Do not press on the zest when straining (or you may extract unpleasant bitterness).

3. Store in an airtight container at room temperature up to 4 weeks, or store in the fridge up to 2 months. Bring to room temperature before using.

MARJORAM OIL

MAKES: 1 CUP

PREPARATION TIME: 30 MINUTES

INGREDIENTS:

1 small bunch (about
½ ounce) marjoram

1 cup extra-virgin olive oil

SPECIAL EQUIPMENT:

1 half-pint jar with airtight
lid, sterilized

1. Wash and dry the marjoram.

2. Add the olive oil and marjoram (leaves and stems) to a heavy-bottom saucepan over medium heat. Bring just to a low simmer, when tiny bubbles begin to appear around the edge of the pot. Let simmer just 1 minute and then remove from the heat.

3. Let the marjoram sit in the warm oil 10 minutes. Strain the marjoram out of the oil and discard, and let the oil cool to room temperature before bottling. Do not press on the marjoram when straining.

4. Store in an airtight container at room temperature up to 4 weeks, and then place in the fridge for longer storage, up to 2 months. Bring to room temperature before using.

BASIL, SAGE & MINT OIL

MAKES: 2 CUPS

PREPARATION TIME: 30 MINUTES

INGREDIENTS:

1 small bunch (¼ ounce)
  mint

1 small bunch (½ ounce)
  basil

1 small bunch (¼ ounce)
  sage

2 cups extra-virgin olive oil

SPECIAL EQUIPMENT:

1 pint jar with airtight lid,
  sterilized

1. Wash and dry the herbs, removing the leaves from the stems. Discard stems.

2. Add the olive oil and herbs to the bowl of a food processor and whiz 20 seconds, just until bright green and well combined.

3. Add the herb-flecked oil to a heavy-bottom saucepan over medium heat. Bring just to a low simmer, when tiny bubbles begin to appear around the edge of the pot. Let simmer for just 1 minute and then remove from the heat.

4. Let the herbs sit in the warm oil 10 minutes. Strain the herbs out of the oil and discard, and let cool to room temperature before bottling. Do not press on the herbs when straining.

5. Store in an airtight container at room temperature up to 4 weeks, and then place in the fridge for longer storage, up to 2 months. Bring to room temperature before using.

GIFT WRAP

Glass bottles

Glass markers

Fill the bottles with infused oil and seal. Write the label directly on the glass.

rhubarb vinegar

MAKES: ABOUT 2 CUPS // PREPARATION TIME: 30 MINUTES ACTIVE TIME
(UP TO 5 DAYS TOTAL TIME)

Though there are a thousand uses for fruity vinegars, I use them in three ways that make them essential to my daily cooking: I drizzle a bit on cooked or raw veggies along with olive oil as a light dressing; I add a splash to any pan sauce to brighten up the flavors in the pan; and I stir the vinegar into club soda with maple or simple syrup to make a shrub. Feel free to pass these ideas along in a little note with your gift.

Rhubarb, my favorite produce in the entire universe, makes a beautiful vinegar. This recipe is created with strong and vibrant rhubarb in late spring. The stalk's flavor is subtler early in the season, so I increase the quantity when I get the first harvest.

For any fruit vinegar, the general ratio of ingredients is one part fruit to one part vinegar, but you can increase the measurements to account for the fruit's flavor and your taste. It's important to strain fruit vinegars. The more fruit particles you extract from the vinegar, the longer it will keep that pure taste. Leftover particles will continue to break down, changing the taste, dulling the color, and shortening the shelf life.

This vinegar can be cooked down further with ¼ cup brown sugar to make a tart glaze, similar to my Balsamic Blackberry Glaze (page 112).

INGREDIENTS:

5 stalks rhubarb (about ½ pound)

2 cups white wine vinegar

SPECIAL EQUIPMENT:

1 large glass jar with airtight lid

Cheesecloth or coffee filters

2 half-pint bottles with airtight lids, sterilized

Narrow-mouth funnel

1. Clean the rhubarb. Chop off about ¼ inch of the tip of each stalk and cut the rhubarb into 1-inch pieces. You will need 2 cups chopped rhubarb.

2. Combine the fruit and vinegar in a medium nonreactive pot over medium heat. Once it warms a bit, stir the mixture, pressing on the fruit a bit to help distribute a little color into the vinegar. Bring to a low boil (the bubbles are tiny around the edge but moving vigorously) and boil 1 to 2 minutes. Remove from the heat and let cool a few minutes.

3. Pour the still-warm vinegar into a large jar and store on a dark shelf 5 days.

4. Strain the fruit from the vinegar, discarding the fruit. If you'd like an even smoother, refined vinegar (which I prefer), strain the vinegar through cheesecloth or a coffee filter to remove extra fruit particles. Funnel the vinegar into newly sterilized jars.

5. Store on a dark shelf and use up to 2 months.

GIFT WRAP

Glass bottle

Tag

String

Fill a clean bottle with the vinegar and seal. Write the label on a tag. Thread string through the tag and tie it around the bottle.

raspberry vinegar

MAKES: ABOUT 2 CUPS // PREPARATION TIME: 30 MINUTES ACTIVE TIME
(UP TO 5 DAYS TOTAL TIME)

Fruity vinegars generally follow a ratio of one part fruit to one part vinegar, but my Raspberry Vinegar is just as good with fewer raspberries, and since they can be expensive, I reduce the amount to 1 cup with lovely results.

It's important to strain fruit vinegars. The more fruit particles you extract from the vinegar, the longer it will keep that pure taste. Leftover particles will continue to break down, changing the taste, dulling the color, and shortening the shelf life.

This vinegar can be cooked down further with ¼ cup brown sugar to make a tart glaze, similar to my Balsamic Blackberry Glaze (page 112). Or you can reduce 1 cup of the finished vinegar on the stove with ½ cup brown sugar, and pour it onto vanilla ice cream. Then, invite me over for dessert.

INGREDIENTS:

1 cup raspberries

2 cups white wine vinegar

SPECIAL EQUIPMENT:

1 large glass jar with airtight lid, sterilized

Cheesecloth or coffee filters

Narrow-mouth funnel

2 half-pint bottles with airtight lids, sterilized

1. Combine the fruit and vinegar in a medium nonreactive pot over medium heat. Once it warms a bit, stir the mixture, pressing on the fruit a bit to help distribute a little color into the vinegar. Bring to a low boil (the bubbles are tiny around the edge but moving vigorously) and boil 1 to 2 minutes. Remove from the heat and let cool a few minutes.

2. Pour the still-warm vinegar into a large jar and store on a dark shelf 5 days.

3. Strain the fruit from the vinegar, discarding the fruit. If you'd like a smoother, refined appearance (which I prefer), strain the vinegar through cheesecloth or a coffee filter to remove extra fruit particles. Funnel the vinegar into newly sterilized bottles.

4. Store on a dark shelf and use up to 2 months.

GIFT WRAP

Glass bottle with airtight lid

Tag

String

Fill a bottle with the vinegar and seal. Write the label on a tag. Thread string through the tag and tie it around the bottle.

balsamic blackberry glaze

MAKES: ABOUT 2 CUPS // PREPARATION TIME: 30 MINUTES

Balsamic vinegar is a staple in my home and, likely, yours. It raises the bar for a simple green salad, but when you reduce it into my Balsamic Blackberry Glaze, its uses multiply. This thick and gooey sauce is divine on pork or chicken. Stunning on a warm beet salad with creamy goat cheese. Oh so sophisticated and special on good vanilla ice cream. It's luxurious brushed onto peaches before a quick grill. As well, this glaze adores clear spirits—a little vodka and bubble water is all it needs to become the hit of your cocktail hour (though extra blackberries for floating are a plus).

Make sure to taste the blackberries beforehand. Extra-sour fruit may require a bit more sugar. A middle of the road balsamic vinegar (not too sour) works fine, but choose a version that's not too sour and not too over-the-top fancy. Though if you want to go all the way fancy, I am not going to stand in your way, ever.

This glaze can be cooked without sugar to make a fruity vinegar, similar to my Rhubarb Vinegar (page 108) and Raspberry Vinegar (page 111).

INGREDIENTS:

2 cups balsamic vinegar

2 cups blackberries

¼ cup light brown sugar, loosely packed

SPECIAL EQUIPMENT:

2 (8-ounce) jars with airtight lids, sterilized

1. In a medium nonreactive pot over medium heat, combine the balsamic vinegar, blackberries, and sugar. Smash up the berries a bit with a wooden spoon to get things started. Bring to boil (watch it closely so it doesn't bubble or foam up too high), then reduce the heat to low.

2. Simmer the mixture, stirring occasionally to continue to smash up the blackberries. The glaze is done when it coats the back of your spoon and reduces in size by about half— about 30 minutes. It won't be super thick like a maple syrup, but thinner, juicier. Let cool a few minutes.

3. Strain the blackberries from the glaze, pressing on the fruit to extract all the liquid. Discard the fruit.

4. While the mixture is still hot, carefully ladle the glaze into jars. Seal and store in the fridge up to 2 weeks. Always bring the glaze to room temperature before using, and stir it with a spoon to loosen it.

GIFT WRAP

Glass bottle with airtight lid

Letter stamps and inkpad (optional)

Tag

String

Brush (optional)

Fill a clean bottle with the glaze. Wipe the rim and seal. Stamp (if using) the label on a tag. Thread string through the tag and tie it around the bottle. Slip a brush (if using) through the string.

vinegar sauce

Barbecuing is the sort of cooking method that works best when you build layers of flavor before you add your ingredients to the open fire or smoker. My husband has taken to barbecuing, and I am, for just those moments, his loyal sous chef, grinding up rubs and whisking together mops (basting liquids). If you or someone you know likes to spend a few hours (or days) on a meaty project, make this vinegar sauce. You can use it for barbecuing or add it to a slow cooker with a pork shoulder for delicious results, or serve it alongside pulled pork.

This Vinegar Sauce is nothing like a traditional tomato-based barbecue sauce. My recipe is inspired by eastern North Carolina–style sauces that cut any fatty meat, mainly pork, with a splash of gussied up vinegar. I prefer to use white wine vinegar, but a high-quality white vinegar or apple cider vinegar works, if just a little sharper in taste.

Add the ingredients to a medium pot over medium-high heat. Whisk to combine. Once it begins bubbling, reduce the heat to low. Let the mixture simmer until the sugar dissolves, about 5 minutes. Let cool to room temperature before using, storing, or gifting. This Vinegar Sauce is great immediately, but the flavor really develops over the course of 2 to 3 days in the fridge. Store in an airtight container in the fridge up to 2 weeks.

GIFT WRAP

Plastic squeeze bottle with airtight lid

Wood tag

String

Fill a plastic squeeze bottle with the sauce and seal. Write the label on a wood tag. Thread string through the tag and tie it around the bottle.

INGREDIENTS:

1 cup white wine vinegar

¼ cup ketchup

¼ cup water

2 tablespoons light brown sugar, loosely packed

1 tablespoon freshly ground black pepper

SPECIAL EQUIPMENT:

1 (12-ounce) squeeze bottle or 3 (4-ounce) jars with airtight lids, sterilized

candied gifts

To be candid, I keep a stash of chocolate and other sweet
confections at the bottom of a secret kitchen drawer
and stuffed into a tiny box near my desk. When I return from
places with unbelievable treats, I also stuff my suitcase to the brim
with exotic sweets. But sometimes, only handmade candy
will do—for your colleague who is a confection connoisseur, for the
kids next door who love chocolate, or as a special
nibble for yourself when you're hand-packing piles of holiday food
gifts for others.

This chapter features my favorite candy recipes for both
celebrations and everyday indulgence. Make them for
your friends and family or for a teacher or the postman. Keep a few
types in your fridge during the winter holidays to
prep last-minute food gift packages or to just get through the
holiday season. Making candy requires a little precision
(and a thermometer), but the rewards are instantly gratifying,
luscious and tasty, and so darn pretty.

◆

chocolate-coconut popcorn // smoky candied popcorn //
how to temper chocolate // chocolate-dipped spoons //
chocolate-dipped everything // homemade bark—fruit
& ginger bark, granola bark // chocolate truffles //
peanut butter balls // graham cracker toffee // chocolate
hazelnut spread // salty dark caramel sauce // jam-swirled
marshmallows // candied blood orange rinds

chocolate-coconut popcorn

MAKES: ABOUT 8 CUPS // PREPARATION TIME: 30 MINUTES ACTIVE TIME
(UP TO 6 HOURS TOTAL TIME)

Popcorn is the great common food denominator: for movie night, a birthday party, or a work event, put a bowl of the freshly popped stuff between us and we'll be fast friends. A quick-to-make sweet and salty snack, my Chocolate-Coconut Popcorn fits the bill for these times and many others. Kids love popcorn plus chocolate, and adults are pleasantly surprised when I set out a dish of it during cocktail hour (with a crisp beer) or bring it as a stand-in for dessert (with a syrupy red wine).

I use unsweetened shredded coconut because milk chocolate is sweet enough. You can also pair it with dark chocolate. This chocolate-coated snack is even better sprinkled with Vanilla Sea Salt (page 93) or sliced almonds, to add more crunch.

INGREDIENTS:

1 cup unsweetened
    shredded coconut

8 cups popped popcorn

2 cups milk chocolate
    chips

1 tablespoon coconut oil

1 teaspoon fine sea salt
    (or try Vanilla Sea Salt,
    page 93)

SPECIAL EQUIPMENT:

Double boiler

1. Preheat the oven to 300°F. On a large (18x13-inch) baking sheet lined with parchment paper, spread the coconut. Bake 7 minutes or until golden brown. Transfer to a small bowl and let cool. Set aside.

2. On another baking sheet lined with parchment, spread a single layer of popcorn. You may need two baking sheets to keep the kernels in a single layer. Set aside.

3. In a double boiler set over medium heat, place a bit of water in the bottom pot—making sure the water doesn't touch the underside of the top pot. Assemble the double boiler. (If you do not have a double boiler, place a metal or glass bowl on top of a medium pot.)

4. Place the chocolate and coconut oil in the top part of the double boiler to melt until reaching a smooth consistency, stirring a few times with a rubber spatula.

5. When you're ready to make the popcorn, set up your work area with the shredded coconut and salt. Pour the melted chocolate into a plastic bag. Cut a tiny corner off of the bag and immediately begin drizzling the chocolate over every single popcorn kernel, until all the chocolate is used. Sprinkle the coconut over the popcorn and chocolate evenly, making sure the coconut attaches to the chocolate. Lastly, sprinkle the sea salt evenly over the popcorn. Do not stir the mixture, or the chocolate will smear up and not form a smooth cover.

6. Let the popcorn sit at room temperature 4 to 6 hours to cool completely. Alternatively, place the tray(s) in the fridge or freezer to quicken the hardening process. Gift or serve immediately. Store in an airtight container in the fridge up to 3 days.

GIFT WRAP

Paper bags

Ribbon

Stapler

Fill a paper bag with (fully dried) Chocolate-Coconut Popcorn. Fold the bag opening over a few times. Fold a length of ribbon into a V shape, place it on the folded edge of the bag, and staple it into place.

smoky candied popcorn

MAKES: ABOUT 8 CUPS // PREPARATION TIME: 30 MINUTES ACTIVE TIME
(UP TO 3 HOURS TOTAL TIME)

This sweet and savory popcorn is coated with an amber-hued caramel touched with a little chili powder. It's not spicy or sweet; it has an irresistible just-right balance. You may be tempted to toss in some peanuts or almonds. I say, go with that feeling.

INGREDIENTS:

8 cups popped popcorn

¾ teaspoon chili powder

½ teaspoon baking soda

½ teaspoon fine sea salt

1 cup sugar

1 tablespoon golden syrup or corn syrup

½ cup (1 stick) unsalted butter

1. Line a large (18x13-inch) baking sheet with parchment paper or a silicone pan liner. Place the popcorn in a large metal bowl. Add the chili powder, baking soda, and salt to a separate tiny bowl and set aside.

2. In a heavy-bottom pan over medium-high heat, combine the sugar, golden syrup, and butter. Cook 10 minutes, occasionally swirling or stirring with a rubber spatula, until it all melts into an amber-hued caramel and pulls away a bit from the side of the pan. This mixture will be super hot, so please don't get any of it on your skin; it will burn. Remove from the heat and carefully whisk in the chili powder, baking soda, and salt—the mixture will bubble up, so be careful.

3. Quickly pour the caramel over the popcorn and toss with a rubber spatula to evenly coat all the popcorn kernels. Once coated, carefully spread the popcorn onto the parchment-lined baking sheet, separating the pieces. Let cool 15 minutes if serving immediately or 2 to 3 hours to cool completely before wrapping and gifting. Store in an airtight container up to 3 days.

GIFT WRAP

Resealable food-grade cellophane bags

Washi tape

Pinking shears

Fill plastic bags with the popcorn and seal. Cut a small piece of tape, and crimp each edge with pinking shears. Apply the tape to the edge of the bag and fold over to the other side.

how to temper chocolate

INGREDIENTS:

2 (3.5 ounces each) dark chocolate bars, 70% to 75% cocoa

SPECIAL EQUIPMENT:

Double boiler

Candy thermometer

Teaspoons

Chocolate is beautiful, rich, silky, and so shiny when melted. Anything covered in chocolate—whether dark, milk, or white chocolate—becomes an instant reason to celebrate, a reason to make some good coffee or pop open a bottle of something special, and is most certainly the ultimate *Food Gift Love*. Once melted, though, chocolate loses its shine and needs a little extra help to keep that shine beyond the initial melt. If you want to dip anything (and everything) in chocolate that will keep its luster beyond the first few days, you'll need to learn how to temper chocolate.

Tempering allows you to modify the crystal molecules in the chocolate by raising and lowering the temperature—this challenges the molecules to break apart and reform into a stable, dense network that creates lustrous, firm chocolate. By adding already tempered chocolate to the melted chocolate, you're essentially providing a template within which the right molecules will come to life. During all the temperature changes, you'll be whisking rigorously to make the chocolate as shiny as possible and aid in the crystallization formation. You'll then want to maintain the temperature—or the state in which these molecules have successfully formed—so that it stays tempered. It may sound complicated, but it's actually fairly easy.

Note that tempering chocolate can be simple, especially after you do it once, but it's a task that requires focus. Do not do anything else when you're tempering. Watch the temperature very closely—an extra 30 seconds could raise or lower the temperature too far and alter your results.

With an inexpensive candy thermometer, you can temper a few bars of chocolate within 20 to 30 minutes so you can dip or coat or frost anything (and everything) in chocolate without worrying about it deteriorating quickly. Once tempered and dried, your chocolate will stay shiny and maintain a nice snappy bite for gifting.

Once your chocolate is tempered, use it to make a myriad of chocolate-covered treats like the Chocolate-Dipped Spoons (page 125), Homemade Bark (page 128), and Peanut Butter Balls (page 132).

1. Make sure your work area is clean and free of any moisture. (Even a few drops of water splashed into the chocolate unintentionally will ruin the chocolate and may cause it to seize.)

2. Chop each chocolate bar separately into ½-inch pieces. Set aside.

3. In a double boiler set over medium heat, place a bit of water in the bottom pot—making sure the water doesn't touch the underside of the top pot. Assemble the double boiler. (If you do not have a double boiler, place a metal or glass bowl on top of a medium pot.)

4. Place half of the chocolate in the top part of a double boiler fitted with a candy thermometer. Don't set the thermometer into the pot—either prop it up with some masking tape, or plan to hold it in place as you go.

5. Turn the heat to medium, and melt the chocolate until it reaches a temperature of 115°F to 120°F, but do not let it go over 120°F. Stir continually to urge the melting along and make sure to test the temperature of the chocolate (not the pot) as you go by ensuring that the tip of the thermometer doesn't rest on the bottom of the pot.

6. Remove the top pot and set it on a thick towel, trivet, or heat pad on a heatproof surface. Add a small handful from the remaining chopped chocolate bar to the melted chocolate. Whisk continually, vigorously, until the temperature decreases to 90°F. Keep adding chocolate, small handful by small handful, until the temperature is reached. And . . . keep whisking; the more you whisk, the better your temper will be and the shinier your chocolate.

7. To test your temper, dip a tiny clean and dry spoon in the chocolate. Let the extra chocolate drizzle off the spoon. Set it on a plate in the fridge for 2 to 3 minutes. If it dries quickly and begins to lose its shine, your chocolate is tempered. If it's streaky or white or soft to the touch, it hasn't tempered and you'll need to start over again—which means, you'll need to reheat and set aside some extra chocolate to bring the temperature down again.

8. While you're testing, you may need to sit the double boiler top back on the double boiler for a few seconds to keep the chocolate at 88°F to 90°F (no higher and no lower)—this temperature range maintains the desired crystallization. But don't leave it on the double boiler for more than a few seconds because if it spikes much higher, the molecules will lose formation and you'll have to start all over again.

9. Once your chocolate is tempered, use as directed in your recipe.

chocolate-dipped spoons

MAKES: 6 TO 8 SPOONS // PREPARATION TIME: 30 MINUTES ACTIVE TIME
(UP TO 90 MINUTES TOTAL TIME)

This recipe produces the sweetest gift for a summer brunch, bridal party, or new baby treat, especially if gifted alongside dainty espresso cups, napkins, and a little coffee. I like to use vintage silver that I find for a buck a piece at antique markets, but wooden or plastic spoons work well, too.

After dipping the spoons, you'll be left with some extra chocolate; I use 2 bars in order to melt enough to dip everything easily. Of course, don't let any extra chocolate go to waste. Keep a few pieces of fruit at the ready to make sure you use up every last drop.

INGREDIENTS:

2 (3.5 ounces each) dark chocolate bars, 70% to 75% cocoa

Extra fruit or salty items to dip

SPECIAL EQUIPMENT:

Small plate

Double boiler

6 to 8 small spoons

1. Make sure your work area is clean and free of any moisture. (Even a few drops of water splashed into the chocolate unintentionally will ruin the chocolate and may cause it to seize.)

2. Place a piece of parchment paper on a small plate. Spray the parchment with just a little nonstick spray.

3. In a double boiler set over medium heat, place a bit of water in the bottom pot—making sure the water doesn't touch the underside of the top pot. Assemble the double boiler. (If you do not have a double boiler, place a metal or glass bowl on top of a medium pot.)

4. Chop each chocolate bar into ½-inch pieces. If you plan to melt the chocolate without tempering, place it all in the top part of your double boiler to melt until it reaches a smooth consistency. However, if you plan to temper the chocolate, place half the chocolate in the top part of a double boiler to melt until a smooth consistency, then proceed to temper the chocolate by slowly adding the reserved chocolate (see "How to Temper Chocolate," page 122).

5. Dip each spoon into the melted chocolate. Let the extra chocolate drip off the spoon. (There will be some extra melted chocolate, so dip several pieces of fruit to coat and place on a separate plate in the fridge to set.)

6. Place each spoon on the parchment-topped plate, and place the plate in the fridge and let chill 1 hour, though tempered chocolate will require less time to chill. Store in an airtight container in the fridge up to 2 weeks. If the chocolate isn't tempered, the color of the chocolate will likely become cloudy or white within 2 to 3 days, but it's still edible and will melt into your coffee just the same.

GIFT WRAP

Small food-grade cellophane bags

Ribbon

Vintage tin

Trim the bags to fit your chocolate-dipped spoons. Slip single spoons—or 2 spoons—into each bag. Tie off and seal the bag with a short piece of ribbon. If gifting multiple spoons, pile them into a vintage tin.

chocolate-dipped everything

MAKES: ENOUGH FOR 3 TO 4 SMALL GIFTS // PREPARATION TIME: 30 MINUTES ACTIVE TIME (UP TO 90 MINUTES TOTAL TIME)

My chocolate escapades are not limited to Chocolate-Dipped Spoons (page 125). In fact, they venture into way deeper territory. Melted chocolate makes me crazy, crazy like I need to use up every last drop because unused melted chocolate is just a waste. To fend off this madness, I keep all sorts of extra eats queued up, ready to dip into leftover melted chocolate. And sometimes I melt chocolate specifically to have a dipping fest with a whole variety of foods, because all types of chocolate-dipped goodies make wonderful gifts. I consider and gather a range of ingredients that make excellent companions to melted chocolate like all the following:

Baked goods: Cookies, pound cake, graham crackers, Rice Crispies treats, shortbread, granola clusters, animal crackers, sourdough bread, challah, baguette, bagel chips, goldfish, muffins, waffles, pancakes, cheese-flavored crackers, saltines, macaroons, and macarons

Dried and fresh fruit: Strawberries, pineapple, pears, bananas, orange slices or segments, kiwifruit, blueberries, grapes, cherries, apricots, peaches, nectarines, mango, ground cherries, figs, and apples

Salty foods and nuts: Popcorn, potato chips, pretzels, bacon, corn chips, pecans, walnuts, brazil nuts, peanuts, cashews, almonds, pumpkin seeds, and sunflower seeds

Sweets and candy: Candy canes, caramels, blobs of jam or marmalade, ice pops, peppermints, honeycomb candy, and leftover cheesecake squares

Recipes from this cookbook: Brown Butter Madeleines (page 151), Candied Blood Orange Rinds (page 142), Candied Ginger (page 215), Candied Jalapeños (page 206), Chocolate Truffles (page 130), and Jam-Swirled Marshmallows (page 140)

And to make these treats *even better*, try topping the nonsalty items with a few grains of my Infused Sea Salts (page 90).

INGREDIENTS:

2 (3.5 ounces each) dark chocolate bars, 70% to 75% cocoa

2 handfuls of whatever ingredients you plan to dip

SPECIAL EQUIPMENT:

Double boiler

Fork

1. Make sure your work area is clean and free of any moisture. (Even a few drops of water splashed into the chocolate unintentionally will ruin the chocolate and may cause it to seize.)

2. Place a piece of parchment paper on a baking sheet. Spray the parchment with just a little nonstick spray.

3. In a double boiler set over medium heat, place a bit of water in the bottom pot—making sure the water doesn't touch the underside of the top pot. Assemble the double boiler. (If you do not have a double boiler, place a metal or glass bowl on top of a medium pot.)

4. Chop each chocolate bar into ½-inch pieces. If you plan to melt the chocolate without tempering, place it all in the top part of your double boiler to melt until a smooth consistency. However, if you plan to temper the chocolate, place half the chocolate in the top part of a double boiler to melt until a smooth consistency, then proceed to temper the chocolate by slowly adding the reserved chocolate (see "How to Temper Chocolate," page 122)

5. One by one, dip your ingredients into the melted chocolate, either by hand or with a fork. Or you can just drop each one in to coat the entire ingredient, then use a fork to fish it out and let the extra chocolate drip off back into the pot.

6. Place each ingredient on the parchment-lined baking sheet and place in the fridge and let chill 1 hour—though tempered chocolate will require less time to chill. Store in an airtight container in the fridge up to 2 weeks. If you tempered the chocolate, the chocolate items will keep at room temperature until gifted.

GIFT WRAP

Parchment paper

Small tin or box

Pinking shears

Ribbon

Trim parchment paper to fit as a liner in your tin and then trim the edges with pinking shears. Layer in the chocolate-dipped pieces. Place the lid on the tin and tie a long piece of ribbon around the tin. If you tempered the chocolate, this treat will keep at room temperature until gifted.

homemade bark

Chocolate bark shines with both high and low ingredients. In the first recipe, I use a combination of dried fruit and candied ginger because it's zippy and fresh and in the second I use my Homemade Granola (page 147) because it provides a salty and wholesome crunch to dark chocolate. Both recipes make major league, professional-level food gifts, the sort you can give to the pickiest food fanatic. Consider, as well, serving them as the final course on a silver platter at a lavish dinner party.

Treat these recipes as blueprints for your own bark creations. Simply press anything you (or they) love into melted chocolate, and watch your recipient feast on every last piece. If you temper the chocolate, the final result will have a nice snap that makes it feel more polished.

GIFT WRAP

Cups
Ribbon
Skewers
Tape

Add the bark pieces to your cups. Cut small ribbon strips, and tie each one in a knot at one end of the skewer for a decorative accent. Trim any excess ribbon. Write the label or recipient name on tape, then cut it and adhere to the cup.

FRUIT & GINGER BARK

MAKES: 12 TO 18 PIECES
PREPARATION TIME: 10 MINUTES ACTIVE TIME
(UP TO 2½ HOURS TOTAL TIME)

INGREDIENTS:

⅔ cup dried fruit (apricots, cherries, cranberries, raisins)

1 tablespoon candied or crystallized ginger

2 (3.5 ounces each) dark chocolate bars, 70% to 75% cocoa

SPECIAL EQUIPMENT:

Double boiler

1. Cut a piece of parchment paper to fit a standard baking sheet. Make a space in your fridge to fit the baking sheet.

2. Chop the dried fruit and candied ginger into a small dice of no larger than ½-inch pieces.

3. In a double boiler set over medium heat, place a bit of water in the bottom pot—making sure the water doesn't touch the underside of the top pot. Assemble the double boiler. (If you do not have a double boiler, place a metal or glass bowl on top of a medium pot.)

4. Chop each chocolate bar into ½-inch pieces. If you plan to melt the chocolate without tempering, place it in the top part of your double boiler to melt until a smooth consistency. However, if you plan to temper the chocolate, place half the chocolate in the top part of a double boiler to melt until a smooth consistency, then proceed to temper the chocolate by slowly adding the reserved chocolate (see "How to Temper Chocolate," page 122).

5. Using a flat rubber spatula, spread the melted chocolate into a 9x9-inch square on the parchment-lined baking sheet. Press the dried fruit and candied ginger evenly across the surface of the chocolate. Place the baking sheet in the fridge and allow 2 hours for the chocolate to firm up.

6. With a sharp knife, slice the bark into your desired size and shape. I typically slice them into rough rectangles or break them up by hand into triangles. Store in an airtight container in the fridge up to 1 week.

GRANOLA BARK

MAKES: 12 TO 18 PIECES
PREPARATION TIME: 10 MINUTES ACTIVE TIME
(UP TO 2½ HOURS TOTAL TIME)

INGREDIENTS:

2 (3.5 ounces each) dark chocolate bars, 70% to 75% cocoa

⅔ cup (½ ounce) granola, store-bought or homemade (see page 147)

SPECIAL EQUIPMENT:

Double boiler

1. Cut a piece of parchment paper to fit a standard baking sheet. Make a space in your fridge to fit the baking sheet.

2. In a double boiler set over medium heat, place a bit of water in the bottom pot—making sure the water doesn't touch the underside of the top pot. Assemble the double boiler. (If you do not have a double boiler, place a metal or glass bowl on top of a medium pot.)

3. Chop each chocolate bar into ½-inch pieces. If you plan to melt the chocolate without tempering, place it in the top part of your double boiler to melt until a smooth consistency. However, if you plan to temper the chocolate, place half the chocolate in the top part of a double boiler to melt until a smooth consistency, then proceed to temper the chocolate by slowly adding the reserved chocolate (see "How to Temper Chocolate," page 122).

4. Using a flat rubber spatula, spread the melted chocolate into a 9x9-inch square on the parchment-lined sheet. Sprinkle the granola evenly across the surface of the chocolate. Place the baking sheet in the fridge and allow 2 hours for the chocolate to firm up.

5. With a sharp knife, slice the bark into your desired size and shape. I typically slice them into rough rectangles or break them up by hand into triangles. Store in an airtight container in the fridge up to 1 week.

chocolate truffles

MAKES: 24 TO 30 TRUFFLES // PREPARATION TIME: 45 MINUTES ACTIVE TIME
(UP TO 4 HOURS TOTAL TIME)

I can't remember where I enjoyed my first great chocolate truffle, but it was probably in France. In Paris, there are entire boutiques dedicated to chocolate in all its lovely forms. I always find myself lingering in those shops for an hour or two, marveling at the variety and creativity of the chocolate shapes and flavors.

I make my own truffles now and the shape is *au naturel* or as you would find in nature. Since my uncomplicated recipe yields rustic-looking truffles, the taste should be outstanding—use the highest-quality ingredients. I prefer dark chocolate, but you can use bittersweet or semisweet. I also use fresh heavy cream from a local dairy.

As for flavoring, this is where you will make the recipe your own. I use Irish cream (my recipe is on page 240). I also enjoy these with Port or Amaretto; Vanilla, Cinnamon, or Hazelnut Extract (pages 101 and 103); or Strawberry Cordial (page 232). Just replace the Irish Cream with your flavor in the same measure.

INGREDIENTS:

8 ounces (60% or higher) dark chocolate

½ cup heavy cream

3 tablespoons Irish cream, store-bought or homemade (see page 240)

About ¼ cup high-quality cocoa powder, for rolling

1. Chop the chocolate into ½-inch pieces. Add it to a medium-size glass, ceramic, or metal bowl (that will fit in your fridge). Set aside.

2. In a saucepan over medium heat, bring the heavy cream and Irish cream just to a boil, and then remove from the heat. This will take no more than 5 minutes.

3. Pour the cream over the chocolate. Give it 2 minutes to melt, then stir vigorously to make sure the cream and chocolate are thoroughly blended. Let the mixture cool. Cover with plastic wrap and let sit in the fridge 2 hours or until firm. If you cannot make the truffles immediately, the mixture will keep, covered, in the fridge up to 1 week.

4. When ready to make the truffles, line a baking sheet with parchment paper. The chocolate will melt in your hands as you go, so work fast and prepare to get dirty. Place the cocoa powder on a large plate and reserve.

5. Drag a small warmed teaspoon (dipped into hot water and then dried) through the truffle mixture to pick up about 2 teaspoons' worth. Using your hands, press and pinch each spoonful into tiny irregular-shaped balls and place on the baking sheet. Don't worry about making them perfect.

6. When all the balls are formed, place the baking sheet in the fridge for 1 hour or the freezer for 10 minutes until firm.

7. Roll the truffles in the cocoa to coat lightly. Package your truffles up as a gift, or store them in an airtight container in the fridge up to 1 week.

GIFT WRAP

Parchment paper

Small plates

Resealable, food-grade cellophane plastic bags—the bags will need to fit the plates

Hole puncher

Ribbon

Cut parchment paper to fit the small plates. Slip your plate with parchment into the plastic bag. Holding one end open, carefully place truffles onto the parchment. Seal the bag. Punch holes in either end of the bag and tie with small bits of ribbon. Make sure to transport level with the floor so the truffles stay in place.

peanut butter balls

MAKES: 60 TO 70 TINY BALLS // PREPARATION TIME: UP TO 3 HOURS

On one of my long stays in Paris, I was invited to a very chic house party in a gorgeous apartment that towered high above Montmartre. In attendance were many Parisians, several Europeans, and a few of us Americans. I was nervous about fitting in because I didn't speak French and I had heard stories about the perfection of Parisian parties. I expected vintage music crooning from an old player and wide floor-to-ceiling windows strung open to let church bells and that perfect Paris light drift all around the fashionable room.

To avoid standing out with an average dish, I timed my arrival just so to buy a fresh apple and rhubarb tart from Les Petits Mitrons, a revered neighborhood bakery. I surmised that a local dessert might make me a hit with the swank crowd. Indeed, my first French house party was exactly how I pictured it. Everyone was terribly cool but also exceptionally sweet. And by the time the dessert offerings were passed, guests grabbed a little bit of everything, including my tart. But the real American victory was yet to be won.

One of the American guests who had lived in Paris for more than a few years began to pass her dessert. She floated about the apartment, her tray floating, too, filled with tiny bites that became fewer in number the closer she got to me. The Parisians clearly loved it. I managed to grab one of the last sweets on the tray and when the maker explained the ingredients, I flipped. As it turns out, the Parisians love peanut butter and chocolate just as much as we Americans. Despite vintage music, Paris light, perfect fruit tarts, and very stylish guests, the biggest hit were these Peanut Butter Balls.

The only change between this recipe and traditional "Buckeyes" is the rice cereal. The crunch cuts some of the sweet peanut butter flavor nicely. Crushed corn flakes work well, too. Because they are so rich, I prefer small pieces—about 1 teaspoon each—but larger or smaller is just fine.

INGREDIENTS:

3/4 cup confectioners' sugar

1 cup peanut butter

3 tablespoons unsalted butter, melted

1 cup rice cereal

2 cups milk chocolate chips

SPECIAL EQUIPMENT:

Double boiler

1. Line a small baking sheet with parchment paper. Set aside.

2. In a medium bowl, add the sugar, peanut butter, and butter. Mix to combine well—until no trace of confectioners' sugar remains in the bowl.

3. Add the rice cereal and mix to combine well—it's easiest to combine with your clean hands.

4. With a measuring spoon or small scooper, form small balls the size of about 1 teaspoon. Use your hands to pinch, press, and roll each into a little ball and place on the parchment-lined cookie sheet.

5. When all the mixture has been formed into balls, place the baking sheet in the fridge overnight or in the freezer for 30 minutes to chill and harden.

6. When ready to coat your peanut butter balls with chocolate, prepare the double boiler. In a double boiler set over medium heat, place a bit of water in the bottom pot—making sure the water doesn't touch the underside of the top pot. Assemble the double boiler. (If you don't have a double boiler, just place a metal or glass bowl on top of a medium pot.)

7. Place the chocolate in the top part of a double boiler to melt until a smooth consistency. You may opt to temper the chocolate (see "How to Temper Chocolate," page 122) instead. If you plan to temper the chocolate, reserve half the chocolate for the tempering part of the process.

8. Roll each ball in the melted chocolate and return to the baking sheet. Let chill in the fridge at least 2 hours or until hard. Store in an airtight container in the fridge up to 2 weeks.

GIFT WRAP

Small bowls
Ribbon

Add the peanut butter balls to bowls. Cut a long length of ribbon and tie it in a knot around each bowl. Trim any excess ribbon. Gift immediately. Wrap in cellophane if gifting later.

graham cracker toffee

MAKES: 48 PIECES // PREPARATION TIME: 45 MINUTES

A traditional holiday treat, Graham Cracker Toffee recipes have been passed between families for generations. It's less toffee and more a delicious hack of graham crackers, butter, and sugar. A dear girlfriend gave me a batch of this toffee, along with the recipe, years ago. In that simple act, she fueled years of effortless holiday food gifts for my friends and family. I slip a few pieces—because a little goes a long way—into my cookie boxes during the winter holidays. They're always the first treats gobbled up.

INGREDIENTS:

12 large graham crackers, broken into halves

1/2 cup (1 stick) unsalted butter

3/4 cup light brown sugar, loosely packed

3/4 cup coarsely chopped walnuts or pecans

3/4 cup semisweet chocolate chips

1 tablespoon coconut oil

SPECIAL EQUIPMENT:

Double boiler

1. Preheat the oven to 350°F. Line 2 baking sheets with aluminum foil, setting 1 aside for later use. Arrange the graham crackers on a lined baking sheet, with each cracker touching the next. Set aside.

2. Melt the butter in a small pot over low heat. Stir in the sugar and simmer (do not boil) about 10 minutes just until the sugar melts. Stir occasionally to help the sugar dissolve. Pour the hot mixture over the graham crackers and spread it evenly to cover all the crackers. Sprinkle the nuts over the graham crackers. Bake about 10 minutes or until their nutty fragrance begins to fill the kitchen. Keep a close eye on them so they don't burn.

3. After 10 minutes, remove the graham crackers from the oven and let cool on a cooling rack 8 to 10 minutes. Remove each cracker to the second lined baking sheet, taking care to make sure the crackers do not touch each other this time.

4. In a double boiler set over medium heat, place a bit of water in the bottom pot—making sure the water doesn't touch the underside of the top pot. Assemble the double boiler. (If you do not have a double boiler, just place a metal or glass bowl on top of a medium pot.)

5. Place the chocolate and coconut oil in the top part of the double boiler. Stir and melt until the chocolate forms drippy ribbons when you lift your rubber spatula from the pot.

6. Pour the melted chocolate into a plastic bag. Cut a tiny corner off of the bag and immediately begin drizzling the chocolate all over the graham crackers (like you're making a Jackson Pollock painting) until all the chocolate is used.

7. Let it harden overnight at room temperature, and store in an airtight container up to 1 week.

GIFT WRAP

Boxes

Tissue paper

Ribbon

Line each box with tissue paper. Place the toffee in the box and seal. Cut a long length of ribbon, and tie in a bow around the box. Cut the loops of the bow to the same size as the extra ribbon.

chocolate hazelnut spread

MAKES: 2 CUPS // PREPARATION TIME: 45 MINUTES

There is very little as mouthwatering as chocolate and hazelnut together, and I sometimes find it hard to part with jars of my Chocolate Hazelnut Spread, but I relent because something this good needs to be shared. My version is nothing like anything else; it's shiny and thick, and you can taste little bits of hazelnuts in every bite.

I favor smooth and sweet milk chocolate, so I've increased the indulgence factor by using high-quality milk chocolate in my recipe. You can, of course, use dark chocolate, but the milk chocolate adds a little more creaminess due to the dairy in it. You can omit the hazelnut extract or try my Homemade Extracts (page 100) to aid your efforts here. I provide two oil options below, and each will impart just a hint of their unique flavors, but both mesh nicely with the other ingredients.

Getting the right texture depends on using a food processor or a powerful blender. Pulverizing hazelnuts is uncertain business and may require extra liquid to achieve the right consistency; add a little additional oil if the spread is not shiny after everything has been blended together.

INGREDIENTS:

2 cups hazelnuts

½ pound milk chocolate chips

5 tablespoons unsalted butter

2 tablespoons coconut oil or extra-virgin olive oil

1 teaspoon hazelnut extract (optional)

½ cup confectioners' sugar

¼ teaspoon fine sea salt

SPECIAL EQUIPMENT:

Double boiler

2 half-pint jars with airtight lids

1. Preheat the oven to 350°F. Spread the hazelnuts into a single layer on a cookie sheet. Roast 10 minutes or until the skins begin to pull away from the nuts and the kitchen smells like roasted nuts. Remove from the oven and let cool 10 minutes. Rub the skins off of the hazelnuts with a kitchen towel until they're mostly removed. Discard the skins.

2. Place the cooled nuts in the bowl of a food processor and process, scraping down the side of the bowl frequently, until the nuts release their heavenly oils. This will take about 5 minutes, but it may take longer in order to achieve a smooth, but still gritty, texture that looks like a smooth peanut butter.

3. Meanwhile, in a double boiler set over medium heat, place a bit of water in the bottom pot, making sure that the water doesn't touch the underside of the top pot. Assemble the double boiler. (If you do not have a double boiler, place a metal or glass bowl on top of a medium pot.)

4. Add the chocolate, butter, coconut oil, and hazelnut extract (if using) to the top of the double boiler and melt until liquefied and well combined, stirring to urge it along. This should take 4 to 5 minutes.

5. To the food processor, add the melted chocolate mixture, confectioners' sugar, and salt. Process until well combined, smooth, and glossy. This spread will still be gritty; that's the nature of homemade nut spreads.

6. Transfer the spread to glass jars—one for you, one for a friend—and store in the fridge up to 1 week. This is best given and eaten immediately, but bring to room temperature before serving or gifting.

Wax paper

Tiny espresso cups

Baker's twine

Tiny spoons (optional)

Trace several circles on the wax paper that are 2 inches larger than the diameter of the espresso cup opening. Cut out the circles and set aside. Pour the spread into the espresso cups. Place a wax paper circle over the opening of each espresso cup and fold the extra paper down to mold to the shape of the cup. Tie it in place with baker's twine wrapped around the cup 3 times. Gift with tiny spoons (if using).

salty dark caramel sauce

MAKES: ABOUT 1¼ CUPS // PREPARATION TIME: 20 MINUTES

I had many food revelations during my travels to Paris. Besides the chocolate and the red wine and the baguettes and the rotisserie chicken, the caramel totally changed my life. Famously made in the Bretagne region of France, good French caramel sauce is very dark, almost burnt in flavor. I don't know how or when American-style caramel sauces, light in color and overly sweet, drifted so far afield from the original, but thank goodness there are several artisans bringing the good stuff back. My vanilla bean ice cream thanks you all.

I make this caramel sauce with either white sugar or natural sugar and love them both. If this is your first time and you're not so sure about noticing color changes to indicate doneness, use the white sugar, as the color change will be more apparent. Though stored in the fridge, this salty dark caramel sauce is a treat best served at room temperature. Here are ten ways your family and friends will love it: spooned over ice cream; swirled into espresso; sandwiched between two cookies; drizzled over pavlovas; stirred into yogurt or pudding; spread on toast; whirred up in a milkshake; baked into brownies; dripped onto fresh bananas; and spread into a s'more.

INGREDIENTS:

1 cup granulated sugar

4 tablespoons (½ stick) cold unsalted butter, cut into tablespoons

½ cup heavy cream

⅛ teaspoon fine sea salt

SPECIAL EQUIPMENT:

Regular-mouth funnel

1 pint glass jar with airtight lid

1. Measure everything out before getting started because this is a recipe that requires your eyes on the pot at all times.

2. Add the sugar in an even layer to a heavy-bottom (about 8-inch) pot over medium-high heat. Shake the pan, as needed, to evenly spread the sugar across the bottom of the pan. When the sugar begins to melt, stir with a wooden spoon to ensure that no hot spots develop and to help the sugar continue to melt. Melt until all the sugar dissolves, the caramel just simmers, and it takes on an amber-like hue. The sugar may crystallize a bit on the side of the pan, but keep stirring.

3. When the sugar starts to simmer, stop stirring; just swirl the pan to urge it along. Stay close to the pot and pay attention to the aroma of the caramel—you want it to melt and darken slightly in color but also take on a dark flavor; you will know that the dark flavor is coming to life when you smell the first almost-burnt scent above the pot. At that moment, remove the pot from the heat and swirl to help maintain the temperature. Place on a thick towel on a heatproof surface.

4. Gradually add the butter, as it will foam up a bit, and stir or swirl to help it melt. Gradually add the heavy cream, as it will foam up a bit too, and stir to combine. Add the salt and stir again to combine. If you have any clumps, feel free to strain it. Carefully ladle the caramel sauce through a funnel into the jar. Let the caramel sauce cool before sealing the jar. Store in the fridge up to 1 week.

GIFT WRAP

Glass jar with airtight lid

Handheld tape embosser (optional)

Fill a glass jar with caramel. Wipe the rim and seal. Type the label on tape with a handheld embosser (if using) and stick it to the jar.

jam-swirled marshmallows

MAKES: ABOUT 32 MARSHMALLOWS // PREPARATION TIME: 60 MINUTES ACTIVE TIME
(UP TO 12 HOURS TOTAL TIME)

I am a sucker for handmade marshmallows. Whether made by a gourmet vendor or simply by me at home, a handmade marshmallow is the tops. It's the finial on a candy crown. It's the one confection that most home cooks avoid, until now, naturally. My Jam-Swirled Marshmallows will exceed your expectations. You'll produce a beautiful vanilla puff that's swirled with fruity syrup. The puffs are sweet, tender, and barely swooshed with bright strawberry red, breaking up the powdery cloud with blazing zing.

The swirl is the magic and completely customizable. Instead of strawberry jam, choose another: peach, apricot, and blackberry are equally transcendent. Just be mindful that every jam has a different viscosity, and you may need to add a little extra water to loosen it up. If you like, swirl in some dense maple syrup or even some chocolate chips (they'll melt with the heat). Instead of vanilla extract, try Coffee Extract (page 102), Cinnamon Extract (page 101), or even peppermint. Don't skimp on the confectioners' sugar because you're going to need it to powder every inch of the marshmallows. Also, keep it handy for powdering your scissors or your hands as you work through trimming the puffs into shape. The making process can be a little messy, but the messy will make it worth it.

INGREDIENTS:

For the swirl:

4 tablespoons strawberry jam
2 tablespoons cold water

For the marshmallow base:

Light nonstick cooking spray, for the dish
1/2 cup and 2 tablespoons cold water, separated
2 packets (1/4-ounce each) unflavored gelatin

1½ cups granulated sugar
½ cup light corn syrup
⅛ teaspoon fine sea salt
1½ teaspoons pure vanilla extract
½ cup confectioners' sugar

SPECIAL EQUIPMENT:

8x8-inch glass dish
Candy thermometer

1. Prepare the swirl: In a medium saucepan over medium-high heat, combine the jam and cold water. Heat until loose and syrupy, stirring constantly, for no more than 5 minutes. Strain through a fine-mesh strainer, pressing the syrup from the fruit pieces. Discard the fruit. Set the syrup aside to let cool and thicken.

2. Prepare the marshmallows: Spray the glass dish very well with cooking spray. Cut a piece of parchment paper to fit the bottom of the dish. Spray the parchment paper well and lay it in the bottom of the dish.

3. In the bowl of a stand mixer with the whisk attachment, add the ½ cup water and the gelatin. Let sit 15 minutes.

4. In a separate medium saucepan over medium-high heat, combine the remaining 2 tablespoons water, the sugar, corn syrup, and salt. Heat until the sugar and salt dissolve, swirling the pan as needed to ensure that it all dissolves. This is going to be very hot, so be very careful. Attach a candy thermometer to the pot. Boil the mixture until it reaches a temperature of 240°F. Remove from the heat and let sit 2 minutes.

5. Turn the mixer on to a low speed. Slowly and very carefully pour the very hot sugar liquid in a steady stream into the stand mixer. Once all the liquid is incorporated, slowly increase the mixer to a high speed. Whisk until thick and opaque, about 12 minutes. The desired texture

will be like marshmallow fluff. Add the vanilla and whisk another minute. Turn the mixer off.

6. Pour 3 tablespoons of the strawberry syrup into the mixer. (Save any remaining syrup for a cocktail.) Mix on low speed for a count of 5 seconds. Turn the mixer off. Using a rubber spatula, pour all the marshmallow into your greased glass dish. Level the marshmallow with your spatula. Let the baking dish sit at room temperature 8 hours or up to overnight.

7. Dust a large baking sheet with half of the confectioners' sugar. Turn the marshmallow out onto the sugar. Dust your clean hands with confectioners' sugar, and remove the parchment paper from the marshmallow. Dust the top of the marshmallow with the remaining confectioners' sugar. Dust kitchen scissors or a pizza cutter with confectioners' sugar, and cut the marshmallow into 2x1-inch pieces. Use any extra sugar to dust every surface of each marshmallow. Store in an airtight container at room temperature up to 1 week.

GIFT WRAP

Glassine bags
Hole puncher
Ribbon

Fill each bag with marshmallows. Fold over the top flap. Punch a hole through both sides. Cut a long length of ribbon, and thread it through the hole. Tie it in a knot and trim any excess ribbon.

candied blood orange rinds

MAKES: ABOUT 250 STRIPS OR ABOUT 1½ POUNDS // PREPARATION TIME: ABOUT 3 HOURS
PASSIVE TIME (UP TO 12 HOURS TOTAL TIME)

The French understand how to preserve citrus with such elegance, and after tasting so many versions of candied rind, in particular, in France, I committed to creating my own recipe. This works just beautifully with oranges and grapefruit, but these Candied Blood Orange Rinds have become one of my signature food gifts. Making them is time intensive but also has honed my multitasking skills: I prepare the fruit while watching a movie and candy the rinds while cooking meals for the week.

The rinds will last a while, but I rarely have any left two weeks later. (My mother, in particular, can magically sniff these out in my home; it's a gift, really.)

INGREDIENTS:

5 blood oranges

2 cups granulated sugar, plus more for dredging

1½ cups water

SPECIAL EQUIPMENT:

Handheld juicer

Drying rack or parchment paper

1. With a sharp knife, score the peel of the blood oranges into four big wedges. Peel the thick skin wedges away from the fruit, discarding any loose pith fibers. Set the skin aside.

2. Slice the blood oranges in half and juice them with a hand juicer. I get about 1 cup of juice; reserve ½ cup for this recipe, and store the remaining ½ cup for another use (like blood orange mimosas).

3. Slice the orange rinds into strips between ⅛ inch and ¼ inch wide. My knives are very sharp, which makes it easy for me to get the ⅛-inch slice, but a ¼-inch slice is good, too. If the peel has a very thick white pith, trim a touch of the white pith away and discard. Do not trim too much, as the pith is what retains the sweetness once candied.

4. Place the rinds in a pot and add enough cold water to cover by an inch. (If you're unsure of how to quantify the water, place the orange rinds in the pot and hold some down with a small measuring cup with a clean ruler placed inside. Add enough water to come up 1 inch on the ruler. Remove the measuring cup and ruler before beginning to cook.) Bring to a boil and then boil 3 minutes. Drain.

5. Repeat this process 3 more times. Boiling the rinds several times helps to remove extra bitterness. On the last drain, put the fruit aside for a moment.

6. In a clean pot, add the sugar, water, and reserved ½ cup blood orange juice. Bring to a boil and then add the rinds. Return to a boil over high heat, and then reduce the heat to medium. Cook the rinds 45 minutes or until the syrup is very thick and the rinds are barely translucent. Do not stir the pot; just keep swirling the liquid in the pot in order to keep the rinds fully submerged. If you smell any sign of burning, immediately reduce the heat to low and swirl, swirl, swirl.

7. When ready, remove the rinds from the syrup (a few at a time) with tongs, and place them on a rack or a simple piece of parchment paper, making sure to not let them touch each other (they'll stick!). Let them dry 4 to 6 hours or up to overnight. If they are still a bit wet, let them dry a little longer. (They will always be just a bit sticky.)

8. When dry, dredge the rinds through sugar. I prefer organic granulated sugar, as the color is a bit more translucent and the rind color shines through, but traditional white granulated sugar is fine, too. You may need to press the sugar up against the rinds to ensure that it sticks well. Alternatively, if you plan to use the rinds in a baked good, omit the sugar altogether.

9. Store in an airtight container at room temperature up to 4 weeks or in the fridge for up to 3 months.

Crimping shears

Paper bags

Stamps and ink pad (optional)

Tags

Hole puncher

Round-head paper fasteners

Crimp the bags to the desired height and fill them with rinds. Write or stamp your label on a tag. With a hole puncher, make a hole through the top of the bag and the top of the tag. Thread a round-head paper fastener through the tag and the bag. Bend the fastener into place.

baked gifts

Baked gifts are probably what come to mind when you think of food gifts. They're the originals, the stalwarts, and I couldn't write a book on food gifts without featuring the magic of cookies, pies, quick breads, and savory baked goods. Perfect for your next bake sale or your new neighbor's welcome package, these recipes will make you very popular.

This chapter features some classic and not-so-classic recipes to impress the baked-treat fans in your life. You may already love to bake, but if you're new to it, you'll find detailed techniques and hidden flavor gems easy to master after just a little practice.

◆

homemade granola, your way

MAKES: ABOUT 7 CUPS // PREPARATION TIME: 45 MINUTES

I didn't have granola for the first time until my freshman year in college. My dorm's cafeteria had large tubs of granola and strawberry yogurt side-by-side in the breakfast buffet. The crunchy sweet and savory texture was a revelation to me.

The moment I figured out how to make my own granola, the revelations continued. It's effortless, but there are so many possible combinations that you may never make the same granola twice. I've created a recipe that produces a very crunchy style where the toasted oats and nuts and seeds are bound into large clusters.

You can alter any element of this recipe—omitting, substituting, or adding ingredients—to reveal your own granola style, but aim to keep the size of the mix-ins similar. Be sure to write down your combination so you can recreate it and share it with your gift recipients.

INGREDIENTS:

3 cups rolled oats (not quick-cooking)

1½ cups pecans, chopped (or nuts of your choice)

1 cup mix of pumpkin and sesame seeds (or seeds of your choice)

½ teaspoon ground ginger (or cinnamon, nutmeg, cardamom, or spice of your choice)

¼ cup extra-virgin olive oil

¼ cup light or dark maple syrup

¼ cup light brown sugar, loosely packed

1 tablespoon citrus zest (optional)

1 teaspoon vanilla extract

½ teaspoon fine sea salt

1 cup semisweet chocolate chips (or chips of your choice)

1 cup dried apricot (or dried fruit of your choice), chopped to match the size of other ingredients

1. Preheat the oven to 350°F. Line a large baking sheet with parchment paper.

2. In a large bowl, mix together the oats, nuts, seeds, and ginger. Spread into a single layer on the baking sheet. Roast 10 minutes until fragrant and warm.

3. In a medium pot over medium heat, mix the olive oil, maple syrup, brown sugar, citrus zest (if using), vanilla extract, and salt. Simmer about 3 to 4 minutes, just until the sugar is dissolved.

4. Carefully remove the baking sheet from the oven and, also carefully, pour the sweet mixture evenly over the granola. With an oven mitt in one hand and a rubber spatula in the other, toss the granola with the sweet mixture until very well coated. I pull all the granola into the center of the baking sheet and mix, mix, mix to coat. Then, spread the mixture back into a single layer on the baking sheet.

5. Return the baking sheet to the oven for 10 minutes until golden brown. Rotate, as needed, to ensure that it all browns evenly. Let the granola cool in the baking sheet to room temperature. Once the granola has cooled completely, pour it into a clean large bowl. Mix in the chocolate chips and the dried apricot.

6. Store in an airtight container at room temperature up to 1 month.

GIFT WRAP

Stamp and ink pad

White bags

Tape

Stamp the label directly on the bag. If using alphabetical stamps, tape them together in a line with masking tape. Fill the bags with granola. Roll down the opening and seal with tape.

roasted banana bread

MAKES: 1 LARGE LOAF OR 3 MINI LOAVES // PREPARATION TIME: 1½ HOURS

Banana bread makes a cameo at every bake sale, potluck, or holiday gathering; it's the steadfast treat in the background, ready in case someone needs a little snack. Instead of waiting for bananas to ripen, I accelerate the process by roasting the fruit. And since my family fights over the warm slice with the most chocolate chunks, I make it easy for them and put the chocolate on the outside. You should, too, only if consuming immediately. After a couple days, the chocolate on the outside turns a bit cloudy.

A couple tips: While you roast the bananas, prepare everything else to save some time. Also, make sure to let the melted butter cool before adding it to the wet ingredients to prevent curdling.

If chocolate isn't your thing, I have also made banana bread studded with chopped ripe pear; it kept the loaf very moist and everyone loved it. If you opt for the pear version, spoon 1 tablespoon melted butter on top of the chopped pear so it browns nicely. Banana and pear and butter, oh my.

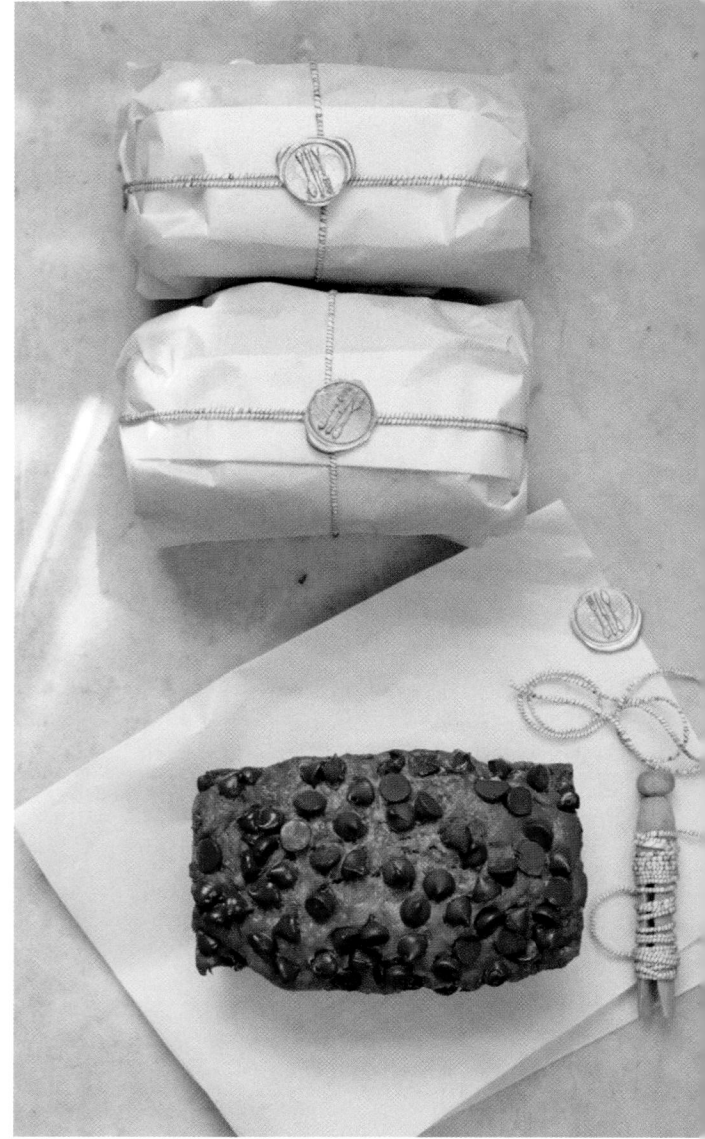

INGREDIENTS:

4 large bananas

2 tablespoons plus ½ cup (1 stick) unsalted butter, melted, cooled, and separated

2 cups all-purpose flour

1 teaspoon baking soda

½ teaspoon fine sea salt

½ cup granulated sugar

½ cup dark brown sugar, loosely packed

1 tablespoon vanilla extract

2 large eggs, beaten

6 ounces coarsely chopped milk, semisweet, or dark chocolate, or large chips or 8 ounces cubed ripe pear

SPECIAL EQUIPMENT:

9x5-inch loaf pan or mini loaf pans

1. Preheat the oven to 400°F. Place the unpeeled bananas, as is, on a parchment-lined baking sheet. Roast 15 minutes.

2. Meanwhile, with a pastry brush, butter the loaf pan with the 2 tablespoons butter. (Or divide the butter among 3 mini loaf pans.)

3. In a small bowl, sift together the flour, baking soda, and salt. Set aside.

4. After you remove the bananas from the oven to cool, reduce the heat to 350°F. Let the bananas cool until just warm to the touch. Remove from and discard the skins, and place the roasted bananas in a large mixing bowl. Mash lightly with a fork.

5. To the bananas, add the sugar, brown sugar, vanilla extract, remaining ½ cup melted butter, and the eggs, whisking together until combined and only a few small lumps remain. Add the dry ingredients to the wet mixture, and stir until just combined.

6. Fill the loaf pan just over halfway up the sides with the batter. Sprinkle the chocolate (or pear) on top of the raw banana mixture, pressing some of it gently into the mixture.

7. Bake 45 to 55 minutes (or 35 to 45 minutes for 3 mini loaves) or until a toothpick poked in the center comes out clean. Let the loaf cool in the pan 5 minutes, and then remove to a cooling rack to come to room temperature. Remove from the pan carefully, holding the sides and avoiding the top, so you don't smear the warm chocolate.

8. Store wrapped in plastic wrap at room temperature up to 1 week.

GIFT WRAP

Parchment paper

Tape

String

Wax and wax sealer (optional)

Once cool, wrap each bread in parchment paper as you would a gift, folding and tucking the ends of each side down under the bread. Adhere the ends with a quick piece of tape. Wrap string around bread, as you would a gift, and tie into a knot. Trim the ends short. Remove the tape. Light a wax stick (if using) to drip over the meeting spot of the string and press the sealer (if using) into the hot wax to form an imprint. Alternatively, make a seal on a separate piece of paper and adhere it to the bread with a touch of glue.

Madeleines

brown butter madeleines

MAKES: ABOUT 12 CAKES // PREPARATION TIME: 45 MINUTES ACTIVE TIME (UP TO 12 HOURS TOTAL TIME)

Madeleines, small, shell-shaped sponge cakes, are the quintessential French treat. Forget macaroons, éclairs, and crepes (at least, for a moment), I prefer the buttery marvelousness of these cakes any day. Madeleines are traditional to the Lorraine region of France and are baked in a special pan. I found my pan in Paris, but they're available online and in most kitchen shops.

I like the nutty flavor that permeates these cakes, along with the almond and vanilla extracts. If browning butter—cooking the butter a little past the melting point to brown the milk solids—worries you, just skip that step. They'll still be cakes filled with melted butter so, in other words, delicious.

INGREDIENTS:

½ cup (1 stick) unsalted butter, plus more for the pan

½ cup all-purpose flour, plus more for the pan

½ teaspoon baking powder

¼ teaspoon fine sea salt

2 large eggs

¼ cup granulated sugar

1 tablespoon almond extract

1 tablespoon vanilla extract

Confectioners' sugar, for dusting

SPECIAL EQUIPMENT:

Pastry brush

Standard madeleine pan (holds 12 cakes)

1. In a saucepan over medium-high heat, melt the butter until it just reaches the browning point. The moment it turns golden brown, about 3 minutes after it first melts, remove it from the heat. Pay attention during this part as there's a fine line between golden brown butter and burnt butter. Some pans hold onto heat for a while, so feel free to pour the brown butter into a clean bowl to cool.

2. In a medium bowl, sift together the flour, baking powder, and salt. Set aside.

3. In the bowl of a stand mixer with a whisk attachment, add the eggs, sugar, and both extracts. Whisk vigorously about 5 minutes until pale yellow, thick, and about double in volume. Remove the bowl from the mixer.

4. With a rubber spatula, fold in the dry ingredients and the melted butter until the flour streaks have disappeared. At this point, you can bake them immediately, but I prefer to place the batter, covered, in the fridge 1 to 2 hours or, even better, overnight to get more lightness in the batter.

5. Position a rack in the center of the oven. Preheat the oven to 350°F. Lightly butter your pan and dust with flour.

6. Divide the batter evenly among the indents in the pan. Bake 14 to 16 minutes or until the cakes become golden brown on the edges and a toothpick inserted in the center comes out slightly moist (but batter free). Pop them out of the pan onto a cooling rack. Serve them warm sprinkled with confectioners' sugar. Wrap and gift once the cakes have cooled.

7. These little cakes keep in an airtight container at room temperature up to 3 days but are best enjoyed immediately, with some tea and a neighbor.

GIFT WRAP

Napkin

Vintage ice tray (or narrow plate)

Tag

Twine

Layer the napkin inside the clean tray. Place the powdered cakes atop the napkin. Write the label on a tag. Thread kitchen twine through the tag and through the hole in the tray, or tuck the twine halfway under the napkin.

sweet & salty pantry cookies

MAKES: 30 TO 36 COOKIES // PREPARATION TIME: 60 MINUTES

This is my go-to cookie recipe. They're crunchy on the outer edges and slightly chewy in the center. The caramel-like flavor makes this a great base to adapt with what you have in your pantry, so feel free to make it your own go-to cookie.

All the pantry elements can be switched up in the same measurements: any chocolate, any nonsweet cereal, and any pretzel-like salty snack. Instead of chopping the pretzels and shredded wheat with a knife, I put them into a resealable plastic bag and crush them with a rolling pin. Measure after they've been chopped. Don't forget the sea salt sprinkle; it's the salty yin to the batter's sweet yang. Consider using my Vanilla Sea Salt (page 93) for the final sprinkle.

INGREDIENTS:

1½ cups all-purpose flour

1 teaspoon baking soda

1 teaspoon baking powder

1 teaspoon fine sea salt

1 cup light brown sugar, loosely packed

½ cup granulated sugar

1 cup (2 sticks) unsalted butter, room temperature

1 large egg

2 teaspoons vanilla extract

1 cup chocolate chips (milk, semisweet, or dark)

1 cup chopped shredded wheat cereal

½ cup chopped pretzel sticks

Coarse sea salt (optional)

1. Position a rack in the center of the oven. Preheat the oven to 375°F. Line a baking sheet with parchment paper.

2. In a large bowl, add the flour, baking soda, baking powder, and fine sea salt, and whisk to combine. Set aside.

3. In a stand mixer, add the sugars and butter. Beat until well blended. Add the egg and vanilla extract, and beat again until well blended.

4. Gradually add the flour mixture, and blend on low to combine until the flour disappears into the batter. With a wooden spoon, stir in the chocolate chips, shredded wheat, and pretzels. Place the batter in the fridge and let chill 10 minutes before baking.

5. Spoon heaping tablespoons onto the baking sheet, leaving 3 inches between each cookie. Sprinkle a few coarse sea salt grains (if using) on each cookie. Bake 9 to 12 minutes or until golden and flat. Keep an eye on these cookies as they bake because the moment between golden and burned is fleeting. Let the cookies cool on the baking sheet 2 to 3 minutes, and then transfer to a cooling rack.

6. Store the cooled cookies in an airtight container at room temperature up to 1 week.

GIFT WRAP

Small glassine bags

Clear tape

Twine

Slip each cookie into a bag. Fold over the top and tape closed. Cut a length of twine, and wrap the bag as you would a square present. Trim any extra twine.

molasses cookies

MAKES: 90 TO 100 COOKIES // PREPARATION TIME: 1 HOUR 15 MINUTES

Molasses Cookies are fall and winter favorites, providing just the sort of comfort and flavors to help us get through tough New England weather. The original recipe was shared by a local chef, but I've altered it over the years to suit my need for more molasses and more spice. I like more of everything, and after you taste these cookies, you will too. The cookies are dairy-free, so they are a flavorful option for folks avoiding the stuff.

Keep a kitchen towel handy as this dough is a little slick. If you have any Cinnamon Sugar hiding in your *Food Gift Love* pantry (or feel like making it, page 96), then roll the dough in that before baking.

INGREDIENTS:

2 large eggs

1½ cups canola oil

¾ cup molasses

1 cup granulated sugar, plus more for rolling

1 cup light brown sugar, loosely packed

4½ cups all-purpose flour

2 teaspoons fine sea salt

1 tablespoon plus 1 teaspoon baking soda

1 tablespoon ground cinnamon

1 tablespoon ground nutmeg

1 tablespoon ground cloves

1 teaspoon ground ginger

1. Cut two large (18x12-inch) sheets of wax or parchment paper. You'll wrap the cookie dough in the paper.

2. In a stand mixer, add the eggs, canola oil, molasses, and both sugars. Beat at medium-high speed until well blended.

3. Add the remaining ingredients to a large bowl, and whisk to combine. Pour the dry ingredients into the mixer, and blend at low-medium speed until combined.

4. Drop the dough onto one sheet of the wax or parchment paper, using your well-floured hands to press any extra dough bits into the big lump of dough, forming a round disk. Using a well-floured knife or pastry cutter, slice the dough in half. Slide one half of the dough onto the second sheet of wax or parchment paper. Shape both doughs into low round disks, and wrap them up in the paper. Place on a plate or in a plastic bag and let chill in the fridge 2 hours or up to overnight. If you'd like to make these in the future, this is the moment to place the dough in the freezer as is or pre-rolled into dough balls (see step 6). (Defrost the dough disks overnight in the fridge before baking, but feel free to bake pre-rolled dough balls from frozen.)

5. Preheat the oven to 350°F. Line cookie sheets with parchment paper (not wax paper). Pour extra sugar onto a large flat plate.

6. Using a spoon, scoop out 1 tablespoon of dough and form into a ball. Repeat until all the dough is used. Roll the dough balls in the sugar until well coated. Place on a cookie sheet about 2 inches apart. Bake 8 to 10 minutes until the cookies have flattened slightly and cracked a bit but are still soft to the touch. Transfer to a cooling rack or new sheet of parchment paper to cool.

7. Store in an airtight container at room temperature up to 1 week.

GIFT WRAP

Parchment paper

Slide box

String

Tag

Stamps and ink pad (optional)

Cut a slip of parchment paper to fit the box. Place the cookies in the box vertically. Slide the box cover closed. Cut a long length of string and wrap it around the box several times. Tie a knot and trim any excess string. Slip a hand-written (or stamped) tag under the string.

nectarine-almond crisp

This is my favorite dessert—really. It's a cross between a crumble and a crisp, packed with tart and sweet stone fruit, crumbly almond meal, crisp rolled oats, and crunchy slivered almonds. The vanilla bean and almond extract mellow out the tart flavors and meld beautifully with ripe nectarines. When I take my first bite, it's a sign that summer is here and there will be a long, happy season of crisps for me and my friends.

If you don't like nectarines, feel free to use another fruit. I've substituted pitted cherries or blueberries for half the nectarines. Instead of slivered almonds, add in chopped pecans or hazelnuts. Consider this recipe yours now and adapt as you like.

This recipe can be gluten free if you use gluten-free oats and dairy-free if you replace the butter with coconut oil.

INGREDIENTS:

- 2 pounds (about 9 to 10) ripe nectarines
- 2 tablespoons cornstarch
- ½ tablespoon almond extract
- ¾ cup granulated sugar
- 1½ cups ground almond meal
- ½ cup rolled oats
- ½ teaspoon fine sea salt
- 1 vanilla bean, split lengthwise
- ½ cup plus ¼ cup slivered almonds, separated
- ½ cup (1 stick) cold unsalted butter, cut into ½-inch cubes

SPECIAL EQUIPMENT:

- 9-inch pie plate or 8x8-inch baking dish

1. Preheat the oven to 375°F. Lightly butter a 9-inch pie plate.

2. There is no need to peel the nectarines. Wash, core, and cut them into thin half-moon slices, about ¼ inch thick, but don't fuss about size too much. Some nectarines "give" when sliced in half, letting the pit easily pop out with a tug. If you have tougher nectarines, just cut around the pit. In a medium bowl, gently toss the nectarine slices with the cornstarch and almond extract. Pile them into the pie plate, mounding them a bit in the center. Set aside.

3. In a large bowl, add the sugar, almond meal, oats, and salt. With a knife, scrape the vanilla beans from the pod and add them to the bowl. Add the ½ cup slivered almonds and the cold butter. With your hands, mash the butter into all the ingredients, carefully distributing the vanilla beans throughout. Mash and press until the butter is well distributed and lots of small bits the size of hazelnuts emerge.

4. Place the pie plate on a baking sheet. Sprinkle handfuls of the crumble mixture all over the top of the fruit, taking care to cover all the exposed fruit. If you have any trouble with crumb mixture falling down or off the plate, just use your hands to press it into place. Pile any extra crumb mixture on the very top.

5. Bake 20 minutes. Remove from the oven and sprinkle the remaining ¼ cup slivered almonds all over the crumb mixture. Return to the oven and bake 20 to 25 minutes longer until the crumble is golden brown and bubbly. Watch it closely during the last 10 minutes to ensure that the almond slivers don't get too brown—cover loosely with foil if you notice any extra browning. Let cool before gifting, naturally.

6. Store covered at room temperature up to 2 days, or a little longer in the fridge.

GIFT WRAP

Large fabric square

Rubber band

Tag

Ribbon

Serving spoon (optional)

Cut a piece of fabric to three times the size of your crisp—30 inches of fabric works for an 8- to 9-inch crisp. Place the crisp in the center of the fabric square. Pull up all the sides and secure them with a rubber band. Write the label on a tag, and thread a piece of ribbon through the tag. Tie the ribbon around the rubber band. Slip a serving spoon through the rubber band (if using).

apple galette

MAKES: 4 TO 6 GENEROUS SERVINGS // PREPARATION TIME: 1 HOUR

A galette is essentially a pie without a pie plate. It's more rustic in form and very forgiving. It's also a speedy dessert to make. With premade dough, this is a baked treat that whips up in less than 20 minutes of hands-on time, which makes it a splendid gift. I probably make and share it a couple dozen times a year.

To keep the rustic look, don't bother peeling your apples. Cut them thinly, but precision is a low priority here as some of them will be tucked underneath the crust. Fold the crust up and over, then pinch and crimp to form your own design. Instead of butter, I use a high-quality extra-virgin olive oil to soften up the apples and add a slightly savory taste that offsets the sugar. Drizzle a little thyme-infused olive oil if you have it.

INGREDIENTS:

2 to 3 Granny Smith apples

½ recipe Pie Dough (page 164)

All-purpose flour, for rolling

¼ cup granulated sugar

3 teaspoons cornstarch

1 teaspoon ground cinnamon

2 tablespoons fresh lemon juice

2 pinches of fine sea salt, separated

1 tablespoon extra-virgin olive oil

1 large egg

1 tablespoon water

1. Preheat the oven to 375°F. Line a baking sheet with parchment paper or a silicone pan liner.

2. Core the apples and slice them into half moons about ¼ inch thick, making about 1½ cups of prepared fruit. (There's no need to peel the apples.)

3. Place the refrigerated single pie dough on a kitchen counter to bring it closer to room temperature. On a well-floured surface and with a well-floured rolling pin, roll out the dough to about a 12-inch circle. Using the rolling pin to help lift the dough, place the dough on the baking sheet. Set aside.

4. In a large bowl, add the fruit, sugar, cornstarch, cinnamon, lemon juice, and a pinch of salt. Stir to coat the apples well. Pile the fruit into the center of the pie crust, leaving 2 to 3 inches of bare dough around the outer edges.

5. Fold the extra dough up and over to cover some of the apples. Pinch and crimp the dough to create a bit of a frame around the apples and to keep the apple mixture inside the dough. Drizzle the olive oil on top of the apples.

6. In a small bowl, beat the egg, the remaining pinch of salt, and the water. Using a pastry brush or your finger, gently brush bits of the egg wash across the exposed dough.

7. Bake about 40 minutes or until the top crust is golden brown and the apples are soft. Serve warm or at room temperature. Let cool completely before gifting.

8. Store, covered, at room temperature up to 2 days, or a little longer in the fridge.

GIFT WRAP

Box, homemade

Parchment paper

Twine

Make a box (see "How to Make a Gift Box," page 160). Line it with parchment paper and carefully lay your galette into the box. Wrap the box with twine several times and tie off in a knot. Trim any extra string.

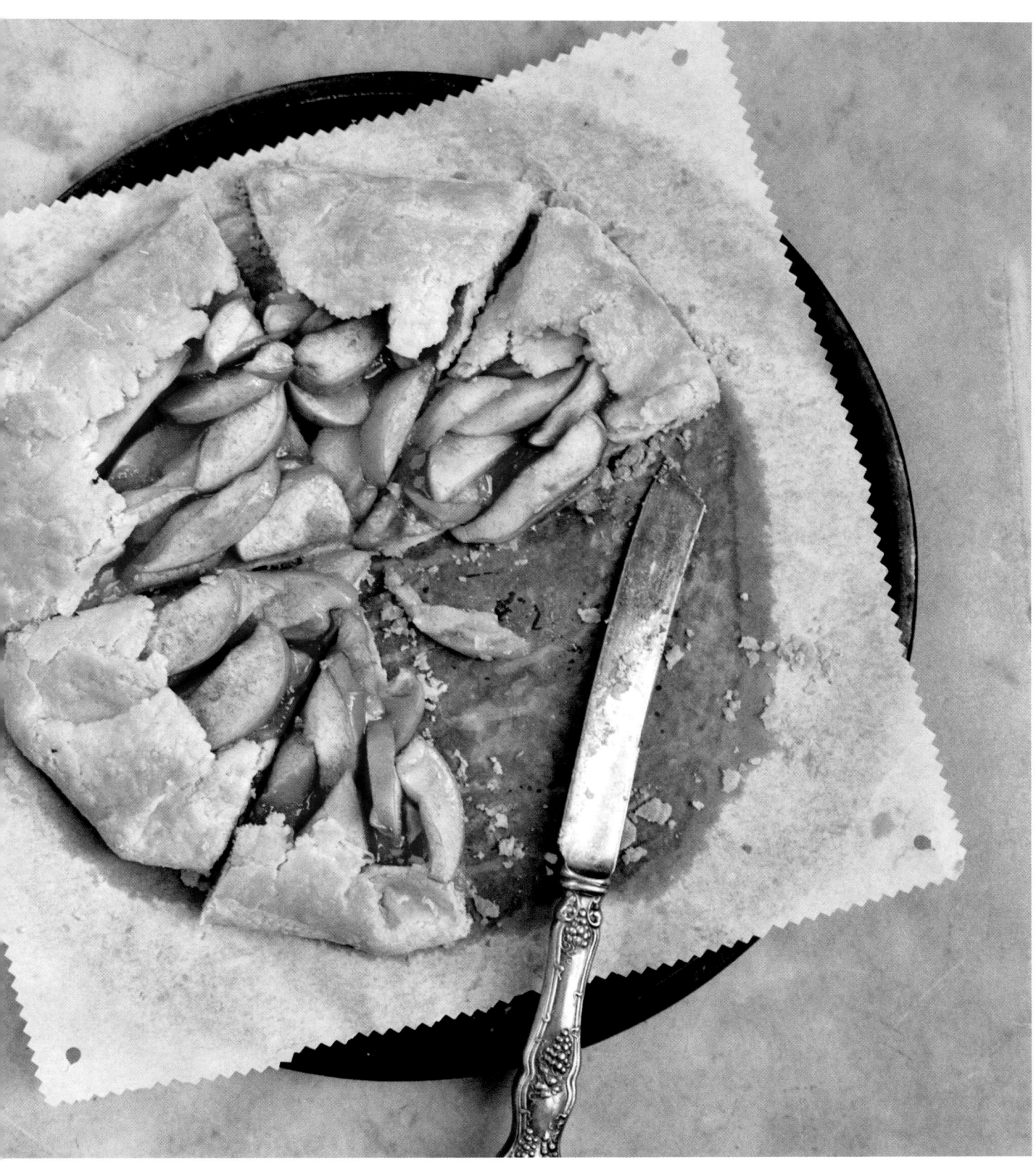

how to make a gift box

Cardboard boxes, in all shapes, sizes, and colors, are critical to my *Food Gift Love* pantry. But sometimes, only the perfectly snug gift box will do. In those cases, I make one from scratch. My version uses just a few cardboard scraps. It takes a little patience, but honestly, you may never go back.

Ruler

Several cardboard pieces

Scissors

Masking tape

Wrapping paper

Clear tape

Parchment paper

String

1. Measure the width and depth of the object you're wrapping—in the photos is a 5x5-inch mini Apple Galette—and trace a cardboard square that's 1 inch larger, so 6 inches by 6 inches. Measure the height of the object you're wrapping—the Apple Galette is 1 inch tall—and trace 4 cardboard rectangles that are ½ inch taller. They should be 6 inches by 1½ inches. Cut out the cardboard square and rectangles with scissors.

2. Lay out all 5 pieces on a flat surface—the square in the center, and each rectangle touching each side of the square. Arrange the pieces so that they're touching each other.

3. Measure all the masking tape needed. You will need 8 pieces of masking tape at 6 inches long and 4 pieces at 1½ inches long. Cut the masking tape to the exact measurements.

4. Adhere a 6-inch length of masking tape such that half of it is on the square piece of cardboard and half of it is on the rectangle piece of cardboard. Repeat for the other 3 sides. Flip one rectangle side up and attach a 6-inch length of masking tape such that half of it is on the square piece of cardboard and half of it is folded up and stuck to the rectangle piece of cardboard. Repeat for the other 3 sides. Adhere a 1½-inch length of tape to the exterior corner where two rectangle cardboard pieces meet. Repeat for other 3 sides.

5. Measure to determine the size of your wrapping paper. Since we know the 1 square bottom (6 inches) and 2 rectangle sides (1½ inches) are

9 inches in total, double that measurement— which equals 18 inches. Trace one side of the wrapping paper to 18 inches. Since this is a square box, the other side of the wrapping paper should be traced to 18 inches as well. Cut out the 18x18-inch piece of paper.

6. Lay out the wrapping paper (pretty side down) on a flat surface. Place your box in the center of the paper. With scissors, cut a straight line in the wrapping paper to every corner of the box. There should be 2 cuts per corner; remove the excess square of paper at each corner after making the cuts. Fold up one side of the paper over and into the box, pushing it snuggly against the interior side. Tape it into place with clear tape. Repeat with the opposite side.

7. Turn the still untaped long side of wrapping paper to be in front of you. Fold both tips over toward each other, taking care to make a crease that leaves 3 inches (twice the size of the height of the box) of the paper unfolded. Fold that piece up, over, and into the box, pushing it snuggly against the interior side. Tape it into place with clear tape. Repeat with the opposite side.

8. Cut a piece of parchment to the exact measurement of the base of the box, which is 6 inches by 6 inches in this case. Press it into the interior of the box.

9. Slide the Apple Galette (or your food gift) into the box. Wrap a long piece of string around the box several times, and tie off into a knot.

spring pie

MAKES: 1 PIE // PREPARATION TIME: UP TO 2 HOURS

Pie is a seasonless dessert, but fruit pies are at their peak with summer's harvest. I can't wait for summer, so my Spring Pie is an ode to spring: filled with bright and tangy fruit, it requires only a little sugar to coax sweetness from the berries and the rhubarb. It may be an homage to spring, but this pie tastes great all summer, too.

I've occasionally altered the ratio of rhubarb to strawberries but always keep the total weight of fruit about the same. The tapioca helps the pie set, and the country girl in me loves tapioca; it's used in both vintage and Latin recipes. The quick-cooking variety is ideal, but if you only have instant tapioca pearls, break them up in a spice grinder before adding to the fruit.

My pie dough is a blend of several recipes at this point. *America's Test Kitchen* replaces the water with vodka, which evaporates upon baking, leaving behind a nice flakey texture. I use vodka, but use all water if vodka isn't your thing.

INGREDIENTS:

4 cups (1½ pounds) strawberries, fresh or frozen

1 pound rhubarb, fresh or frozen

1 tablespoon fresh lemon juice

¼ cup quick-cooking or minute tapioca

½ cup granulated sugar

All-purpose flour, for dusting

1 recipe Pie Dough (recipe follows)

1 large egg

1 tablespoon water

Pinch fine sea salt

SPECIAL EQUIPMENT:

9-inch pie plate

1. Preheat the oven to 400°F. Wash the fruit. Hull and quarter the strawberries. Chop the rhubarb into ½-inch pieces. Place all the fruit in a large bowl. Add the lemon juice, tapioca, and sugar. Fold gently until all the fruit is coated. Let sit 15 minutes, or longer to sync up with the time it takes to roll out your dough—the sitting time is important, it softens the tapioca.

2. On a well-floured surface and with a well-floured rolling pin, roll out one pie dough to a 12-inch circle that's about ⅛ inch thick. Using the rolling pin to help lift the dough, place the dough in the pie plate, taking care to mold the crust to the shape of the plate. With a knife, trim the excess dough that hangs over the edge of the pan.

3. Pour the fruit mixture into the prepared pie plate. Level out the fruit to ensure that it's evenly distributed, and pile it a bit higher in the center.

4. Roll out the second pie dough on a well-floured surface to a 12-inch circle that's about ⅛ inch thick. With a pizza wheel, cut the dough into very narrow triangles. Place the pointy side of each triangle in the center of your filled pie and lay them gently out toward the edge of the pie plate. Keep a little water on hand to dot the dough along the rim, ensuring that it sticks to each dough triangle. Overlap many of the triangles, but leave a few gaps for fruit to bubble up through the cracks. Place a small circle of pie dough in the center over all the triangle tips. Trim any extra dough from the dough triangles. (Reserve all extra dough by rolling into a new ball and freezing.)

5. Beat the egg, water, and salt in a small bowl. Let sit 2 to 3 minutes. Using a pastry brush or your finger, gently brush bits of the egg wash across the finished top crust.

6. Place the pie on a baking sheet. Bake about 20 minutes. Reduce the temperature to 350°F and bake 50 to 60 minutes longer until the top crust is golden brown and bubbly. If your crust is darkening too quickly, cover it loosely with a little aluminum foil for part of the baking.

7. Let cool completely before wrapping and gifting.

8. Store covered at room temperature for up to 2 days.

◆
PIE DOUGH

MAKES: 2 PIE DOUGHS FOR 9-INCH PIES
PREPARATION TIME: 1 HOUR 30 MINUTES

INGREDIENTS:

1 cup (2 sticks) unsalted
butter

6 to 10 tablespoons ice-
cold water or vodka

2¼ cups all-purpose flour

1 teaspoon fine sea salt

1 tablespoon granulated
sugar

1. Cut the butter into ½-inch cubes and place in the freezer
   until ready to use. Make sure your water or vodka are ice
   cold by adding a few ice cubes if necessary.

2. In the bowl of a food processor, add the flour, salt, and
   sugar. Pulse a few seconds to combine.

3. Add the butter cubes and pulse about 10 seconds or until
   the butter has incorporated into the flour and the flour
   resembles large bread crumbs. With a spatula, swipe
   down the side of the bowl to redistribute everything. Pulse
   another few seconds to evenly incorporate.

4. Add 6 tablespoons ice-cold water or vodka to the food
   processor, pulsing a few times until the mixture begins
   to clump together. Test the texture of your dough: it
   should hold together when you press it together. If it
   doesn't, gradually add another tablespoon or 2 (or up to
   4 tablespoons) of liquid and pulse again. Add the liquid
   slowly; you want to add as little liquid as possible because
   too much will make the dough tough. You shouldn't need
   more than 10 tablespoons of liquid in total.

5. When your dough holds together when pressed, turn it
   out onto a clean surface. Gently shape the dough into
   2 disks, pressing it together. Avoid overkneading as
   that will make the dough tough, too. Wrap each disk in
   plastic wrap and place in the fridge 1 to 2 hours or up to
   overnight. Alternatively, you may freeze at this stage for
   future use; thaw in your fridge overnight before using.

6. Remove the dough from the fridge and let it sit at room
   temperature 10 to 15 minutes before rolling for your pie.

GIFT WRAP

Extra large
fabric square

Twine

Pie server
(optional)

Cut a piece of fabric to three times the
size of your pie—30 inches of fabric
works for an 8- to 9-inch pie. Place your
pie in the center of the fabric. Pull up all
the sides and hold them together with a
length of twine tied into a bow. Gift with
a pie server (if using).

petite pavlovas

MAKES: ABOUT 8 PAVLOVAS // PREPARATION TIME: 3 HOURS 30 MINUTES ACTIVE TIME (UP TP 12 HOURS TOTAL TIME)

My Petite Pavlovas are much smaller than typical pavlovas but are more than enough to satisfy. They're crisp on the outside and a little marshmallow-like inside. To achieve that texture, make them the night before you need them with room-temperature egg whites. I make them when I have extra egg whites on hand. I also freeze egg whites throughout the year expressly for this recipe.

I use homemade Vanilla Extract (page 101) in my pavlovas, but you may substitute whatever tempts you, like Almond Extract (page 102), orange blossom or rose water, or even Coffee Extract (page 102). It's also lovely with the beans of an entire vanilla pod scraped into the meringue.

Petite Pavlovas with Vanilla Whipped Cream and Meyer Lemon Curd (page 70) is the ultimate combination. If you're short on time, serve these with whipped cream and fresh fruit like cherries, berries, or passion fruit. Avoid making pavlovas on humid or rainy days; the moisture in the air doesn't play well with meringue.

INGREDIENTS:

Meringues:

6 egg whites, at room temperature

2 teaspoons white wine vinegar

2 tablespoons sifted cornstarch

1 cup granulated sugar

1 tablespoon vanilla extract

Vanilla Whipped Cream:

2 cups heavy cream

1 tablespoon sifted confectioners' sugar

1 tablespoon vanilla extract

Assembly:

8 meringues

1 batch Meyer Lemon Curd (page 70)

1 batch Vanilla Whipped Cream (recipe above)

1. Prepare the Meringues: Rearrange the racks in your oven to ensure that one (or both) are as close to the center as possible. Preheat the oven to 200°F. Line large baking sheets—at least 18 inches by 13 inches—with parchment paper to fit, spray with cooking spray, and set aside. (I can make them all fit on a single baking sheet, but prep 2 just in case.)

2. Place the egg whites, vinegar, and cornstarch in the bowl of a stand mixer with the whisk attachment. Whisk about 4 to 5 minutes on low-medium speed until a thick, loose meringue forms. You can test the texture by stopping the mixer, pulling the bowl down, and watching how the egg whites loosen from the whisk attachment. At this point, it should be thick but still loose.

3. Add the sugar and vanilla extract, and turn the mixer up a few notches to medium-high and whisk 4 to 5 minutes until stiff peaks form when the whisk is lifted. The mixture should be glossy and shiny, and the tips of each peak shouldn't fall, but stand alert. You can test this by pausing the whisking and pulling the whisk from the mixture. If stiff peaks form, you're done.

4. Spoon the mixture into small mounds, about 4 inches wide by 3 inches high, using about ⅛ of the mixture for each petite mound. Using the back of a spoon, make a small well in the center of each mound. (You may wish to fill a pastry bag or plastic bag with the egg whites and pipe them onto the parchment to make perfect mounds, but I find this step fussy and unnecessary. One of the appeals of these pavlovas is in their natural curves.)

5. Bake 2 hours and 45 minutes, checking on them once or twice to ensure that they haven't fallen flat. (If it's raining or humid where you live, or if your kitchen has a high level of moisture, the meringues will be temperamental and either may not form stiff peaks or may fall flat in your oven.)

6. The meringues are ready when they gain a touch of color (though they'll stay fairly white) and are firm-ish to the touch. Turn the oven off and let the meringues sit in the oven all day or overnight (about 8 hours) to adequately dry. If your oven runs hot, leave the oven door open a bit for this drying period.

7. Prepare the Vanilla Whipped Cream: Add the heavy cream to the (very clean) bowl of a stand mixer with the whisk attachment. Whisk until loose peaks form.

8. Add the confectioners' sugar and vanilla extract. Whisk until luscious firm peaks form.

9. Store covered in the fridge until ready to use. This can be made 1 day in advance.

10. Assemble the Petite Pavlovas: On a single baking sheet or large, long plate, make 2 rows of 4 meringues each.

11. Place a healthy spoonful of curd in the well of each meringue.

12. Place a healthy dollop of whipped cream on top of the curd.

13. Serve with extra curd or whipped cream, as needed. Alternatively, you can arrange each meringue on individual plates.

GIFT WRAP

Glass jars with airtight lids

Plastic wrap

Rubber band

Parchment paper

Tray

Transfer the whipped cream and the curd into clean jars. Wipe the rims and seal either with lids or with plastic wrap and a rubber band. Trim a piece of parchment to fit your tray. Place the jars on the tray. Pile the pavlovas on the tray. Cover the entire tray with plastic wrap during transport, but gift immediately.

tomato tart

MAKES: 10 TO 12 SERVINGS, AS AN APPETIZER // PREPARATION TIME: 1 HOUR

Every potluck needs a beautiful appetizer to get people started, and this Tomato Tart provides that temptation for the cocktail hour; it's the perfect companion to a glass of sparkling wine or a light beer, as the puff pastry provides both lightness in its thin layers and a heartiness in the flour and butter combo that matches up to aperitif-style drinks.

While this dish makes the most of in-season, perfectly ripe tomatoes, you can top the puff pastry with almost any vegetable, like sautéed zucchini, thinly sliced asparagus, or just-roasted red bell peppers or eggplant slices—just squeeze the excess water from cooked veggies before topping the dough. A sprinkle of freshly grated parmesan cheese, goat cheese, or even one of my Infused Sea Salts (page 90) will up the decadence factor, but believe me, the tart shines just as it is.

The deliciousness of this dish is dependent on very good ingredients. Use the best puff pastry you can find—Dufour is my favorite. If you cannot find a large 14-ounce dough, use two doughs of lesser weight and crimp them together with a little water and your fingers to fill an 18x13-inch baking sheet.

INGREDIENTS:

1 (14-ounce) puff pastry dough, thawed according to package's instructions

1 pound cherry tomatoes

½ teaspoon fine sea salt plus a pinch of fine sea salt, separated

All-purpose flour, for dusting

2 tablespoons extra-virgin olive oil

12 thyme sprigs, leaves removed

Pinch of freshly ground black pepper

1 large egg

1 tablespoon cold water

1. Preheat the oven to 400°F. Line a baking sheet with parchment paper. Remove the puff pastry from the fridge.

2. Slice the cherry tomatoes in half or, if they are large, into several slices, and place them in a large bowl. Sprinkle with the ½ teaspoon salt, and toss gently to coat well. Set aside to permit some liquid to drain from the fruit.

3. Dust your work surface with a bit of flour. Unfold the pastry dough on top of the floured surface. Using a floured rolling pin, roll the dough just a few times to add an extra 1 to 2 inches in length and width; it should be about 12 inches by 17 inches. Fold the dough loosely over your rolling pin and gently transfer the dough onto your baking sheet, taking care to lay it flat and even across the pan.

4. With a knife, lightly trace a 1-inch border along the outside edge of the dough, creating a space for the tomatoes to nest and defining the edge that will puff up; don't skip this step. Using a fork, lightly poke divots all across the inner large rectangle, taking care not to poke holes that go all the way through the dough. This will help keep the center of the dough from puffing up. Set aside.

5. Drain the liquid that has gathered in the bowl of tomatoes (or reserve it for another use that day, such as a salad dressing). Drizzle the tomatoes with the olive oil and toss gently to coat. Place each tomato cut side up within the large rectangle on the pastry dough. Sprinkle the thyme leaves on every single tomato and then sprinkle the entire tart with the remaining pinch of salt and the pepper. In a small bowl, beat together the egg and water. Brush lightly all over the border of the puff pastry.

6. Bake at least 40 minutes or until golden brown and cooked through, taking care to notice when the tomatoes are slightly roasted (drying them out a bit concentrates the flavor). Remove from the oven and let cool a few minutes.

7. Slice into rectangle-shaped pieces and serve immediately. If transporting, cover with a clean kitchen towel and reheat 10 minutes at 250°F at your destination.

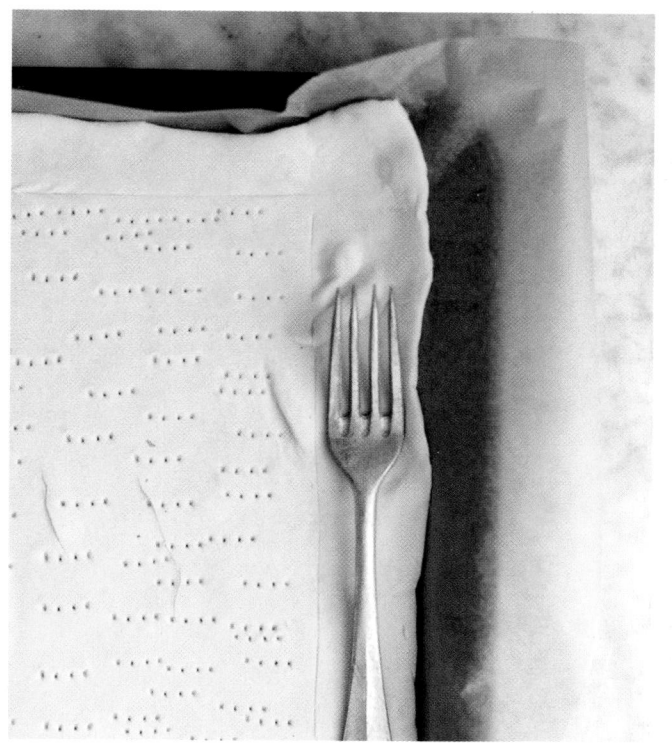

GIFT WRAP

Cardboard

Dish towel

Rectangular basket (optional)

Cut a piece of cardboard to the size of your Tomato Tart. Lay a dish towel over the cardboard cutout. Lift the tart by opposite ends of the parchment paper and, carefully, place on top of the towel. Gently pull the parchment paper out from under the tart. Gift as is, or slide into a large rectangular basket (if using).

savory cheese-plate quick bread

MAKES: 1 LOAF // PREPARATION TIME: 1 HOUR 15 MINUTES

A cheese plate, overflowing with luscious cheeses, roasted nuts, and dried fruit is a glorious thing at the start of a house party. By midnight though, it's been picked apart, leaving leftover bits here and there. Wrap up those bits, especially the goat cheese, for this savory cake. Not at all sweet except for a trace amount of honey, my Savory Cheese-Plate Quick Bread is lovely for a picnic or wonderful warmed through for breakfast with a little jam. You can also serve lightly fried slices with a thick sweet wine on the side for an after-dinner treat. It's good warm because the cheese softens a little, improving the texture and flavor.

You can alter the fruit, nuts, and even the herbs as you wish. Stick with the goat cheese; it holds up surprisingly well when baked, and the tang is refreshing.

INGREDIENTS:

½ cup extra-virgin olive oil, plus more for the pan

1 cup all-purpose flour, plus more for dusting

½ teaspoon baking powder

½ teaspoon baking soda

1½ teaspoons fine sea salt

½ teaspoon freshly ground black pepper

1 teaspoon thyme leaves, fresh or dried

1 (6-ounce) goat cheese log, cut into ½-inch pieces

½ cup roughly chopped pistachios

½ cup roughly chopped dried apricots

2 large eggs

½ cup full-fat or low-fat Greek yogurt

1 tablespoon light or dark honey

SPECIAL EQUIPMENT:

10x5-inch bread pan (a little smaller or larger is fine)

1. Place an oven rack in the middle position. Preheat the oven to 350°F. Grease and flour the bread pan.

2. In a large bowl, add the flour, baking powder, baking soda, salt, pepper, and thyme, and whisk to combine. Add the goat cheese, pistachios, and apricots. Toss gently with a rubber spatula to coat.

3. In another large bowl, add the eggs, oil, yogurt, and honey. Whisk vigorously to blend well. The yogurt may separate from the eggs and the oil, but if you whisk it vigorously enough, it will blend to form a beautiful pale yellow color.

4. Add the wet ingredients to the dry ingredients, and fold gently with a rubber spatula just to combine and until most of the flour streaks have disappeared into the batter. Pour into the prepared bread pan.

5. Bake 40 minutes or until the cake becomes golden brown and a toothpick inserted in the center comes out clean. Let the cake cool in the pan 10 minutes. Remove to a cooling rack to cool completely.

6. Store in an airtight container in the fridge up to 1 week. Bring to room temperature before serving.

GIFT WRAP

Napkin

Basket

Twine

Tag

Slip a napkin in to line the basket. Nestle the bread into the napkin and fold the napkin over bread. Cut a long length of twine and wrap around the bread several times. Tie a knot and trim any excess twine. Slip a hand-written gift tag under the twine.

pizza rolls

MAKES: ABOUT 10 SERVINGS (1-INCH SLICES) // PREPARATION TIME: 1 HOUR 15 MINUTES

My Pizza Roll is actually called pepperoni bread to folks back home in New Jersey. It's a mishmash of a British-style sausage roll and an Italian calzone, which my family considers a bit of super-indulgent bliss served for only special occasions. It intermingles cheese and spicy meat in between layers of a bread-like pizza dough. Once baked, the pepperoni almost melts into the dough to form a spicy oil. If you don't eat pepperoni, replace it with a cup of leftover cooked green vegetables and 2 to 3 tablespoons of pesto; you'll get great results. Also, try stuffing it with mortadella or peppery salami. And if you like a dipping sauce, I make a thin pesto with whatever herbs, oil, nuts, and citrus zest I have on hand.

While you can use any store-bought dough for this recipe, my Quick Pizza Dough recipe follows. It makes enough for 2 pizza rolls or two 14-inch pizzas. Don't roll it too thin, or it will pierce during baking and the cheese will ooze out and brown up; it's a delicious mistake but makes the roll less cheesy.

INGREDIENTS:

1 Quick Pizza Dough (recipe follows; use only 1 of the 2 doughs) or store-bought dough

All-purpose flour, for dusting

¼ pound provolone cheese, thinly sliced (about eight 4-inch slices)

¼ pound pepperoni, thinly sliced (about fifteen to twenty 3-inch slices)

1 large egg

1 tablespoon water

Pinch of fine sea salt

SPECIAL EQUIPMENT:

Pastry brush

1. Preheat the oven to 350°F. Line a large (18x13-inch) baking sheet (or one larger than the dough) with parchment paper.

2. Dust your work surface with a hefty dose of flour, and dust the top of your dough and rolling pin. Roll the dough out into a single, long oval that is about 14 to 16 inches long by 10 to 12 inches wide and ½ inch deep (make sure it will fit your baking sheet), adding more flour to your rolling pin and dough, as needed. Press your fingers lightly across the dough, as if giving it a light massage, creating divots.

3. Leaving a 2-inch border of dough cheese free, place a single layer of cheese evenly across the dough. Place a single layer of pepperoni evenly over the cheese layer, retaining that 2-inch border. Brush a bit of water on the 2-inch border of dough.

4. Starting with the longer end in front of you, roll the dough into a thick log. Work slowly, pulling up the dough an inch at a time, from left to right. When you get to the end, stretch up the extra uncovered dough and, if dry, brush it with a bit more water. Tuck it over the top, pressing gently, and roll the dough over so that the seam edge is on the bottom. Tuck each end of the dough under as well, to prevent cheese from oozing out when baked. With flour on your hands, gently transfer the roll onto your prepared baking sheet. In a small bowl, beat the egg and water. Brush all over the pizza roll. Sprinkle with the pinch of salt.

5. Bake about 45 minutes or until golden brown and fragrant like hot pepperoni pizza. To check if it's ready, tap the top of the roll carefully; if it springs back, bake 5 to 10 minutes longer. The roll is done when it's crispy on the outside and doesn't spring back so easily. Serve immediately. If transporting, wrap in foil and reheat 10 minutes at 250°F at your destination.

QUICK PIZZA DOUGH

MAKES: 2 SMALL DOUGHS
PREPARATION TIME: 2 HOURS

INGREDIENTS:

4 cups all-purpose flour, plus more for dusting

2 teaspoons fine sea salt

2 cups warm water (95°F to 110°F)

2 teaspoons active dry yeast

2 tablespoons light brown sugar, loosely packed

¼ cup olive oil

Extra-virgin olive oil, for greasing

SPECIAL EQUIPMENT

Candy thermometer

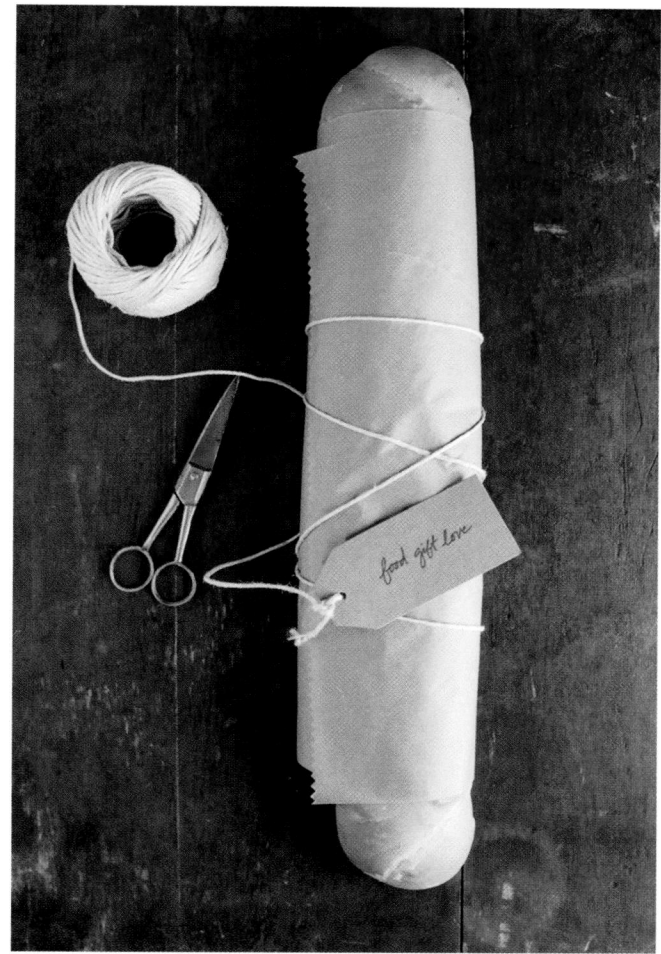

1. Place the flour and salt in a deep bowl. Set aside.

2. Place the warm water in a large glass. Sprinkle the yeast on top of the water, and add the brown sugar; whisk slightly. Let sit to foam up 10 minutes. After the liquid has become a little foamy with bubbles, whisk in the olive oil.

3. Pour the liquid into the dry ingredients, and stir the dough until a sticky dough ball is formed. Flour a clean surface, and turn the dough out onto the flour. Knead the dough 10 minutes, adding extra flour liberally to make it less sticky. (If you don't know how to knead: push the dough away from you with the floured heel of your hand, and then turn and pull the far end of the dough toward you with your floured hand, then repeat.)

4. Place the dough in a large bowl that's been well-oiled. Cover with plastic wrap and let sit in a warm part of your kitchen (about 70°F to 75°F) to rise 2 hours. If you want to make the dough ahead of time, it can sit for an additional 4 hours at room temperature or in the fridge overnight.

5. Turn the dough out onto a very well-floured surface and knead 3 minutes or until the dough is not sticky, adding extra flour as needed, and until it holds a round shape. Let the dough rest on a floured surface 5 minutes.

6. With a floured knife, divide the dough in half. Flour each dough well and use immediately or freeze, wrapped in plastic wrap, up to 2 months.

GIFT WRAP

Parchment paper

Pinking shears

String

Tag

Cut a piece of parchment to just shy of the length of your Pizza Roll. Using pinking shears, trim off each shorter end of the paper to create a scalloped edge. Place the Pizza Roll on one of the scalloped edges and roll it up until all the parchment is wrapped around the Pizza Roll. Wrap string around the roll at least 3 times to hold the paper in place. Tie off into a knot and trim any extra string. Write the tag on a label and slip into the end of the string.

preserved gifts

To make a preserved food gift is to capture a moment,
a memory, a flavor that can be shared and enjoyed days, weeks,
or even months later. These recipes are the epitome of
consideration. When you gift Rhubarb-Vanilla Jam, you are
saying "Don't worry about changing your schedule (or menu
or diet) to eat this right now, just enjoy it when you have a few
moments to yourself." A food gift that's coupled with that
mindful regard is the sweetest sort.

This chapter is filled with what some consider traditional or
quintessential food gifts, and they are the centerpieces
of a *Food Gift Love* pantry. Each recipe here, though, offers a fun
twist on classic preserves and a joyous excuse to
spend an afternoon in the kitchen demonstrating your proficiency
as a masterful food gifter.

◆

citrus crisps

MAKES: 24 TO 30 SLICES // PREPARATION TIME: 20 MINUTES ACTIVE TIME
(UP TO 18 HOURS TOTAL TIME)

This straightforward recipe for preserving citrus will make them last almost indefinitely. Citrus Crisp uses are endless, so they're a permanent fixture in my *Food Gift Love* pantry, to gift and to decorate food gifts. They are the food gift that truly keeps on gifting.

Citrus Crisp slices are wonderful in drinks, for the presentation and the tart aroma that drifts around the glass. Lemon crisps mingle well in a pitcher of lemonade, along with a handful of mint or thyme. Meyer lemon crisps are beautiful decorations on cakes, and, when served with marmalade, my Panna Cotta Cups (page 78) get an orange crisp for garnish. Enhance a fresh-from-the-oven lemon-roasted chicken with lemon crisps and fresh herbs, or serve alongside cheese and nuts as makeshift crackers. Nonfood uses are plentiful as well. My holiday tree always gets the year's remaining Citrus Crisps in the form of a garland—just weave twine or wire through each slice and hang.

Humidity is the prevailing challenge to Citrus Crisps. Moist days or climates will require a little more cooking—just make sure they're completely dry before storing. Use firm fruit and don't stop at lemons. All citrus dries well; the larger the fruit, the longer the bake.

INGREDIENTS:

3 Meyer lemons (or regular Eureka lemons, navel oranges, or limes)

SPECIAL EQUIPMENT:

Glass jar with airtight lid

1. Preheat the oven to no lower than 150°F (or the lowest possible temperature, such as 170°F). Line a large baking sheet with parchment paper.

2. Slice the lemons into ⅛-inch slices with a very sharp knife. If you come across any seeds, discard them. Place the slices on the baking sheet, about an inch apart.

3. Bake at least 3½ hours, flipping the slices 1 to 2 times during cooking. Be mindful of the hot spots in your oven, and turn your sheet as needed to evenly distribute the heat. Turn off oven when the slices feel dry-ish to the touch, and let sit in the oven 2 to 4 hours longer, until cooled to room temperature.

4. Remove from the oven and let sit at room temperature 12 hours or overnight to ensure that the fruit is completely dry. Sometimes, I leave the slices out for a couple days to make sure every bit of moisture is gone.

5. Gently peel the slices from the parchment. Store in a clean glass jar up to 1 year.

GIFT WRAP

Ribbon

Ceramic container or box

Parchment paper

Pinking shears

Straight pin

Tag

Cut a length of ribbon and place it across the container, pressing it inside. Trim a piece of parchment paper, enough to line your container with enough overhang to enclose the crisps. Crimp the edges with pinking shears and place in the container over the ribbon. Add your crisps and fold the paper over to cover. Tie a loose knot in the ribbon and pin to secure. Write the label on a tag and slide it under the ribbon.

preserved lemons

MAKES: ABOUT 5 CUPS // PREPARATION TIME: 30 MINUTES ACTIVE TIME
(PLUS 3 WEEKS TOTAL TIME)

When I think that a dish needs just a little something special and bright, I turn to my stock of Preserved Lemons. They work beautifully as a gift for a seasoned home cook or someone who likes to add new flavors to her or his daily cuisine. I use them for everything from jazzing up salad dressings to slivering in with cooked green vegetables. And they are very nice chopped and stirred into my Lemony Bean Dip (page 42). They give a lift to anything that needs a little acid and a little salt. They're salty, no doubt, but it's the salt, a natural food preserver, that keeps citrus season rolling through the months.

Typically, Preserved Lemons are made in single large jars, making it oh-so-hard to gift easily. My recipe makes 5 half-pint jars that you can store in the fridge, ready for gifting.

Meyer lemons produce lots of juice and have a sweet richness that just seems worth preserving. If Meyer lemon season is short in your area, use regular Eureka lemons, but make sure they're super juicy (they should feel soft and almost bursting at the touch, not hard). Larger lemons go further, so you may need additional jars. Rinse each slice before using in a recipe to pull out a bit of the salt.

INGREDIENTS:

13 small Meyer lemons, preferably organic, washed and dried

1 regular Eureka lemon (keep 2 to 3 on hand, if needed at 5-day test)

2 cups plus 5 tablespoons fine sea salt, separated

SPECIAL EQUIPMENT:

5 half-pint jars with airtight lids, sterilized

1. Sterilize 5 half-pint jars and airtight lids (for sterilizing, see "Cleaning Your Jars," page 183).

2. Juice 2 Meyer lemons and 1 Eureka lemon into a bowl, straining out any seeds. Dispose of the rinds and set the juice aside. You should be left with at least 8 tablespoons juice, but may get a bit more—save it for the 5-day check.

3. Slice the remaining 11 Meyer lemons in half vertically. Slice each half into 3 equally sized wedges. Place the Meyer lemon wedges into a large mixing bowl. Add the 2 cups salt, and stir gently until all parts of the exposed fruit are covered in salt.

4. Place 1 tablespoon of the remaining salt into the bottom of each jar. Stack and press about 15 lemon wedges into each jar, adding extra salt from the bowl between each layer. My lemons were small, so 15 slices squeezed into each jar; if your lemons are larger, slice, salt, and stack only half of them to start—add more as needed to fill the jars. Top each lemon-wedge-filled jar with extra salt from the bowl, using up all the salt.

5. Pour 1½ to 2 tablespoons of the mixed lemon juice into each jar, leaving about ¼ inch of headspace. Wipe the rims clean and seal the jars.

6. Shake each jar to create more juice and distribute the juice and salt well. Leave the jars on the counter at room temperature 5 days, shaking a little each day. Your salt and juice may separate a bit—that's okay—just keep shaking to aid distribution. After 5 days, check the jars—open them up—to ensure that most of the lemons are covered in juice. If more than a sliver of Meyer lemon is exposed, add more lemon juice to make ¼ inch of headspace. Wipe the rims and reseal.

7. Place the jars in the fridge for 3 weeks. The lemons are ready to use at that point and will keep in the fridge for an additional 4 months. I've had jars that have been beautifully kept for more than 6 months.

GIFT WRAP

Tag
String

Write the label on a tag. Cut a length of string and wrap it around the jar several times. Tie a knot and thread the tag onto the string. Tie another knot to hold the tag in place, and trim any extra string.

sweet & sour cranberries

MAKES: ABOUT 6 CUPS // PREPARATION TIME: 30 MINUTES ACTIVE TIME
(UP TO 1 HOUR TOTAL TIME)

These gems make for an unexpected holiday gift. They're excellent as is or dropped onto a cheese plate near some sharp white cheddar. Their delight only transcends when spread into a sandwich or dabbed onto some roast pork or a Thanksgiving turkey. And the sweet, tart liquid that results can be served at the bottom of a flute—topped with champagne, of course—at any holiday party. Float a few cranberries in the glass, for sure.

INGREDIENTS:

4 cups cranberries, fresh or frozen

1³⁄4 cups apple cider vinegar

1³⁄4 cups granulated sugar

2 cinnamon sticks

1⁄2 heaping teaspoon allspice berries (or ground allspice)

1⁄2 heaping teaspoon whole cloves

1⁄2 heaping teaspoon black peppercorns

1⁄2 heaping teaspoon juniper berries (optional)

SPECIAL EQUIPMENT:

Spice bag or cheesecloth (optional)

3 pint jars with airtight lids, sterilized

Wide-mouth funnel

1. Wash the cranberries and pick over them for any stems or bad berries. If you are using frozen cranberries, just open the bag(s) and use them directly from the freezer; add a few minutes to the cooking time.

2. Combine the vinegar and sugar in a medium saucepan over medium-high heat and begin to bring to a boil. When the liquid begins to boil, add the cinnamon. If using ground allspice (instead of allspice berries), add that now, too.

3. Place the allspice berries, whole cloves, black peppercorns, and juniper berries (if using) in a spice bag (if using) or tie them up in a length of cheesecloth (if using). (Alternatively, you can just add them directly to the pot, but wrapping in cheesecloth makes for a cleaner gift.) Add the spice bag to the pot.

4. Bring the mixture to a boil. Once the mixture is boiling vigorously, add the cranberries. Stir to make sure each cranberry is well coated and cook 5 to 7 minutes, until the cranberries begin to pop and the mixture has returned to a rolling boil.

5. After most of the cranberries have popped, remove the saucepan from the heat. Pull out the spice bag, but leave the cinnamon sticks in because they're so darn pretty.

6. Ladle the cranberries into sterilized glass jars through a funnel, distributing them into each jar evenly and topping with only as much liquid as needed. (Save the remaining liquid for your cocktail bar or other use.) Let the jars cool to room temperature, and then store in the fridge up to 1 month.

GIFT WRAP

Vintage glass jar with lid

String

Stamp and ink pad

Fabric

Tape (optional)

Add your cranberries to a clean vintage jar. Wipe the rim and seal. Wrap layers of string around the jar, tie into a knot, and trim any excess string. Stamp the label on a small square of fabric. Slip it under the string or adhere it with tape.

how to preserve

Homesteading—which means leading a life of self-sufficiency—is experiencing a modern-day renaissance. Even if you have no plans to raise hens or grow heirloom vegetables or explore your own back-to-the-land thing with expert-level proficiency, the act of preserving foodstuffs is the foundation of a *Food Gift Love* pantry. If you know how to preserve, your homesteading potential is certainly exponential, but on a basic level, your pantry will never be empty.

The following equipment and six techniques are the key parts of preserving food in jars for long-term enjoyment.

PRESERVING EQUIPMENT

These are the main types of equipment required to properly preserve jars of food for long-term storage. You can purchase all of these items brand-new online, but I've also suggested some easy alternatives to get you started. Once you fall in love with preserving, you should buy the setup that works best for you.

Stainless steel pot—There's no hack here. You need a deep pot that will fit a canning rack, your jars, plus 4 inches or so of water and space to avoid a boil-over situation.

Canning rack—You'll need to elevate the jars off the bottom of the pan. I started by using a thick dish towel and then a small cooling rack, but now I use a proper canning rack.

Jar lifter—I improvised early on with regular kitchen tongs (be careful), but I purchased a real jar lifter quickly thereafter.

Headspace tool—You need space between the top of the food and the rim of the jar. I have a headspace tool but find a wooden chopstick works just as well.

Magnetic lid lifter—I used tongs before getting my lid lifter.

Regular-mouth funnel—This is not a narrow-mouth funnel, but one with a much wider opening at the downspout. There's no reliable replacement, so this was my first canning purchase.

Canning ladle—Use a regular soup ladle.

CHOOSING JARS

Brand-new glass jars are the bee's knees, and there's a list of jar sources on page 249. They come with so much potential, a blank slate ripe for your food projects right now. If you preserve a lot, always using new jars becomes a luxury; reusing old jars is just fine. However, examine them for nicks, dents, or cracks—signs that they may not produce a safe, secure seal. Any damaged jars should be reserved for another use (like flowers) or tossed.

Most American-style canning jars generally have three parts: the jar, the lid with the sealing compound, and the band. The Weck jars used throughout this cookbook are produced in Germany and popular in preserving across Europe. They have four parts: the jar, the lid, the rubber ring (which is equal to the American-style lids with the sealing compound), and the clamps.

Whether the jars are new or old, new lids with the sealing compound or new rubber rings must be used every time. If using the jars that have two pieces—a lid and a band—the bands can be reused as well, but examine them and toss any rusted or bent bands as they may also affect whether you get a proper seal.

CLEANING (STERILIZING) YOUR JARS

All jars need to be cleaned well prior to being filled with any kind of preserves. Jars that will be processed for 10 minutes or longer in boiling water simply need a good wash in hot, soapy water just before being filled. Wash them well and let them air dry on a clean towel.

Jars that will be processed for less than 10 minutes or used for long-term storage require a stronger sterilization path. You can clean them in one of three ways: wash them in hot soapy water and dry them in a low oven; run them through a full dishwasher cycle; or fully immerse them in a deep pot of water and boil 10 minutes. The latter is my preferred method—it ensures full sterilization—and it's best to heat the jars just before you're ready to fill them.

Weck rubber rings need to be warmed in boiling water 10 minutes just prior to filling your jars to heat up the sealing compound. American-style canning lids with the sealing compound do not need to be warmed in this manner—just clean them in hot, soapy water and keep them at room temperature until you need them.

FILLING YOUR JARS

When you're ready to fill your jars, focus on one jar at a time. Place a regular-mouth funnel on the jar to help target your pouring or ladling. Add the hot preserves to the warmed jar and pay close attention to the headspace—the space between the top of the food and the rim of the jar. The just-right amount of space is needed to allow for expansion of food as it's processed and to ensure that a vacuum forms when the jars cool. The *Ball Bluebook Guide to Preserving* recommends allowing ½ inch of headspace for high-acid foods like tomatoes, pickles, and relishes and ¼ inch of headspace for jams and jellies. In my experience, these measurements hold true and make a big difference in the long-term preservation of your food.

Once filled, you must remove air bubbles from the food packed into the jar. There are two ways to remove air bubbles: you can run a plastic spatula or wooden chopstick inside the jar between the food and the side of the jar, or you can lift the rim of the jar with protected fingers and tap the jar up and down on the counter, careful to not splatter any hot preserves. The latter technique requires some experience, so start with the former.

Wipe the rim of your jars with a clean, damp cloth or paper towel. Removing any extra sticky particles will support a good seal during processing. With American-style jars, place the lid on the jar rim and screw the band into place until it's fingertip tight—until you just begin to feel resistance—to ensure that the air bubbles have a way to escape the jar during the hot-water-bath canning process. Don't screw it too tight as then air bubbles won't be able to escape during processing. With Weck jars, place the rubber ring on the lid and then place on the filled jar. Snap both clamps into place on opposite ends of the jar.

PROCESSING YOUR JARS

All the preserved recipes in this cookbook follow the water-bath-canning method. The proper setup requires a stainless steel or aluminum pot that's deep enough to hold the jars you're processing plus 2 inches of water to cover the jars and an additional 2 inches to prevent the boiling-over scenario, which happens; it also requires a rack to elevate the jars off the bottom of the pan. Fill your pot with water and get it boiling when you're about 20 to 30 minutes away from processing your jars. Place your sealed jars onto the rack in the pot with your jar lifter (or tongs) and process your jars from the moment the water has returned to a boil. The water must maintain a rolling boil for the entire processing period.

Let's get mathematical for just a moment: The times required for processing that are quoted in this cookbook are what the USDA recommends for preserving at or below 1,000 feet above sea level, which applies to where I live in New England. You may live at a higher elevation than 1,000 feet; if so, you should plan to increase the time by 1 additional minute for every 1,000-foot increase in elevation.

Once processing is complete, turn the heat off and let your jars rest in the water 5 minutes. Remove the jars from the pot with your jar lifter (or tongs) and set them upright on a dry towel somewhere out of the way. Do not touch the jars or lids during this cooling time. Let the jars cool 12 to 24 hours.

Check to ensure that your jars have sealed properly. There are two ways to do this, and performing both of them gives me confidence that the seal is secure: you may press the center of the lid to determine if it's concave, and you may remove the band or clamps and try to lift the lid off with your fingertips. If the center of the lid doesn't pop back up and the lid stays in place, you have achieved a good vacuumed seal. Any jars without a good seal should go into your fridge for immediate enjoyment only.

LABELING YOUR JARS

All preserved food in jars should be labeled with the name and the date it was made. Between markers, stickers, and tags, there are so many ways to do this these days, and you'll see an array of ideas for labeling throughout this cookbook. But don't stick a label on a hot jar because you may get burned and the heat may prevent the label from sticking—let the jar cool down completely before trying to adhere a label.

STORING YOUR JARS

Before storing your filled and cooled jars, remove the band or the clamps that you used to hold the lid in place. The band sure is pretty but may corrode or even get rusty from any lingering water under it. The clamps will also make it hard to stack the jars. Finally, you'll want to wash the lid and the entire outer surface of the jar to remove any residue or sticky stuff that lingered during the processing phase. Rinse and dry.

To ensure the longest possible shelf life, your food in jars should be stored out of direct sunlight and at room temperature, somewhere between 50°F and 70°F. If you live in a colder climate, don't let the jars freeze or the seal may break. If you live in a warmer climate, don't let the jars get too warm as the seal may break from the heat.

In this cookbook, you'll notice that I showcase some food in jars on open bright shelves. I do sometimes rotate pretty preserves onto exposed shelves for a few days at a time to photograph for the website or cookbook. And then, like clockwork, I promptly put them back into a dark pantry for long-term storage.

quick strawberry jam

MAKES: ABOUT 1½ CUPS // PREPARATION TIME: 30 MINUTES

This jam is just wonderful as a simple, special gift. Just pour it into a jar and gift immediately, advising the recipient to store it in the fridge up to 2 weeks. It's also the perfect accompaniment to Panna Cotta Cups (page 78).

INGREDIENTS:

1½ cups quartered strawberries, cleaned and hulled

¾ cup granulated sugar

2 tablespoons lemon juice

SPECIAL EQUIPMENT:

1 glass jar or plastic container with airtight lid

1. In a medium pot over medium-high heat, combine the strawberries, sugar, and lemon juice. While the fruit mixture cooks, stir and crush the fruit bit by bit. Once the fruit mixture has reached the boiling stage, reduce the heat to medium and cook 10 minutes. Stir every 30 seconds to ensure that the mixture doesn't burn. Skim the foam that forms, if desired.

2. Let the mixture cool in the pot 2 to 3 minutes. Pour into the desired glass container, or let cool 15 to 20 minutes longer before spooning into a plastic container.

GIFT WRAP

Ribbon

Wrap a length of ribbon around the rim of the jar.

minty pickles

MAKES: ABOUT 4 CUPS // PREPARATION TIME: 20 MINUTES

My garden grows pickling cucumbers and varieties of mint—spearmint, peppermint, chocolate mint, apple mint, you name it—like it grows weeds. Each harvest, I'm left with pounds and bunches, respectively. One season, I paired them together and the refreshing combo rejuvenated ordinary pickles. These Minty Pickles complement all sorts of cuisine—from beef burgers to lamb burgers to hot dogs, sandwiches, and really spicy food (they're great with fiery Indian food). They add a unique spark to a typical taco bar—toss them into soft corn tortillas filled with beans or roasted meat. Equally wonderful, these pickles provide joy eaten from the jar during snack time.

To create a sleek visual effect, stack the cucumber slices in the jars in an orderly design, either all vertically or in a pattern. When herb season is in your favor, switch up the mint for a few springs of thyme or oregano or fennel fronds. By playing with the herb accent, you can customize them for your table or your recipient.

INGREDIENTS:

3 (about 1 pound) pickling cucumbers, washed

2 to 4 sprigs mint, rinsed and patted dry

2 cups white wine vinegar

½ cup granulated sugar

1 tablespoon white, pink, or black peppercorns

1 tablespoon yellow mustard seeds

1 scant tablespoon cumin seeds

1 tablespoon fine sea salt

SPECIAL EQUIPMENT:

2 pint jars with airtight lids, sterilized

Wide-mouth funnel

1. Slice the cucumbers into ⅛-inch slices (up to ¼ inch is fine too) and divide them evenly between your jars. Nestle 2 sprigs of mint into each jar, or nestle only 1 sprig if you're leery of too much mint intensity. One sprig is refreshing, and 2 sprigs is very minty (in a good way).

2. In a medium pot over medium-high heat, combine the white wine vinegar, sugar, peppercorns, mustard seeds, cumin, and salt. Bring to a boil and, once the sugar has dissolved, remove from the heat.

3. Place a funnel on each cucumber jar and ladle enough liquid into each jar to leave ¼ inch of headspace—be careful, it's hot. Tap the jar a few times to loosen any air bubbles. Top off with any extra liquid. If you have a little leftover liquid, pickle some veggies hanging out on your counter (Swiss chard stems, perhaps?) or discard.

4. Seal the jars and place in the fridge to marinate at least 3 days, then they're ready to eat. These pickles keep in the fridge up to 3 months or longer.

5. Alternatively, you can process these immediately after sealing in a water-bath canner 10 full minutes and store up to 1 year in your pantry.

GIFT WRAP

Glass jar with airtight lid

Rubber band

Paper

Pickle fork (optional)

Add your pickles to a clean jar. Wipe the rim and seal. Slip a rubber band around the jar. Write a label on a paper rectangle, and slide it between the rubber band and the jar. Add a pickle fork (if using).

rhubarb-vanilla jam

MAKES: ABOUT 2 CUPS // PREPARATION TIME: UP TO 45 MINUTES

If I ever had a signature fruit, rhubarb—tart and sweet but mostly tart—is mine. It doesn't really require much to make it agreeable. Just a bit of sugar, lemon, and vanilla will smooth out the tangy flavor. Rhubarb-Vanilla Jam is not only great on toast, but it's perfect to top pancakes, oatmeal, vanilla ice cream, or teacake. No big surprise, it also makes a great base for a mean cocktail. Instead of making a single big batch, I stockpile a couple jars for my *Food Gift Love* pantry each spring weekend, extending my rhubarb enjoyment as long as possible, and then I dole it out to friends and family throughout the year.

Making jam makes some people nervous, but do try this first-timer's jam. Several of my recipe testers had never made jam before this one, and it was a snap for them. So if you're new to it, too, just take it slow.

INGREDIENTS:

18 ounces rhubarb, chopped into 1-inch pieces (2¼ cups)

1¼ cups granulated sugar

2 tablespoons fresh lemon juice

½ teaspoon vanilla extract

1 vanilla bean, split lengthwise

SPECIAL EQUIPMENT:

2 half-pint glass jars with airtight lids, sterilized

Wide-mouth funnel

1. If you're preserving/canning your jam for long-term storage (see "How to Preserve," page 182), start with step 1a. If you're not preserving the jam (if it's your first jam experience and you're wary), you can skip to step 1b.

   a. Sterilize your canning jars and prepare your water-bath-canning pot.

   b. Place a small plate with 4 to 5 small spoons in a flat space in your freezer.

Now let's make jam:

2. In a wide nonreactive 5-quart pan over medium-high heat, combine the rhubarb, sugar, lemon juice, vanilla extract, and vanilla bean. Stir a few times with a rubber spatula and bring to a boil. Once the mixture has come to boil, reduce the heat to medium and cook at least 15 minutes, stirring occasionally, but it could take up to 30 minutes. Pay close attention to this jam, please, as it tends to burn easily if not stirred.

3. Cook the mixture until all the moisture has evaporated and you're left with a very thick, hot syrup. The thicker it gets, the more you will need to stir to ensure that it doesn't burn or stick to the bottom of the pan. At this point, begin checking for doneness.

4. Here are the signs that your jam is ready: the mixture looks glossy and shiny; the mixture begins to thickly coat the back of your spoon; the rhubarb has become very stringy and almost translucent; and the mixture has darkened in color. If all signs point to done, conduct a spoon test.

5. Remove from the heat to slow down the cooking each time you test the jam. Place 1 teaspoon of the mixture on 1 of your frozen spoons and quickly return to the plate in the freezer. After 2 minutes, check to see if the jam has thickened on the frozen spoon by rocking it from side to side. If it's very loose and runny, return to medium heat and continuing boiling the mixture and stirring. When it runs very slowly, it's done. This jam won't really set completely—it has a loose texture. When it's ready, remove from the heat and do not stir it any further. Remove the vanilla bean once the jam has cooled, before storing.

6. If you're not preserving/canning the jam, allow the mixture to cool and then store in the fridge up to 2 weeks in a sealed container.

7. If you are preserving the jam, ladle your jam through a funnel into your prepared sterilized jars, leaving ¼ inch of headspace. Tap the jar a few times to loosen any air bubbles. Wipe the rims and seal carefully, as the jars will be hot. If you're canning according to my water-bath-canning directions, place the jars in a single layer in your pot of boiling water. Once the water bath boils again, process these jars 10 full minutes. Store for up to 1 year in a dark pantry.

GIFT WRAP

Ribbon

Tape

Wrap a length of ribbon around your jar vertically. With a small piece of tape, adhere the ribbon to the underside of the jar.

pear-pineapple-ginger jam

MAKES: ABOUT 6 CUPS // PREPARATION TIME: 2 HOURS

My Pear-Pineapple-Ginger Jam is one of my favorites; it is deep, sweet, and packed with a heavy dose of ginger spice. It perks up anything it touches, like a pile of fluffy pancakes, pound cake, or a runny cheese, and it has the perfect consistency for whisking into cocktails. For a sweet-and-savory thing, slide a bit into a chicken sandwich, glaze a duck breast, or slip it into a first-rate grilled cheese sandwich. While this process requires a bit of technique, it's a wonderful way to spend an afternoon. Once made, you'll have mastered one of the quirkier jam processes—the sort that requires pureeing the fruit during the cooking phase.

Two big lessons to take away here: First, the most direct way to success with any fruit preserve is to weigh the fruit and the sugar with a kitchen scale. The right proportions will ensure that your gift is safe to sit in a pantry. I prefer a 2 parts fruit to just over 1 part sugar ratio, and that's generally perceived as the minimum sugar required for long-term preservation. Second, pureeing hot fruit, whether with an immersion blender or food mill, lets you achieve a texture to match the tastes of your family and friends.

INGREDIENTS:

4½ cups ½-inch dice Bosc pears (about 10 medium pears)

2½ cups ½-inch dice fresh pineapple

1 (1-inch) piece ginger, peeled

5 cups granulated sugar

½ cup fresh lemon juice

3 tablespoons finely chopped crystallized ginger

1½ tablespoons vanilla extract

SPECIAL EQUIPMENT:

Kitchen scale

6 half-pint glass jars with airtight lids, sterilized

Cheesecloth

Immersion blender, food processor, or food mill

Wide-mouth funnel

1. Weigh your prepared fruit. The prepared pear and pineapple, in total, should weigh about 4 pounds.

2. If you're preserving/canning your jam for long-term storage (see "How to Preserve," page 182), start with step 2a. If you're not preserving the jam, you can skip to step 2b.

   a. Sterilize your canning jars and prepare your water-bath-canning pot.

   b. Place a small plate with 4 to 5 small spoons in a flat space in your freezer.

Now let's make jam:

3. Wrap your ginger knob in a bit of cheesecloth; this will make it easier to avoid when pureeing and easier to extract from the pot later.

4. Add the fruit, sugar, lemon juice, gingers, and vanilla to a nonreactive pot that's both wide and deep (a 10-inch or 12-inch diameter is ideal), and stir to combine. Place over medium-high heat. Bring to a boil and then reduce the heat slightly.

5. During the first 45 minutes of cooking, your jam will have large bubbles and create lots of foam—do not stir the jam during this stage; let it continue to cook past the foaming stage. After the foaming has subsided, stir your jam a few times to keep things moving.

6. After 45 minutes of total cooking, remove from the heat and carefully puree about half the jam, avoiding the ginger knob, with an immersion blender. If you don't have an immersion blender, carefully puree 1 to 2 cups in the bowl of a food processor. (A food mill works well, too.) Everything will be very hot, so please be very careful. Add this pureed fruit back to the pot.

7. Place the pot again over medium-high heat, and watch your jam closely as it will be ready within the next 15 to 20 minutes or so. Stir it every few minutes to keep things moving and prevent burning. Once all the moisture has evaporated and you're left with a very thick, hot syrup, begin checking for doneness.

8. Here are the signs that your jam is ready: the mixture looks glossy and shiny; the mixture begins to thickly coat the back of your spoon and the bottom of the pan; and the mixture has darkened slightly in color. If all signs point to done, conduct a spoon test.

9. Remove from the heat to slow down the cooking each time you test the jam. Place 1 teaspoon of the mixture on 1 of your frozen spoons and quickly return to the plate in the freezer. After 2 minutes, check to see if the jam has thickened on the frozen spoon by rocking it from side to side. If it's very loose and runny, return to medium heat and keep boiling and stirring the mixture. When your jam barely moves on the spoon, it's ready. When it's ready, remove from the heat and do not stir it any further. Carefully remove the ginger from the jam and discard.

10. If you're not preserving/canning the jam, allow the mixture to cool and then store in the fridge up to 4 weeks in a sealed container.

11. If you are preserving the jam, ladle your jam through a funnel into your prepared jars, leaving ¼ inch of headspace. Tap the jar a few times to loosen any air bubbles. Wipe the rims and seal carefully, as the jars will be hot. If you're canning according to my water-bath-canning directions, place the jars in a single layer in your pot of boiling water. Once the water bath boils again, process these jars 20 full minutes. Store up to 1 year in a dark pantry.

GIFT WRAP

Tag

Rope

Write the label on a tag. Wrap a length of rope around the jar and slip the tag through the rope. Tie a knot and trim any excess rope.

fig-rosemary jam

MAKES: ABOUT 4 CUPS // PREPARATION TIME: 1 HOUR 30 MINUTES

This jam is inspired by late September days in northern California. The wine harvest is in full swing, the rosemary is heady, and the figs are fat, juicy, and bursting from the trees. Figs are also more affordable in peak season, and I often want to buy them all. During my visits, I borrow a pot from a friend and source jars at the hardware store. In a short afternoon, relaxed and enjoying some local red wine, I make souvenirs for all my friends. This recipe is effortless, especially if you skip the canning part. But preserve at least one jar for later when you'll want to enjoy this perfect memory of late summer in a jar.

The takeaway here is that time improves most things—just like wine—and a little counter time coaxes the sweetness from the figs and allows you some time to enjoy your wine (or take care of other things).

INGREDIENTS:

3 pounds (about 30) ripe Mission figs

3½ cups (about 1½ pounds) granulated sugar

3 (4-inch) strips lemon zest

1 (6-inch) sprig rosemary

½ cup fresh lemon juice

SPECIAL EQUIPMENT:

Kitchen scale

8 quarter-pint glass jars with airtight lids, sterilized

Wide-mouth funnel

1. Wash, de-stem, and slice the figs into quarters.

2. If you're preserving/canning your jam for long-term storage (see "How to Preserve," page 182), start with step 2a. If you're not preserving the jam, you can skip to step 2b.

   a. Sterilize your canning jars and prepare your water-bath-canning pot.

b. Place a small plate with 4 to 5 small spoons in a flat space in your freezer.

Now let's make jam:

3. Add the figs, sugar, and zest to a large, nonreactive bowl or the nonreactive pot you will use to cook it in. Stir to combine and let sit at room temperature 1 hour or up to several hours. You may also pack them in a sealable container and store in the fridge up to 2 days before proceeding.

4. Place the mixture in a nonreactive pot that's both wide and deep (a 10-inch or 12-inch diameter is ideal) and set it over medium-high heat. Add the rosemary and lemon juice. Bring to a boil and then reduce the heat slightly, to just above medium. Cook at a low but rolling boil until all the moisture has evaporated and you're left with a very thick, hot syrup.

5. During the first 20 minutes of cooking, your jam will have large bubbles and create some foam—do not stir the jam during this stage, let it continue to cook past the foaming stage.

6. At the 20-minute mark, start watching your jam closely as it will be ready within the next 10 minutes or so. Stir it every few minutes to keep things moving and prevent burning. Begin checking for doneness.

7. Here are the signs that your jam is ready: the large bubbles have become very tiny; the mixture looks glossy and shiny; the mixture begins to thickly coat the back of your spoon and the bottom of the pan; and the mixture has darkened slightly in color. If all signs point to done, conduct a spoon test.

8. Remove from the heat to slow down the cooking each time you test the jam. Place 1 teaspoon of the mixture on 1 of your frozen spoons and quickly return to the plate in the freezer. After 2 minutes, check to see if the jam has thickened on the frozen spoon by rocking it from side to side. If it's very loose and runny, return to medium heat and keep boiling the mixture. When your jam barely moves on the spoon, it's ready. It will continue to thicken as it sits. When it's ready, remove from the heat and do not stir it any further. Carefully remove and discard the rosemary sprig.

9. If you're not preserving/canning the jam, allow the mixture to cool and then store in the fridge up to 4 weeks in a sealed container.

10. If you are preserving the jam, ladle your jam through a funnel into your prepared jars, leaving ¼ inch of headspace. Tap the jar a few times to loosen any air bubbles. Wipe the rims and seal carefully, as the jars will be hot. If you're canning according to my water-bath-canning directions, place the jars in a single layer in your pot of boiling water. Once the water bath boils again, process these jars 10 full minutes. Store up to 1 year in a dark pantry.

GIFT WRAP

Masking tape

Glue (I prefer Mod Podge)

Glitter

Fig leaf (optional)

Washi tape

Once the jar has cooled completely (at least 24 hours after making), place a piece of masking tape around the lower ½ inch of the jar. Apply glue below the tape line on the jar. Sprinkle with glitter and turn upside down to dry. Once dry, adhere a small fig leaf (if using) to the jar with washi tape.

orange-cinnamon marmalade

MAKES: ABOUT 5 CUPS // PREPARATION TIME: 3 HOURS ACTIVE TIME (UP 12 HOURS TOTAL TIME)

Sweet and slightly bitter, my Orange-Cinnamon Marmalade is my most requested food gift. One friend sends me a little alert (a text or photo) when scraping the last spoonful from the jar, in case I have extras that need a new home, pronto.

Orange marmalade may put fear in the hearts of many home cooks, but you can do this. Your success here depends on three things: having the right size pot, weighing your ingredients (like a professional), and paying close attention to signs that indicate when your marmalade is ready. Use a pot close to the size specified. Buy a scale to weigh your prepared fruit. Watch your marmalade as the cooking time winds down. After 2 days of (really, quite fun) work, you'll have 10 half-pint jars of the purest *Food Gift Love*.

Cara Cara oranges have few to no seeds and thin rinds, so they make a fine marmalade. Other navel varieties work, too, though the marmalade may be a touch more bitter. Either way, your kitchen will fill with the sweetest scent. One recipe tester said the aroma should be bottled and sold as an *eau de parfum*.

INGREDIENTS:

4 pounds (about 8 or 9) Cara Cara oranges, preferably organic

2¼ pounds (about 5 cups) granulated sugar

½ cup fresh lemon juice

3 (4-inch) cinnamon sticks

SPECIAL EQUIPMENT:

Kitchen scale

Candy thermometer (optional)

10 half-pint glass jars with airtight lids, sterilized

Wide-mouth funnel

Day 1:

1. Wash and dry the oranges and slice off and discard the nubby stem end. Using a very sharp knife, cut the oranges into quarters, and then slice each quarter into ⅛-inch wedge-shaped slices crosswise. Quarter-inch slices are okay, too—you'll just have thicker rinds in your marmalade.

2. Place the oranges in a large nonreactive pot that's both wide and deep (a 10-inch or 12-inch diameter is ideal), and add enough cold water to cover by 1 inch. (If you're unsure of how to quantify the water, place your orange slices in the pot and hold some down with a small measuring cup with a clean ruler placed inside. Add enough water to come up 1 inch on the ruler. Remove the measuring cup and ruler before beginning to cook.)

3. Bring to a boil over high heat, and then reduce the heat to medium-high, cooking 45 to 55 minutes until the fruit is tender. Check for tenderness by sticking a fork into a few orange rinds. If it pierces easily, it's done. Remove from the heat and let cool to room temperature. Cover and let rest at room temperature 8 hours or up to overnight.

Day 2:

4. If you're preserving/canning your jam for long-term storage (see "How to Preserve," page 182), start with step 4a. If you're not preserving the jam, you can skip to step 4b.

   a. Sterilize your canning jars and prepare your water-bath-canning pot.

   b. Place a small plate with 4 to 5 small spoons in a flat space in your freezer.

5. Add the sugar, lemon juice, and cinnamon sticks to the pot with orange-water mixture, and stir to combine.

6. Place the pot over medium-high heat. Bring to a boil, then reduce the heat slightly, and cook until all the moisture has evaporated and you're left with a very thick, hot syrup.

7. During the first 60 minutes of cooking, your marmalade will have large bubbles and create some foam—do not stir the marmalade during this stage, let it continue to cook past the foaming stage.

8. After the first 60 minutes of cooking, start watching your marmalade closely as this jam tends to burn easily if not watched. It will be ready within the next 15 to 30 minutes, depending on your stove and pot size. Stir every few minutes to keep things moving and prevent burning. At the 75-minute mark, begin checking for doneness.

9. Here are the signs that your marmalade is ready: the large bubbles have become very tiny; the mixture looks glossy and shiny; the mixture begins to thickly coat the back of your spoon and the bottom of the pan; and the mixture has darkened slightly in color. For those of you with a candy thermometer, your marmalade is ready at 220°F. If you don't have a thermometer and all signs point to done, conduct a spoon test.

10. Remove from the heat to slow down the cooking each time you test the marmalade. Place 1 teaspoon of the mixture on 1 of your frozen spoons and quickly return to the plate in the freezer. After 2 minutes, check to see if the marmalade has thickened on the frozen spoon by rocking it from side to side. If it's very loose and runny, return to medium heat and keep boiling the mixture. When your marmalade barely moves on the spoon, it's done. When it's ready, remove from the heat and do not stir it any further.

11. Remove the cinnamon from the marmalade and discard.

12. If you're not preserving/canning the marmalade, allow the mixture to cool and then store in the fridge up to 4 weeks in a sealed container.

13. If you are preserving the marmalade, ladle your marmalade through a funnel into your prepared jars, leaving ¼ inch of headspace. Tap the jar a few times to loosen any air bubbles. Wipe the rims and seal carefully, as the jars will be hot. If you're canning according to my water-bath-canning directions, place the jars in a single layer in your pot of boiling water. Once the water bath boils again, process these jars 10 full minutes. Store up to 1 year in a dark pantry.

GIFT WRAP

Craft paper

Stamp and ink pad

Tape

Twine

Lay craft paper flat on a table. Stamp your message or design all over the paper. Once the paper has dried, wrap each jar as you would a present, taping the ends into place. Cut a length of twine and wrap it around the jar a few times. Tie a knot and trim any excess.

grapefruit-elderflower marmalade

MAKES: ABOUT 4 CUPS // PREPARATION TIME: 3 HOURS ACTIVE TIME
(UP TO 10 HOURS TOTAL TIME)

After you conquer this Grapefruit-Elderflower Marmalade, you'll never look at the store-bought stuff the same. This elegant recipe balances simplicity with professional-like skills. It does require 2 days to come to life, but your morning toast, baked goods, and cocktails will glow with every spoonful. My friends rarely buy or make anything with grapefruit, so I love to surprise them with jars of this sweet-tart treat for their pantries.

Just like with the Orange-Cinnamon Marmalade (page 194), your success here depends on having the right size pot, weighing your ingredients, and paying close attention to signs that illuminate when your marmalade is ready. This recipe intentionally makes a very large batch. After 2 days of my attention, 8 half-pint jars are the right reward, but 4 pint jars would be nice, too.

Elderflower liqueur is the most heavenly liquid, but it can be expensive. If you like, replace it with elderflower syrup or something equally heady like orange liqueur or dark rum. If you buy a bottle of elderflower liqueur, the rest of it won't go to waste. Try this: pour 2 tablespoons into a flute and fill with sparkling wine. If you like that, try my Sparkling Elderflower Punch (page 222), and serve it at the marmalade party you'll host next week because you're an expert now.

INGREDIENTS:

3¹/2 pounds (about 4) grapefruit, preferably organic

2 pounds (about 4¹/2 cups) granulated sugar

¹/2 cup fresh lemon juice

¹/2 cup elderflower liqueur (or elderflower syrup)

SPECIAL EQUIPMENT:

Kitchen scale

Manual or automatic juicer

Candy thermometer (optional)

8 half-pint jars with airtight lids, sterilized

Wide-mouth funnel

Day 1:

1. Cut the grapefruits in half and juice each half, reserving the juice for later (so cover the juice and put in the fridge).

2. Place the grapefruit halves in a large nonreactive pot that's both wide and deep (a 10-inch or 12-inch diameter is ideal), and fill with enough cold water to cover the fruit by 1 inch. (If you're unsure of how to quantify the water, place your grapefruit halves into the pot and hold some down with a measuring cup with a clean ruler placed inside. Add enough water to come up 1 inch on the ruler. Remove the measuring cup and ruler before beginning to cook.) Bring to a boil over high heat and cook 5 minutes.

3. Drain the water from the pot, and again add enough cold water to cover the fruit by 1 inch. Bring to a boil over high heat and let cook 45 to 60 minutes until the fruit is tender, adding water as needed to keep the fruit fully submerged. Check for tenderness by sticking a fork into a few grapefruit rinds. If it pierces easily, it's done. Remove from the heat and let cool to room temperature. Cover and let rest at room temperature 8 hours or up to overnight.

continued

Day 2:

4. If you're preserving/canning your jam for long-term storage, start with step 4a; if you're not preserving the jam, you can skip to step 4b.

  a. Sterilize your canning jars and prepare your water-bath-canning pot (see "How to Preserve," page 182).

  b. Place a small plate with 4 to 5 small spoons in a flat space in your freezer.

5. Lay down several kitchen towels under your work area to absorb any liquid, and have a sharp knife and cutting board handy. Remove the grapefruit from the liquid and place on the towels (set the pot and liquid aside for now). Using a spoon, clean the inner white pith from your grapefruit—remove (but reserve) the inner pith and the remaining segments, and scrape out any extra white pith to ensure that the rind is of a uniform thickness of about ⅛ inch thick.

6. Chop up all the pith and segments into small chunks and add to the pot with the cooking liquid in which it sat overnight.

7. With a sharp knife, slice the rind halves into 4 equal segments and then slice the segments into ⅛-inch-thick strips. Return the rinds to the cooking liquid. Add the reserved grapefruit juice, sugar, and lemon juice to your grapefruit rind-pith-water mixture, and stir it to combine. Place the pot over medium-high heat. Bring the mixture to a boil, then reduce the heat slightly, and cook until all the moisture has evaporated and you're left with a very thick, hot syrup.

8. During the first 30 minutes of cooking, your marmalade will have large bubbles and create some foam—do not stir the marmalade during this stage, let it continue to cook past the foaming stage.

9. After the first 30 minutes of cooking, start watching your marmalade closely as it will be ready within the next 15 to 30 minutes, depending on your stove and pot. Stir it every few minutes to keep things moving and prevent burning. Don't be afraid to reduce the heat a bit to prevent burning. Add the elderflower liqueur when you feel the marmalade is close to done. Let's check for doneness.

10. Here are the signs that your marmalade is ready: the large bubbles have become very tiny; the mixture looks glossy and shiny; the mixture begins to thickly coat the back of your spoon and the bottom of the pan; and the mixture has darkened in color. For those of you with a candy thermometer, your marmalade is ready at 220°F. If you don't have a thermometer and all signs point to done, conduct a spoon test.

11. Remove from the heat to slow down the cooking each time you test the marmalade. Place 1 teaspoon of the mixture on 1 of your frozen spoons and quickly return to the plate in the freezer. After 2 minutes, check to see if the marmalade has thickened on the frozen spoon by rocking it from side to side. If it's very loose and runny, return to medium heat and keep boiling the mixture. When your marmalade barely moves on the spoon, it's done. When it's ready, remove from the heat and do not stir it any further.

12. If you're not preserving/canning the marmalade, allow the mixture to cool and then store in the fridge up to 4 weeks in a sealed container.

13. If you are preserving the marmalade, ladle your marmalade through a funnel into your prepared jars, leaving ¼ inch of headspace. Tap the jar a few times to loosen any air bubbles. Wipe the rims and seal carefully, as the jars will be hot. If you're canning according to my water-bath-canning directions, place the jars in a single layer in your pot of boiling water. Once the water bath boils again, process these jars 10 full minutes. Store up to 1 year in a dark pantry.

GIFT WRAP

Masking tape

Twine

Fabric

Tape

Write the label on a piece of masking tape. Once the jar has cooled completely, stick the label to the jar. Cut a length of twine and set aside. Trim a square piece of fabric about 2 inches larger than the diameter of your jar. Place it on the top of the jar (use tape on the underside to hold it in place). Wrap the twine around the fabric a few times, tie a knot, and trim any excess twine.

ground
cherry
chutney

ground cherry chutney

MAKES: ABOUT 1 CUP // PREPARATION TIME: 30 MINUTES

Ground cherries look like currants except they're golden and encased in a husk that peels off easily when ripe. They taste like a cross between a pineapple and a cantaloupe—light, tropical, tart, and mellow. A chef friend of mine once heated up this chutney, thinned it with water, and then drizzled it over a pan-seared scallops dish—it was a dazzling finish.

Customize your chutney by adding ½ teaspoon of your favorite spice, such as ground ginger, ground allspice, or ground mustard to add even more zest.

INGREDIENTS:

1 cup golden ground cherries

1 cup granulated sugar

2 tablespoons water

½ cup minced white onion

¼ cup apple cider vinegar

Pinch of fine sea salt, to taste

Pinch freshly ground black pepper, to taste

SPECIAL EQUIPMENT:

Wide-mouth funnel

1 half-pint jar with airtight lid, sterilized

1. Husk and wash the ground cherries. Set aside.

2. Add the sugar and water to a medium pot set over medium heat. Bring to a low boil; this should take 3 to 5 minutes. Swirl (do not stir), until the sugar is gooey, sticky, and golden.

3. Carefully add the white onion and apple cider vinegar to the pot, as the mixture will boil up a bit and bubble. The fumes are potent, so stand back a little. Stir just to combine everything and let the onions cook 2 to 3 minutes longer, until they begin to become translucent.

4. Add the ground cherries. Stir and cook the mixture until the cherries pop and collapse against the syrup, about 5 to 10 minutes. Remove from the heat and stir in the salt and pepper.

5. Ladle through a funnel into your sterilized jar and store in the fridge up to 3 weeks.

GIFT WRAP

Glass jar with airtight lid

Marker

Ribbon

Vintage knife (optional)

Pour the chutney into a clean jar. Wipe the rim and seal. Write the label on the lid of the jar. Cut a length of ribbon and tie it around your jar, trimming any excess ribbon. Slip a knife (if using) through the ribbon.

maple walnut syrup (wet walnuts)

MAKES: ABOUT 2 CUPS // PREPARATION TIME: 20 MINUTES

Without a doubt, I got my palate, my sense of taste from my father—one hundred percent. He ate anything and always had a fondness for foods that were nontraditional and full of texture. These Wet Walnuts—a favorite treat of mine growing up in New Jersey—are all those things and more. They're gooey, sticky, crunchy, sweet, and a perfect match for vanilla bean ice cream. Gift them with other sundae bar fixings like my Salty Dark Caramel Sauce (page 139) or as a topping with pancake mix.

The golden syrup helps bind the flavors nicely. Pecans as a substitute for the walnuts are a lovely alternative.

INGREDIENTS:

½ cup plus 2 tablespoons walnut halves or pieces

1 cup dark, robust maple syrup

4 tablespoons golden syrup or corn syrup

1 teaspoon vanilla extract

2 tablespoons water

2 teaspoons cornstarch

2 tablespoons bourbon (optional)

⅛ teaspoon fine sea salt

SPECIAL EQUIPMENT:

1 pint jar with airtight lid, sterilized

1. Preheat the oven to 350°F. Line a baking sheet with parchment or a silicone pan liner. Spread the walnuts out on the parchment and roast 10 minutes or until lightly toasted. Set aside and let cool.

2. In a medium pot over medium heat, combine the maple syrup, golden syrup, and vanilla extract. Bring to a low boil; this should take 3 to 5 minutes. Watch carefully as the mixture may bubble over—if this happens, just reduce the heat.

3. Meanwhile, in a tiny bowl, mix the water and cornstarch together until lump free and milky looking. This is called a slurry.

4. Once the maple syrup mixture boils, stir in the slurry and watch carefully. After 3 to 5 minutes, the mixture will return to a low boil and may foam up or begin to edge up the side of the pan. Add the bourbon (if using) to the mixture and stir just a couple times, being careful not to drip any of the bourbon near your flame as it may ignite. Cook just another 1 to 2 minutes and then remove from the heat, as this will continue to thicken up as it cools.

5. Stir in the walnuts and salt to coat and let cool a few minutes. Transfer to a jar to cool completely, and store in the fridge up to 2 weeks. Bring to room temperature before serving.

GIFT WRAP

Glass jar with airtight lid

Parchment paper

Twine

Washi tape

Pour the syrup into a jar. Cut a round of parchment paper and place it over the jar's opening. Wrap the twine around the paper a few times and make a knot. Trim any excess twine. Write the label on washi tape and adhere it to the jar.

honeyed kumquats

MAKES: ABOUT 4 CUPS // PREPARATION TIME: 1 HOUR 30 MINUTES

I have a friend who munches on kumquats like he does popcorn, popping them back one by one as a snack. I agree that the tart taste is addictive. Kumquats are not always easy to source, but when I find them, I relish the task of preserving a tiny crop of kumquats in syrup form. I gift these Honeyed Kumquats as is or with a round of cheese, for a special appetizer, or with a bottle of sparkling wine, for a memorable cocktail hour.

The syrup is half-honey, half-sugar so it's fairly sweet. But as one of my European recipe testers put it, this recipe is good for someone without a "sweet tongue"—as the resulting syrup elevates a purely tart thing into something still bitter but with glorious sweet balance. These jars are mostly infused syrup; the kumquats are distributed evenly between them. Use a very light honey, like clover, so the kumquat flavor persists, and reserve a few extra kumquats, if desired, for garnishing the gift.

INGREDIENTS:

2 cups kumquats, washed and stemmed

1 cup granulated sugar

1 cup light honey

2 cups water

3 tablespoons finely diced candied crystallized ginger

1 tablespoon lemon juice

SPECIAL EQUIPMENT:

Candy thermometer (optional)

Wide-mouth funnel

2 pint jars or 4 half-pint jars with airtight lids, sterilized

1. Slice the kumquats horizontally into three to four ¼-inch slices. Remove and discard the seeds as you go. Set aside.

2. In a medium pot over medium-high heat, combine the sugar, honey, water, ginger, and lemon juice. Bring to a boil, watching closely so the pot doesn't overflow with foam. This should take about 10 minutes. Add the kumquats to the pot, stirring quickly just to ensure that they are coated with the syrup.

3. Return to a boil over medium-high heat and then reduce the heat to medium. Let simmer until the kumquats become translucent and the syrup becomes thicker, 30 to 45 minutes. The consistency will be similar to a thicker maple syrup, but it won't be dense or jam-like. On a candy thermometer (if using), the kumquats are ready when the temperature reaches 220°F. Remove from the heat.

4. If you're not preserving/canning the kumquats, allow the mixture to cool and then store in the fridge for up to 3 weeks in a sealed container.

5. If you are preserving the kumquats, ladle the kumquats and syrup evenly through a funnel into your sterilized glass jars. Tap the jar a few times to loosen any air bubbles. Wipe the rims and seal carefully, as the jars will be hot. If you're canning according to my water-bath-canning directions (see "How to Preserve, page 182), place the jars in a single layer in your pot of boiling water. Once the water bath boils again, process the jars 10 minutes. Store up to 1 year in a dark pantry.

GIFT WRAP

Ribbon

Tag

String

Soft, mild cheese (refrigerated until ready to gift)

Spoon

Fresh kumquats

Wood box

Wrap a piece of ribbon around the jar. Write the label on a tag, and thread the ribbon through the tag. Wind a piece of string around the cheese several times, looping the string around the spoon. Slip the jar, the cheese, and the extra kumquats into a small wood box.

candied jalapeños

MAKES: ABOUT 3 CUPS // PREPARATION TIME: 30 MINUTES

I grew up in a household of women who filled warm corn tortillas with nothing but sliced jalapeños and a squeeze of lemon. I watched as a child thinking these women were absolutely crazy. Turns out that they were on to something. I transformed that memory into something a little more palatable by adding vinegar and sugar. These Candied Jalapeños offer balance to my Smoky Chicken Soup (page 62), fancy up cream cheese and crackers, or satisfy simply tucked into a plain corn tortilla for a quick snack.

I use this same recipe to make jalapeño simple syrup, which, combined with lime juice and Orange Cordial (page 235), makes a spicy (and memorable) Margarita.

INGREDIENTS:

1 pound jalapeños, washed and dried

3 cups (about 1½ pounds) granulated sugar

1 cup apple cider vinegar

1 (4-inch) cinnamon stick

3 whole cloves

1 star anise pod

SPECIAL EQUIPMENT:

Kitchen scale

Rubber gloves

3 half-pint glass jars with airtight lids, sterilized

Wide-mouth funnel

3. Add the jalapeños and simmer 3 to 4 minutes, watching very closely. When the first jalapeño begins to lose its bright green color, remove all of them from the pot quickly with a slotted spoon and place them in a medium bowl. Then, distribute the jalapeños among the sterilized jars. Remove the cinnamon stick from the pot and discard, but leave the rest of the spices in the syrup.

4. Return the syrup to a boil over medium-low heat and cook 5 minutes longer, stirring occasionally to help the foam subside. Remove from the heat.

5. Ladle the hot syrup through a funnel into the jalapeño jars, leaving ¼ inch of headspace. Let the cloves and star anise pod find a home in the jars. Tap the jars a few times to loosen any air bubbles. Wipe the rims and seal carefully, as the jars will be hot.

6. If you're not preserving/canning the jalapeños, allow them to cool completely and then store in the fridge up to 3 weeks.

7. If you're preserving the jalapeños according to my water-bath-canning directions (see "How to Preserve," page 182), place the jars in a single layer in your pot of boiling water. Once the water bath boils again, process the jars 10 minutes. Store up to 1 year in a dark pantry.

1. Prepare the jalapeños: To avoid burning your skin or eyes, wear rubber gloves when working with jalapeños. Slice them horizontally into ¼-inch rounds. Discard the stem end, and gently pull or slice out the seeds; use a little water to help clean them out completely. If you prefer more heat, leave the seeds just where they are. (I love heat, but for some, it's just a bit too hot.) Set aside.

2. In a medium pot over medium-high heat, combine the sugar, apple cider vinegar, cinnamon stick, cloves, and star anise. Bring to a boil, then reduce the heat to medium and cook 5 additional minutes.

GIFT WRAP

Glass jar with airtight lid

Wax paper (optional)

Rubber band (optional)

Tag

Twine

Pour your jalapeños into a jar. Wipe the rim and seal with a lid, or cover the jar with a slip of wax paper and a rubber band (if using). Write the label on a tag, and thread a piece of twine through the tag. Tie it to the jar and trim any excess string.

spirited gifts

A gift full of spirit—booze, hooch, liquor, hard stuff—is
the kind of gift that gets the party started. These tipples will tempt
the mixologist who shakes up ever-changing refreshments, the
teetotaler who searches for flavored-soda sweeteners, and anyone
who just wants a swig of something special on a Tuesday.

This chapter offers the essential finishing touches to
a *Food Gift Love* pantry. Libations are always required, and these
recipes embody the ease and gratification that so many
of the previous chapters showcased. The only stipulation here is
the need for patience. Some of these recipes come
to life in a flash, but others require a little brewing time. I promise,
they're worth the wait.

◆

cucumber-lime pitcher // infused simple syrups—
rhubarb-rosemary simple syrup, lemon-rosemary simple
syrup, ginger simple syrup, black tea simple syrup, raspberry-
rose simple syrup // cider-chai syrup // grenadine // bourbon-
vanilla cherries // sparkling elderflower punch // vin d'orange //
limoncello // basilcello // rhubarb cordial // strawberry
cordial // orange cordial // margarita mix // cold-brew
coffee // irish cream // rompopo

cucumber-lime pitcher

MAKES: ABOUT 2½ CUPS // PREPARATION TIME: 1 HOUR 15 MINUTES

This Cucumber-Lime Pitcher is an easy-to-love, easy-to-make (and easy-to-adapt) drink to gift to a party. Since it's nonalcoholic (to start), it's become my go-to drink for family-style dinner parties. It takes moments to assemble and gets better as it sits on a buffet table. It should be made not more than a few hours before serving; an overnight steep is too long because it will pull all of the bitterness from the pith.

For a potluck, take along a little maple syrup—just 1 to 2 tablespoons per 8-ounce serving—to sweeten cupfuls for the kids. For the adults, take a bottle of gin (or vodka)—add a shot per glass, or as I prefer, let the drinker make a cocktail that suits her or his taste. Sometimes, I create a do-it-yourself cocktail bar with bowls of fresh blackberries, strawberries, or basil for muddling into pours from the pitcher.

INGREDIENTS:

½ cup thinly sliced English (seedless) cucumbers

½ cup lime juice plus 3 more limes, thinly sliced

½ liter club soda plus ½ liter club soda, separated

About 4 cups ice, for serving

SPECIAL EQUIPMENT:

1 (2-liter) glass jar or transportable pitcher

1. To your glass jar or pitcher, add the cucumbers, lime juice, and sliced limes.

2. Pour in ½ liter of the club soda. Stir and let sit in the fridge at least 1 hour.

3. Transport as is; add the remaining ½ liter club soda and ice just before serving.

GIFT WRAP

Cheesecloth
String
Straws (optional)

Cut a piece of cheesecloth to fit over the opening of the pitcher. Drape over the top and tie with a length of string. If you'd like, tie up a small bunch of paper straws (if using) as a supplemental gift. Alternatively, you may use a plastic container instead of a glass pitcher.

infused simple syrups

An infused simple syrup can be as simple as equal parts water combined with equal parts sugar or honey. It can also be as gussied up and elevated as my favorite five Simple syrup recipes, which follow:

Rhubarb-Rosemary Simple Syrup: When rhubarb is in season in early spring, I rush to preserve it a hundred different ways, including using this easy method. Rhubarb stalks vary from green to speckled light pink all the way to bright red. Choose the dark-red rhubarb stalks for the syrup; the color doesn't change the tart flavor much, but it does turn the syrup into a beautiful, gift-worthy pinkish hue. Put this syrup to work mixed with vodka, club soda, and a squeeze of lemon or lime. If you prefer wine, add 2 tablespoons to a flute and fill her up with the dry sparkling stuff. Garnish either drink with rosemary or a long, thin slice of freshly cut rhubarb.

Lemon-Rosemary Simple Syrup: A simple syrup filled with the purest essence of lemon and rosemary perk up the longest, snowiest winter. Serve it as a hot tea (add 1 tablespoon to boiling water), in a bright gin cocktail (add 2 tablespoons to a few fingers of gin and club soda), or even drizzled onto a hot bundt cake (oh, yes). I prefer Meyer lemons because they have a more floral scent, but regular Eureka lemons work just fine.

Ginger Simple Syrup: Ginger root is used frequently in international cuisine, especially Asian, Mediterranean, and Caribbean dishes, but it also is believed to soothe what ails you. So, it stands to reason that mixing it into cocktails basically makes cocktails healthy. If you're candying the ginger slices as suggested in my note, use fresh young ginger. Younger ginger is mild and has a very thin skin that's less flawed in its appearance. You can find younger ginger at many Asian markets, as they turn it over more frequently. Older ginger is thick-skinned and fibrous, and it makes for very stringy candied slices that are not worth the extra effort. So with younger ginger, make syrup and candy. With older ginger, just make syrup.

Black Tea Simple Syrup: Black tea syrup makes many people so happy mixed into gin and soda or into an amped-up lemonade. Because this syrup is indeed simple, the quality of the tea leaves is very important. While it's ideal to use the best you can afford, instead, I recommend the following compromise: use whatever you have in your everyday cocktails and source a few bags of much nicer tea when making this as a gift. My favorite high-quality black tea is usually blended with a floral element—like cornflower or rose.

Raspberry-Rose Simple Syrup: A little fancy and over the top, my Raspberry-Rose Simple Syrup uses dried culinary (edible) rose petals and fresh raspberries to make something that tastes like a rose garden wedged up against a raspberry bush. It's sweet, floral, and made for adding to a glass of sparkling wine or cocktail mixer, or drizzling over fancied crepes. Reserve a bottle for yourself—this recipe makes two—and add a shot to a glass of club soda, with a squeeze of lime and ice. Savor and don't forget to smell the . . .

RHUBARB-ROSEMARY SIMPLE SYRUP

MAKES: ABOUT 3 CUPS
PREPARATION TIME: 30 MINUTES

INGREDIENTS:

½-pound fresh red rhubarb (5 stalks), chopped into 1-inch pieces

2 cups water

2 cups granulated sugar

1 (6-inch) sprig rosemary, stem and leaves

SPECIAL EQUIPMENT:

3 half-pint glass bottles with airtight lids, sterilized

Narrow-mouth funnel

1. In a medium saucepan over medium-high heat, combine the rhubarb, water, sugar, and rosemary. Bring to a boil, stirring or swirling the pan every now and then to help the sugar dissolve. Once the boil is reached, reduce the heat to medium and keep the mixture at a low boil 5 minutes. Remove from the heat.

2. Let the syrup steep 10 minutes. Strain, discarding the rhubarb and rosemary. Let the syrup cool at room temperature before bottling. Store in glass bottles in the fridge up to 2 weeks.

GIFT WRAP

Glass bottle with airtight lid

Tag

Twine

Transfer the syrup to a clean pretty bottle. Write the label on a tag—or find a cutout of a capital *R*—and thread kitchen twine through the tag. Wrap the twine around the bottle to secure.

LEMON-ROSEMARY SIMPLE SYRUP

MAKES: ABOUT 2 CUPS
PREPARATION TIME: 20 MINUTES

INGREDIENTS:

4 large lemons

1½ cups water

2 cups granulated sugar

1 (5-inch) piece rosemary, stem and leaves

SPECIAL EQUIPMENT:

Glass bottles with airtight lids, sterilized

Narrow-mouth funnel

1. With a vegetable peeler, peel the zest (avoiding the white pith) into ten 3-inch strips, from 1 or 2 lemons. Slice all the lemons in half and squeeze the juice; strain to remove the seeds. Measure ½ cup lemon juice for this recipe, and reserve the rest for another use.

2. In a saucepan over medium-high heat, combine the juice, zest, water, sugar, and rosemary. Bring to a boil, stirring or swirling the pan every now and then to help the sugar dissolve. Once the boil is reached, reduce the heat to medium and keep the mixture at a low boil 5 minutes. Remove from the heat.

3. Let the syrup steep 10 minutes. Strain, discarding the zest and rosemary. Let cool at room temperature before bottling. Store in glass bottles in the fridge up to 2 weeks.

GIFT WRAP

Glass bottle with airtight lid

Paper bag

Hole punch

Rosemary branch

Transfer the syrup to a clean pretty bottle. Write the label on a paper bag and place the bottle in the bag. Fold the top of the bag down and punch two holes equidistant from the top. Pull some of the leaves from the rosemary branch and thread it through both holes to seal the bag.

GINGER SIMPLE SYRUP

MAKES: ABOUT 3 CUPS
PREPARATION TIME: 1 HOUR

INGREDIENTS:

½ pound fresh ginger

4 cups water

2 cups granulated sugar

SPECIAL EQUIPMENT:

Glass bottles with airtight lids, sterilized

Narrow-mouth funnel

1. With a vegetable peeler or a spoon, scrape the peel off the ginger. Slice into ⅛-inch or thinner slices.

2. In a medium saucepan over medium-high heat, combine the ginger, water, and sugar. Bring to a boil, swirling the pan every now and then to help the sugar dissolve. Once the boil is reached, reduce the heat to medium and simmer 45 minutes or until the liquid is reduced by about half. Remove from the heat.

BLACK TEA SIMPLE SYRUP

MAKES: ABOUT 2 CUPS
PREPARATION TIME: 30 MINUTES

INGREDIENTS:

2 cups water

2 cups granulated sugar

⅓ cup loose black tea leaves

SPECIAL EQUIPMENT:

Glass bottles with airtight lids, sterilized

Narrow-mouth funnel

1. In a medium saucepan over medium-high heat, combine the water, sugar, and tea leaves. Bring to a boil, swirling the pan every now and again to help the sugar dissolve. Once the boil is reached, reduce the heat to medium and keep the mixture at a low boil 5 minutes. Remove from the heat.

2. Let the syrup steep 10 minutes. Strain, discarding the tea leaves. Let the syrup cool to room temperature before bottling. Store in glass bottles in the fridge up to 2 weeks.

3. Let the syrup steep 15 minutes. Strain, discarding the ginger. Let the syrup cool to room temperature before bottling. Store in glass bottles in the fridge up to 2 weeks.

Candied Ginger: If you'd like to make candied ginger, boil the Ginger Syrup an extra 15 to 20 minutes until the syrup reaches 220°F on a candy thermometer. Strain, let cool to room temperature, and bottle the syrup. Place the ginger slices on parchment paper to dry 4 hours, though they'll remain a little sticky and shiny. Roll in extra sugar and let sit overnight or longer until completely dry.

GIFT WRAP

Glass bottle with airtight lid

Tag

Twine

Transfer the syrup to a clean pretty bottle. Write the label on a tag. Wrap the twine around the neck of the bottle several times and tie it in a knot. Slip the tag on and tie another knot. Trim any excess twine.

GIFT WRAP

Glass bottle with airtight lid

Wrapping paper

Tape

Leather rope or twine

Transfer the syrup to a clean pretty bottle. Roll the bottle in a rectangular piece of wrapping paper, taping the bottom under the bottle. Fold the top over once and tape. Wrap the leather rope around the wrapped bottle and tie it in a knot. Trim any excess rope.

◆

RASPBERRY-ROSE SIMPLE SYRUP

MAKES: ABOUT 2 CUPS

PREPARATION TIME: 30 MINUTES

INGREDIENTS:

2 cups water

2 cups granulated sugar

1 cup (30 grams) culinary dried rose petals

1 cup raspberries

SPECIAL EQUIPMENT:

Glass bottles with airtight lids, sterilized

Narrow-mouth funnel

1. In a medium saucepan over medium-high heat, combine the water, sugar, rose petals, and raspberries. Bring to a boil, swirling the pan every now and again to help the sugar dissolve. Once the boil is reached, reduce the heat to medium and simmer 10 minutes. Remove from the heat.

2. Let the syrup steep 10 minutes. Strain, discarding the rose petals and fruit. Let the syrup cool at room temperature before bottling. Store in glass bottles in the fridge up to 2 weeks.

GIFT WRAP

Glass bottle with airtight lid

Sticker

Transfer the syrup to a clean pretty bottle. Write the label on a sticker and stick to the bottle.

cider-chai syrup

MAKES: ABOUT 3 CUPS // PREPARATION TIME: 45 MINUTES

Apples and chai spices may seem an unlikely combination, but it works gloriously, especially when enjoyed in front of a fire. Add 2 tablespoons to a cup of boiled water for a drink that warms you. Add 1 tablespoon whiskey for a makeshift hot toddy that also warms you, perhaps even a bit more. Process these jars in a water bath to preserve the goodness for gifting all year. This thickish syrup separates a bit once it sits, but a good shake brings it back together.

My preferred chai tea is a high-quality assam black tea seasoned with ginger, cinnamon, cardamom, nutmeg, black pepper, and cloves. Use a loose-leaf tea for this recipe; bags always seem like a convenient idea, but in practice, they tear apart during the simmering.

INGREDIENTS:

4 cups (32 ounces) apple cider

4 tablespoons loose chai tea

1 cup light brown sugar, loosely packed

SPECIAL EQUIPMENT:

Cheesecloth

Glass bottles or jars with airtight lids, sterilized

Coffee filter

Narrow-mouth funnel

4. The syrup can be stored in the fridge up to 1 week. Alternatively, you may process the syrup in small jars according to my water-bath-canning directions (see "How to Preserve," page 182); store up to 6 months in a dark pantry.

1. Place the apple cider and chai tea in a medium saucepan over medium-high heat. Bring to a boil and let boil until the liquid is concentrated and reduced by half, about 30 minutes.

2. Strain out the chai tea through the cheesecloth and return the cider to a cleaned saucepan. Add the sugar to the cider and boil over medium-high heat until dissolved, about 10 minutes. Remove from the heat.

3. Let the syrup cool at room temperature before bottling. Strain it through a coffee filter 1 or 2 times to remove any extra tea or spice bits for the cleanest presentation.

GIFT WRAP

Glass bottle with airtight lid

Ribbon

Wax and wax sealer (optional)

Transfer the syrup to a clean pretty bottle. Wipe the rim and seal. Lay the bottle on its side. Place a length of ribbon across the neck of the bottle. Light a wax stick (if using) to drip over the meeting spot of the ribbon and press the sealer (if using) into the hot wax to form an imprint. Alternatively, make a seal on a separate piece of paper and adhere it to the bottle with a touch of glue or tape.

grenadine

MAKES: ABOUT ⅔ CUP // PREPARATION TIME: 15 MINUTES

Grocery store grenadine doesn't compare to the indie versions available today. And one sip of my homemade version shows that our parents wasted time filling their Singapore Slings, Tequila Sunrises, and Shirley Temples with the high-fructose, artificially flavored stuff.

This is a no-cook recipe. Just shake up the ingredients until the sugar dissolves. The shake retains the tang and the color. (And kitchen exercises strengthen our cocktail-lifting muscles naturally.) You can size this up as required to fill the perfect bottle.

Orange-blossom water can be found in the specialty section at some grocery stores or online. You can substitute the same amount with lemon juice or orange juice. Either will add its own unique perk to the final syrup.

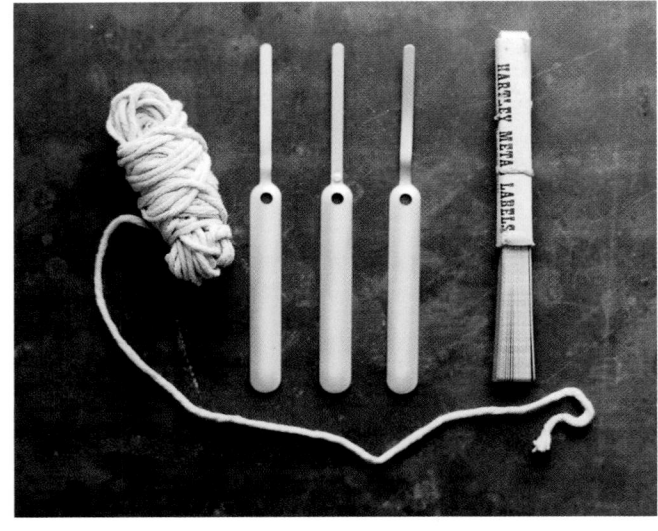

INGREDIENTS:

⅔ cup pomegranate juice

⅔ cup sugar

½ teaspoon orange-blossom water or lemon juice

SPECIAL EQUIPMENT:

Glass bottle with airtight lid

Narrow-mouth funnel

1. Place the pomegranate juice, sugar, and orange-blossom water or lemon juice into a bottle that holds at least 2 cups liquid. Shake 10 minutes or until the sugar is completely dissolved.

2. Store in fridge up to 2 weeks.

GIFT WRAP

Glass bottle with airtight lid

Newspaper

String

Garden tag

Transfer the grenadine to a clean pretty bottle. Wipe the rim and seal. Place the bottle in the center of a single piece of newspaper. Fold the paper up to meet above the bottle. Fold the remaining sides over the sides of the bottle and scrunch the paper to mold to the shape of the bottle. Wrap string around the bottle a few times and tie it in a knot, leaving a little extra. Write the label on a garden tag or regular tag. Thread the string through the tag. Tie another knot and trim any excess string.

bourbon-vanilla cherries

MAKES: 2 CUPS // PREPARATION TIME: 30 MINUTES

As I get older, my taste for spirits changes. I started with clear liquids (white wine, vodka, white rum) and then moved onto reddish liquids (red wine, ports, cordials), and now I crave brown liquids (whiskey, scotch, bourbon). In fact, Fridays require a stirred Old Fashioned trimmed with two of these cherries.

Of all possible cocktail garnishes, these are the easiest. When the jar is empty, I swirl the vanilla bean into my rocks glass. Use a sweeter bourbon of good-enough quality, a brand that you would enjoy drinking.

INGREDIENTS:

1 heaping cup (about 6 ounces) Bing cherries, fresh or frozen and with or without stems

1 cup bourbon

3 tablespoons granulated sugar

1 vanilla bean, split lengthwise

SPECIAL EQUIPMENT:

Cherry pitter (optional)

Glass jar with airtight lid, sterilized

Wide-mouth funnel

1. Wash the cherries and pit them, if desired. Whether fresh or frozen, place the cherries and vanilla bean in a jar and set aside. (Do not thaw frozen cherries. There's no need to pit the cherries.)

2. In a medium pot over medium-low heat, combine the bourbon, sugar, and vanilla bean, being careful not to spill any bourbon over the flame as it might ignite. Bring the mixture just to a simmer (not a boil), and swirl until the sugar dissolves, about 5 minutes. Remove from the heat.

3. Ladle the hot liquid through a funnel set over the jar of cherries. Wipe the rim and seal. Place in the fridge.

4. The cherries will be ready to use in 3 days but will taste better after 1 week. Store in the fridge up to 2 months.

GIFT WRAP

Glass jar with airtight lid

Vintage drawer or box

Bourbon

Cocktail shaker

Tag

Pour the cherries into a jar. Wipe the rim and seal. Place the jar in a drawer along with a bottle of bourbon and a cocktail shaker. Write the label on a tag and slip into the drawer.

sparkling elderflower punch

MAKES: ABOUT 5 TO 6 SERVINGS // PREPARATION TIME: 20 MINUTES

Whether for a backyard picnic or a fancy house party, this snappy punch is lively, fresh, and channels tropical, warm-weather flavors. Sometimes I make this punch during the thickest and snowiest of New England winters to remind myself that this, too, shall pass.

The base of the recipe is a vanilla and lemon simple syrup that has countless uses—topping fruit salad, drizzling over teacake. It keeps in the fridge up to 2 weeks. To make the punch by the glass, simply add 2 tablespoons of the syrup and 1 tablespoon elderflower liquor to a flute and top with a few ice cubes, sparkling wine, and a lemon slice.

I use St. Germain elderflower liqueur and sparkling wine here, but you could replace both with nonalcoholic elderflower syrup (sold in some international food stores and online) and sparkling water, respectively.

INGREDIENTS:

½ cup lemon juice

½ cup water

½ cup granulated sugar

1 vanilla bean, split lengthwise

½ cup elderflower liqueur

2 medium lemons, thinly sliced

1 (750-milliliter) bottle dry sparkling wine

About 4 cups ice, for serving

SPECIAL EQUIPMENT:

1 (2-gallon) glass jar, transportable pitcher, or punch bowl

1. In a medium pot over medium heat, combine the lemon juice, water, sugar, and vanilla bean. Cook until the liquid reaches a low boil and the sugar dissolves, about 5 to 7 minutes. Remove from the heat, and let the syrup cool to room temperature.

2. To your large glass jar, add the elderflower liqueur, lemons, and the cooled syrup. Transport, as is, to a potluck; add sparkling wine and ice just before serving.

GIFT WRAP

Glass jar with airtight lid

Box

Sparkling wine

Ice

Pour the cooled syrup, elderflower liqueur, and lemons into a large jar. Wipe the rim and seal. Place the jar in a box along with the sparkling wine. Transport with a bag of ice and assemble at your destination.

vin d'orange

MAKES: ABOUT 6 TO 7 (750-MILLILITER) BOTTLES // PREPARATION TIME: 15 MINUTES ACTIVE TIME (UP TO 21 DAYS TOTAL TIME)

Vin d'Orange is a fortified, fruity wine that takes up significant space in my pantry. I make a big batch every winter, just when Seville oranges begin to show up at the local shops and I'm dreaming of hot summer nights, when the finished product is the very best refreshment.

Traditionally, oranges infuse the wine for 40 or more days to reach peak flavor. After making so many Vin d'Orange batches, I consider the infusion process to be a conversation between me and the wine. Every 1 or 2 days, I taste to determine the just-right amount of bitterness. I take a sip, remove 1 sour orange, take a sip, remove 2 or 3 sour oranges, and take more sips. By the 3-week point, the Vin d'Orange is bottled and added to my pantry for long-term aging where it just gets better.

If 5 bottles of rosé wine is just too much, cut it down to 2 bottles with these adjustments: use 4 Seville oranges, 1 navel orange, 1 lemon, 1 cup sugar, ½ vanilla bean, and 1 cup vodka. Also, if you'd like, replace the Seville oranges and use only navel oranges (such as Cara Cara or Valencia) or try blood oranges. The resulting libation won't be as bitter and that's just right for some.

INGREDIENTS:

12 sour Seville oranges, preferably organic

2 navel oranges (Cara Cara or Valencia), preferably organic

1 lemon, preferably organic

2½ cups granulated sugar

2 vanilla beans, split lengthwise

¾ liter vodka

5 (750-milliliter) bottles crisp rosé or white wine

SPECIAL EQUIPMENT:

2-gallon (or larger) glass jar or food-safe bucket with airtight lid

Cheesecloth

Narrow-mouth funnel

1. Wash all the citrus well, and cut it all into quarters.

2. Place the citrus, sugar, vanilla beans, and vodka into your glass jar, being careful not to squeeze juice from the fruit; the extra juice may make the final Vin d'Orange a bit cloudy.

3. Empty the wine from each bottle into the glass jar. Reserve the empty wine bottles for your final bottling. Stir briefly to help dissolve the sugar, then cover and store in a cool, dark place in your kitchen for 14 days. (I use a dark corner of my kitchen—it's just too pretty to hide away in a cabinet and will brighten your day like a bouquet of flowers.)

4. Rinse your wine bottles and allow to air dry. Store until ready to use.

Now let's begin our conversation with our Vin d'Orange . . .

5. Once your Vin d'Orange has infused for 14 days, start checking on it every 1 to 2 days. With tongs, remove a few pieces of sour orange if it's getting too bitter. This process can take up to 40 days, depending on the sweetness of your fruit and conditions in which the jar is stored, but I like the style and flavor profile of my Vin d'Orange at the 21-day mark.

6. After your Vin d'Orange is as you like it, remove the solids with tongs and strain the Vin d'Orange through cheesecloth. Using a funnel placed in each bottle, pour the Vin d'Orange into the reserved wine bottles, being careful not to add any sediment. You will have started with 5 bottles, but you'll most likely have to add 1 to 2 extra bottles to hold the extra wine that's come about during the infusion process.

7. Seal the bottles and store the Vin d'Orange at room temperature up to 1 year. As it ages, the Vin d'Orange strengthens in flavor and deepens in color.

8. Serve well chilled or over a couple ice cubes, with a twist of orange or lemon, if you wish.

GIFT WRAP

Glass bottle with airtight lid

Hole puncher

Orange crisp (see Citrus Crisps, page 177)

Ribbon

Pin

Transfer the Vin d'Orange to a clean pretty bottle. Wipe the rim and seal. Punch a hole in an orange crisp. Thread the end of the ribbon through the hole and make a thick knot. Wrap the ribbon around the bottle a few times, positioning the orange crisp in the front. Stick a pin through the ribbon to hold it in place.

limoncello

I remember my initial sip of homemade limoncello—a lemon liqueur. It was my very first spirit project, and the cordial's big reveal was at a backyard picnic with a few European friends—it's clear that I'm the risky type. I knew that my version tasted better than the store-bought kind, but three Italians (loyal to their mama's recipe) would make the final call. One staunch southern Italian, determined to share the truth, said, "This is not right, it's just too good." His mama's limoncello always offered a strong burn as it went down. He poured himself shot after shot, blaming my version's perfection.

Although traditionally made with pure grain alcohol, I used vodka. He said the vodka conspired to keep him wanting more. And the hue, more like thick olive oil due to the organic sugar, made him miss his family's olive groves. In those moments, on the receiving end of his complimentary critique, I felt like a superhero. Nowadays, I add this limoncello to martinis and sorbet, but I remain devoted to serving it in small cordial glasses, ice cold.

I prefer organic vodka, but use whatever you can afford. Don't bother with a top-shelf vodka as it gets overtaken with bright lemon flavor.

INGREDIENTS:

1 (750-milliliter) bottle vodka

8 lemons, preferably organic

For simple syrup (made 4 weeks later):

3 cups granulated sugar

3 cups water

SPECIAL EQUIPMENT:

1 large wide-mouth glass bottle or jar with airtight lid, sterilized, for infusing

Cheesecloth or coffee filters

2 (750-milliliter) glass bottles with airtight lids, sterilized

Narrow-mouth funnel

1. Pour the entire bottle of vodka into the wide-mouth bottle.

2. Peel the thin yellow layer of zest off each lemon, making sure to avoid taking up any of the white pith. Place the zest strips in the same bottle that holds the vodka. Cover and hide it away in your cupboard at least 4 weeks. Every few days, shake the bottle up a bit.

3. Strain the limoncello, discarding the zest. Strain the limoncello again through cheesecloth or coffee filters. Using a funnel, evenly divide the vodka between 2 bottles.

4. Prepare the simple syrup: Combine the sugar and water in a saucepan over medium heat. Bring to a gentle boil, swirling the pan to help the sugar dissolve. This should take about 10 minutes. Once the sugar has dissolved, remove from the heat and let the syrup cool 15 to 20 minutes. The resulting simple syrup yields about 4 cups.

5. Using the funnel, distribute 1 cup of the simple syrup into each of the bottles, separately. The bottles shouldn't be filled to the top; you want to be able to shake the concoction. Cover, shake, and taste. If it's sweet enough for you, reserve the remaining simple syrup for weekend cocktails. If it's not sweet enough, add another ½ cup to 1 cup of simple syrup to each bottle.

6. Cover and gently shake both bottles and put the bottles back in your cupboard 2 weeks longer. (The Limoncello is perfect right now, but let it sit longer to get smoother.)

7. Store in the cupboard or in the fridge up to 1 year. You can also put it in the freezer 30 minutes before serving to ensure that it's ice cold.

GIFT WRAP

Glass bottle with airtight lid

Masking tape

Transfer the Limoncello to a clean pretty bottle. Wipe the rim and seal. Write the label on a piece of masking tape and adhere it to the bottle.

basilcello

The basil variety of limoncello delights the die-hard basil fans in my Italian-loving circle. This version is strong but adds a punch to the end of a meal and just the right sort of strength to a scoop of delicate lemon sorbet.

Don't skip the blanch; it helps to preserve some of the green color.

INGREDIENTS:

2½ cups vodka

50 (about ½-ounce) basil leaves, preferably organic

Water, for blanching

For simple syrup (made 1 week later):

½ cup granulated sugar

½ cup water

SPECIAL EQUIPMENT:

1 large wide-mouth bottle or jar with airtight lid that holds at least 1 liter, cleaned and sterilized, for infusing

Cheesecloth or coffee filter

1 (750-milliliter) bottle with airtight lid, cleaned and sterilized

Narrow-mouth funnel

1. Pour the vodka into a glass bottle or jar and set aside.

2. Prepare an ice-water bath by filling a large bowl halfway with water and plenty of ice (20 to 24 cubes). Then add several inches of water to a medium pot and set over medium-high heat. Bring to a boil.

3. Blanch the basil leaves by placing them into the boiling water 30 seconds. Carefully transfer the leaves with a slotted spoon to the ice-cold water bath 1 minute. Drain the leaves in a fine-mesh strainer, gently squeezing to remove extra water. Then pat dry with a paper towel until as dry as possible.

4. Place the drained leaves into the jar of vodka. Cover and let sit in a cool, dark place 1 week, shaking gently every other day. After 1 week, the infusion should take on an olive green hue. Strain the infusion and discard the basil leaves. Strain again through cheesecloth or a coffee filter. Pour into a clean 750-milliliter bottle and seal. Set aside.

5. Prepare the simple syrup: Combine the sugar and water in a medium pot over medium-high heat. Bring to a low boil until the sugar dissolves, swirling the pot to help the mixture along. This should take about 10 minutes. Once the sugar has dissolved, remove the mixture from the heat and let it cool 15 to 20 minutes.

6. Add the simple syrup to the Basilcello. It's ready to drink immediately but tastes better after at least 1 week in a cool, dark place. Serve ice cold. Store at room temperature up to 1 year. You can also put it in the freezer 30 minutes just before serving to ensure that it's ice cold.

GIFT WRAP

Glass bottle with airtight lid

Masking tape

Transfer the Basilcello to a clean pretty bottle. Write the label on a piece of masking tape and adhere it to the bottle.

rhubarb cordial

MAKES: 1 LITER (ABOUT 4 CUPS) // PREPARATION TIME: 20 MINUTES ACTIVE TIME
(UP TO 14 DAYS TOTAL TIME)

After one bite of rhubarb (in a strawberry-rhubarb pie), I was hooked. The tart tang was exactly what I wanted in a drink too. This Rhubarb Cordial has become my signature infusion. Serve well chilled on its own in a tiny cordial glass or as a base to a little sparkling wine cocktail.

Consider this recipe your starting point for any fruit-based cordial—though absolutely try rhubarb. Certainly, some adjustments may be required if the blueberries are very sweet or the blackberries are early and sour, but the adjustment process involves daily sampling until it feels just right to you, and that will be fun.

INGREDIENTS:

1¼ pounds rhubarb (15 stalks)

1 cup granulated sugar

1 liter vodka

SPECIAL EQUIPMENT:

1 glass jar that holds at least 2 quarts with airtight lid, sterilized

Cheesecloth or coffee filter (optional)

3 (375-milliliter) glass bottles with airtight lids, sterilized

Narrow-mouth funnel

1. Trim the dry ends of the rhubarb, discarding the tips, and then chop the rhubarb into 1-inch pieces. Pile the rhubarb into your clean glass jar. Add the sugar and vodka. Stir to combine.

2. Store in a cool, dark spot in your kitchen and stir every 3 to 4 days. The sugar will dissolve over the next 2 weeks.

3. After 14 days, open your jar and taste. The sugar should be dissolved, and the taste should be sweet and tart. Strain the liquid from the rhubarb. If you'd like to remove any tiny particles, strain again through cheesecloth or a coffee filter (if using).

4. Pour the Rhubarb Cordial into clean glass bottles and store at room temperature up to 6 months. You can also put it in the freezer 30 minutes just before serving to ensure that it's ice cold.

GIFT WRAP

Glass bottle with airtight lid

Paper

Tape

String

Transfer the cordial to a clean pretty bottle. Fold or cut a strip of paper wide enough to form a band around the bottle. Wrap the paper around the bottle and tape it in place. Wrap string around the paper a few times and tie it in a knot.

strawberry cordial

MAKES: 1 (750-MILLILITER) BOTTLE // PREPARATION TIME: 15 MINUTES ACTIVE TIME (UP TO 7 DAYS TOTAL TIME)

After putting up plenty of preserves with wild early summer strawberries, I turn my attention to this Strawberry Cordial. It's quite similar to my Rhubarb Cordial (page 231) but requires less time infusing since strawberries tend to give up their essence rather quickly, fresh little things. Drink it over ice or mix it into a strawberry-infused sparkling sangria; use it to enhance a fruit salad or drizzle over ice cream.

For another flavor idea, consider adding lemon slices or rosemary sprigs. Also, try supplementing the infusion with other berries—raspberries, blackberries, and blueberries all mesh well with strawberries—or try another spirit like white rum or gin.

INGREDIENTS:

2 pints (about 1 pound) strawberries, washed

1 cup granulated sugar

1 (750-milliliter) bottle vodka

SPECIAL EQUIPMENT:

1 glass jar that holds at least 2 quarts with airtight lid, sterilized

Cheesecloth or coffee filter (optional)

1 (750-milliliter) glass bottle with airtight lid, sterilized

Narrow-mouth funnel

1. Hull the strawberries, removing and discarding the green core and green leaves. Pile the strawberries into your clean glass jar. Add the sugar and vodka. Stir to combine.

2. Store in a cool, dark spot in your kitchen and stir every 3 to 4 days. The sugar will dissolve over the next week.

3. After 7 days, open your jar and taste. The sugar should have dissolved, and the taste should be sweet. Strain the cordial, discarding the strawberries. If you'd like to remove any tiny particles, strain again through cheesecloth or a coffee filter (if using).

4. Pour your Strawberry Cordial into a new glass jar, or divide among several small ones, and store at room temperature up to 6 months. You can also put it in the freezer 30 minutes just before serving to ensure that it's ice cold. Serve on its own in a tiny cordial glass, or use as a base to a little sparkling wine cocktail.

GIFT WRAP

Glass bottle with airtight lid

Masking tape

String

Transfer the Strawberry Cordial to a clean pretty bottle. Wipe the rim and seal. Write the label on masking tape and adhere it to the bottle. Wrap string around the bottle a few times and tie it in a knot. Leave the string long so the recipient may reuse.

orange cordial

MAKES: ABOUT 3½ CUPS // PREPARATION TIME: 1 HOUR ACTIVE TIME
(UP TO 18 DAYS TOTAL TIME)

Since Margaritas are a "thing" in my household, a homemade Orange Cordial was decidedly necessary—it's one of the main ingredients in the famous cocktail. My version is less sweet and stronger than the store-bought variety but all the better for your cocktail creations. Use this Orange Cordial as you would Triple Sec or Cointreau in cocktails and martinis.

When using in a mixed drink, definitely taste and alter the final product with additional sweetener, if needed.

INGREDIENTS:

3 large Navel oranges, preferably organic

1 tablespoon dried bitter orange peel

1 tablespoon orange-flower water

1 cup brandy

2 cups vodka

For simple syrup
(18 days later):

½ cup water

½ cup granulated sugar

SPECIAL EQUIPMENT:

1 glass jar that holds at least 2 quarts with airtight lid, sterilized

Cheesecloth or coffee filter (optional)

3 (375-milliliter) glass bottles with airtight lids, sterilized

Narrow-mouth funnel

1. With a vegetable peeler, strip off the zest from the oranges, making sure to avoid the white pith. Set the zest aside and reserve 1 orange for another recipe or your breakfast the next day. Remove the extra white pith from the remaining 2 oranges, and then slice the oranges horizontally into ½-inch-thick slices.

2. In the sterilized jar, add the orange zest, orange slices, dried bitter orange peel, orange-flower water, brandy, and vodka and seal. Let sit in a dark location at room temperature 18 days.

3. Strain the liquid into a new sterilized glass jar (or re-sterilize the jar used during the infusion). If you'd like to remove every bit of extra material to lengthen shelf life, strain again through cheesecloth or a coffee filter (if using). Discard the oranges, peel, and zest.

4. Prepare the simple syrup: Combine the water and sugar in a small saucepan over medium heat. Bring to a low boil, swirling the pan to help the sugar dissolve, about 5 to 7 minutes. Once the sugar has dissolved, remove from the heat and let the syrup cool to room temperature.

5. Using a funnel, add the simple syrup to your orange cordial mixture and stir. Divide the mixture evenly among 3 (375-milliliter) bottles and store at room temperature up to 6 months. You can also put it in the freezer 30 minutes just before serving to ensure that it's ice cold. Serve on its own in a tiny cordial glass, or use as a base to a little sparkling wine cocktail.

GIFT WRAP

Glass bottle with airtight lid

Tag

Ribbon

Transfer the Orange Cordial to a clean pretty bottle. Wipe the rim and seal. Write the label on a tag. Thread ribbon through the tag. Wrap ribbon around the bottle and tie it in a knot. Leave the ribbon long so the recipient may reuse.

margarita mix

My sister is the mixologist in the family. I love all types of booze, and while I prefer to manipulate a recipe, my sister is keen on following a recipe faithfully. Thank goodness for that because cocktail hour depends on her good memory; she's my Friday night call when I need the perfect Margarita. Between my creative infusions and her ratio prowess, we make an excellent team, gifting signature drinks for family celebrations.

This margarita ratio is not at all standard, but rules and recipes are made to be broken. It's a 2-1-1 ratio of tequila to my Orange Cordial (page 235) to freshly squeezed lime juice. If using store-bought orange liqueur, decrease the maple syrup. Speaking of, light maple syrup is my go-to simple syrup on the fly as it's always there and instantly adds "New England style" to any drink. Tequila is a personal choice, but I use 100% pure agave white tequila. For a party, set up your Infused Sea Salts (page 90) to rim the glasses. Important note: this recipe doubles and triples easily.

INGREDIENTS:

3/4 cup Orange Cordial (page 235) or Cointreau

3/4 cup freshly squeezed lime juice (about 6 to 8 limes)

3 tablespoons light maple syrup

1½ cups 100% pure agave white tequila blanco

Ice, for serving

SPECIAL EQUIPMENT:

1 glass bottle that holds at least 4 cups with airtight lid

1. To a glass bottle, add the Orange Cordial, lime juice, and maple syrup. Seal and shake, shake, shake. If taking to a party, transport as is with a bottle of tequila and a bag of ice on the side.

2. If serving immediately, add the tequila and shake again. Fill glasses with ice. Pour a margarita for each person, and enjoy. This mix will keep in the fridge up to 3 days. Shake well before serving.

TIP: *For serving, put out several plates of infused sea salts (lime, lemon, and orange zest sea salts, do well with this cocktail), see page 90; and lime wedges. Before filling up the glasses, encourage guests to rub the rim of the glass with a lime wedge, dip the glass edge into an infused sea salt, fill the glass with ice, and pour in the Margarita. It's an on-the-spot Margarita Bar.*

GIFT WRAP

Glass bottle with deep rim with airtight lid

Wire

Tag

Wrap a length of wire to sit snugly in the bottle's rim. Twist to secure and trim the extra wire. Cut 2 long lengths of wire to use as a handle. Twist one end to secure the wire around the wire on the rim, shape the wire into a handle, and twist the other end to the other side of the wire on the rim. Repeat with the second length of wire, ensuring they remain the same size. Write the label on a tag. Thread a small length of wire through the tag. Twist to secure the tag to the wire on the rim. Pour the drink into the bottle and seal or serve.

cold-brew coffee

MAKES: 4 CUPS // PREPARATION TIME: 10 MINUTES ACTIVE TIME
(JUST OVER 24 HOURS TOTAL TIME)

A true coffee fan gets surprising delight from something as simple as a well-made cup of coffee. I'm lucky enough to live with one such fan, and he has sampled every coffee ever offered in the Eat Boutique shop and has met many of the makers when on my scouting trips, gleaning valuable tips for making hot and cold coffee. When the weather heats up, he makes Cold-Brew Coffee. Inspired by the Japanese style of cold-brew poured directly over ice, this Cold-Brew Coffee recipe should become a part of your weekly repertoire.

Use the best beans possible. I've made this with the best coffee beans in the country and organic beans from the grocery store—they're both good, but the former is just a touch better. Ordinary light-roast coffee beans may taste a bit watered down in a cold brew, so choose medium or darker beans for strong and robust notes. The grocery store will grind the beans for you.

We take our coffee black for the purest flavor, but by all means indulge by adding a little dairy. Sometimes, we do treat ourselves to a splash of sweet condensed milk or homemade Irish Cream (page 240) swirled into tiny cups of this brew.

1. If you're grinding the coffee beans yourself, grind them into a fine grind—the finer, the better. It should be far finer than a typical French Press coffee grind. If using a Burr grinder, aim for a fine setting.

2. Add the ground coffee and water to your glass jar. Stir vigorously 10 seconds. Seal the jar and let it sit in your fridge 24 hours. After 24 hours, stir the coffee and water mixture once again for 10 seconds. Let rest at room temperature 20 minutes.

3. Place a coffee filter in a strainer fitted into a large, clean jar. Strain the coffee mixture through the filter. Feel free to walk away for a few minutes while it filters. It will take a few pours of the coffee to finish filtering the entire volume and 15 to 20 minutes to filter it all. Store in the fridge up to 1 week.

4. To serve, pour the coffee over a few ice cubes into a glass and add a pinch of sea salt.

GIFT WRAP

Glass jar with airtight lid

Tag

Twine

Pour the finished coffee into a clean jar. Wipe the rim and seal. Write the label on a tag and attach it to the jar with twine.

INGREDIENTS:

⅓ cup medium- to dark-roast coffee beans, finely ground

4 cups filtered water, room temperature

Pinch of fine sea salt, to serve

SPECIAL EQUIPMENT:

1 or 2 large glass jars that hold at least 4 cups each, with airtight lids

Coffee filters

irish cream

MAKES: ABOUT 4 CUPS // PREPARATION TIME: 5 MINUTES

Between my parents' diverse backgrounds, our dinners when I was growing up overflowed with amazing Latin and Italian food. Sweet plantains were served with finger-thick slices of whole-milk mozzarella, and homemade refried beans were sprinkled with Parmesan cheese. Distinct foods from their cultures mingled quite happily.

My husband, born in America but of Irish descent, added yet another unique food history to the mix. Alas, Irish cream wasn't one of them. Only created in the 1970s in Dublin, Ireland, the whiskey and cream–based liqueur is rather young by spirit standards. Anecdotally, it's considered a ladies' drink, but in my family, Irish cream ends practically every celebration and remains the nightcap of choice.

A holiday party is a success if everyone leaves with a tiny bottle of my Irish Cream. It's thick and extravagant, whether made with whole milk or coconut milk. Choose your favorite whiskey and don't make it too fancy. If a bottle of Amaretto is more than you need, buy a small nip behind the liquor store counter.

INGREDIENTS:

1¾ cups (14 ounces) sweetened condensed milk

1 cup whole milk (or unsweetened coconut milk)

1 cup good whiskey

1 tablespoon pure vanilla extract

1 tablespoon Amaretto

2 tablespoons chocolate syrup

2 teaspoons instant coffee

2 large eggs

SPECIAL EQUIPMENT:

4 (8-ounce) glass bottles with airtight lids, sterilized

Narrow-mouth funnel

1. Place all the ingredients in the container of a blender. Blend 30 seconds or until the chocolate syrup streaks disappear in your blender.

2. Funnel into small glass bottles and store in the coldest part of your fridge, ready to give away to guests. Store up to 2 weeks in the fridge.

GIFT WRAP

Glass bottle with airtight lid

Masking tape

Ribbon

Transfer the Irish Cream to a clean pretty bottle. Wipe the rim and seal. Write the label on a piece of tape and adhere it to the bottle. Trim a small length of ribbon, fold it in half, and wrap it around the neck of the bottle, tucking the tips through the loop.

rompopo

This Latin-style eggnog is a family heirloom. The original recipe, which I've adapted, was in a vintage cookbook published by the wives of the lawyers of Tegucigalpa, Honduras, in the 1970s. It was a wedding present to my mother from a family friend and is now a little piece of our history.

My mother was born in a small Honduran municipality called El Porvenir. Translated, *El Porvenir* literally means "to come" or "the future." She bravely relocated to New York City in the 1960s with dreams of being a singer. While that never took shape, she still took center stage in our family home, especially around the holidays. She'd sip Rompopo, hum along to old music, and reminisce. My mother makes her own private stash of this eggnog today, maybe filled with a bit more rum than most might expect. But watching her sip and sing puts us all in the best mood.

Use the freshest eggs available here and do not discard the egg whites. Divide them equally into 2 freezer-safe bags for future Petite Pavlovas (page 166) or other recipes.

INGREDIENTS:

1 cup granulated sugar

1 cup cold water

4 cups whole milk

1 (4-inch) cinnamon stick

1 vanilla bean, split lengthwise

Pinch of ground nutmeg

12 large egg yolks (reserve egg whites for another use)

2 cups white rum

1. Add the sugar and water to a medium pot over medium heat. Bring to a low boil to dissolve the sugar and make a simple syrup. This should take no more than 10 minutes. Remove from the heat and set aside to let cool.

2. Add the milk, cinnamon stick, vanilla bean, and ground nutmeg to a clean medium pot over medium heat. Heat until just before scalding—you do not want the milk to boil. Remove from the heat and allow the mixture to steep 15 minutes. Discard the cinnamon stick and vanilla bean.

3. Prepare an ice-water bath: Fill a large bowl halfway up the side with water and add plenty of ice. Set aside.

4. In a medium bowl, whisk the egg yolks until very thick and creamy. Ladle about ¼ cup of the simple syrup into the eggs while continuing to whisk vigorously in order to temper the eggs. Once well combined, whisk in the remaining simple syrup. Place the bowl in the ice-water bath for a few moments to bring the temperature down quickly.

5. Remove the bowl to a clean towel set on the counter. Quickly add 1 cup of the milk to the egg mixture while whisking vigorously. Once combined, whisk in the remaining milk. Set the bowl back into the ice-water bath to quickly bring down the temperature. Strain the Rompopo through a fine-mesh strainer to remove any extra bits.

6. When the mixture is cooled, add the rum. Transfer to a large bottle and store in the fridge up to 2 weeks.

GIFT WRAP

Glass bottle with airtight lid

Tag

Vintage ribbon

Pin

Transfer the spirit to a pretty bottle. Wipe the rim and seal. Write the label on a tag and set aside. Wrap a length of vintage ribbon around the rim of the bottle. Tie in a loose knot. Slip the tag into place and pin.

gift collections

After many years of creating and sourcing food gift collections through Eat Boutique, I've observed first-hand the flavor pairings or food types that resonate with gifters and giftees alike. Those lessons have fed into the recipes I make for my gift recipients and for this cookbook as well as into the gift collections throughout this chapter. Sometimes a single food gift alone doesn't relay the entirety of your intended message, and that's when a collection of related or thematic foods takes the gift to a new, glorious level.

Here are eight collections that are representative of the most popular gifts ordered by my clients and my family and friends. They are styled to inspire your own endless combinations.

COOKIE SWAP
GIFT COLLECTION

It should be no surprise that groupings of cookies are one of the most desired food gifts, especially by families at winter holiday gatherings. Create your collection filled with these three recipes. Make the Molasses Cookies and Pantry Cookies a day or two in advance so you can focus on the Madeleines at the last moment.

Brown Butter Madeleines (page 151)
Sweet & Salty Pantry Cookies (page 152)
Molasses Cookies (page 155)

A few tips: While each of these cookies could be packed together in a single box or basket, I prefer to wrap each recipe individually—to make them look even more impressive. Wrap the Madeleines as a bunch, since they are best eaten immediately, and wrap the Sweet & Salty Pantry Cookies individually so they can be packed up in the week's lunches. Consider using a vintage cookie tin instead of a box or basket.

COFFEE & CAKE GIFT
COLLECTION

Together, coffee and cake make the sort of gift all of your colleagues will jump to sample. Place it in a central room in your office, like the kitchen, at the start of the day and watch it disappear in minutes. Many clients request sweet treat collections to be filled with coffee, a popular staple at the office. Make this collection with the following recipes:

Cold-Brew Coffee (page 239)
Roasted Banana Bread (page 148)
Individual Apple Galettes (page 158)

A few tips: Tuck a bag of fresh coffee beans into the collection, to keep the good-morning times flowing for the rest of the week. When I share this collection at Saturday morning girlfriend get-togethers, I add in something they can hold onto beyond our meeting, like a vintage knife or new kitchen towel.

BREAD & BUTTER
GIFT COLLECTION

Bread, salt, and wine are traditionally offered as housewarming gifts or even as wedding presents. This collection takes that up a few levels with flavorful accompaniments that can be eaten immediately or over a period of time, nurturing that new-home feeling for weeks. Grab a baguette, a bottle of wine, and add in these recipes.

Homemade Butter (page 64)
Infused Sea Salts (page 90)
Grapefruit-Elderflower Marmalade (page 197)

A few tips: A few vintage spreaders, wrapped with a length of ribbon, add to a permanent collection and will be your memory once the food is gone. Instead of parchment, consider wrapping the baguette with a set of dinner napkins.

CHOCOLATES
GIFT COLLECTION

A gift of chocolate is the ultimate celebration and, when handmade, it's the most impressive. Husbands send chocolate to wives; girlfriends send it to boyfriends; and with these recipes, you can share it with everyone.

Chocolate Truffles (page 130)
Peanut Butter Balls (page 132)
Granola Bark (page 129)

A few tips: When I open a beautiful bar of chocolate, I save the clean foil wrappers to wrap my own chocolate collections. Chocolate is great in a box or piled high in a jar, but consider scouring antique markets for inexpensive little plates. Always write a little note that says, "Best enjoyed at room temperature."

APÉRO HOUR GIFT COLLECTION

Every time I get a dinner party invite, I ask the host what I can contribute, and the most frequent reply is "please bring appetizers." I respond by delivering a combination of sweet and savory snacks in the form of this gift collection. It's varied with the following recipes to please most palates and already packed with a bottle of something strong to get the party started.

A few tips: On their own, these recipes are stunning, but sometimes I deliver a little kitchen goodie that the host can also enjoy later as a party memory. Consider adding a small serving bowl to hold these homemade snacks or a few petite wine glasses for the spirits. Keep it handmade by cutting fabric remnants into 4-inch squares to make coasters or 8-inch squares to become napkins.

PANTRY GIFT COLLECTION

When a couple starts a new life together, a young person moves into a first apartment, and someone moves to a new town, a little help and love can come in the form of a pantry gift collection. The recipes in this grouping fill an empty kitchen with basic ingredients. The gift can be customized to the giftee's passions, so, if she or he is a baker, swap in citrus sugar and infused sea salt.

A few tips: Make the pantry items in big batches, tucked in the back of your larder, and portion out small jars as the need arises. The infused oils, however, should be made right before you need them so they're super fresh. Add a little recipe or list of uses to each jar to increase the gift's usefulness.

COCKTAIL BAR
GIFT COLLECTION

Ever the most popular gift collection on Eat Boutique, this grouping offers the following recipes as additions or starters to a homemade cocktail bar. Filled with both boozy and nonalcoholic libations, this collection of recipes pleases the person looking for something juiced-up and also includes infused drink syrups that mix well with club soda.

Ginger Simple Syrup (page 212)
Orange Cordial (page 235)
Rhubarb Cordial (page 231)
Bourbon-Vanilla Cherries (page 221)
Basilcello (page 228)

A few tips: This gift should be handled with care and delivered in person because it's glass laden. If using a box or a basket, make sure to include a lot of tissue or crinkle paper to keep the bottles from banging against each other. Add in well-wrapped cocktail glasses and your favorite cocktail recipe cards to up the fancy factor.

GOODNIGHT
GIFT COLLECTION

This special gift collection, only passed around at the holidays in my circle, is the sweet way to cap off a lovely evening. Keep molasses cookie dough, already formed into balls, in your freezer during the winter, so these cookies are never more than a few minutes away.

Molasses Cookies (page 155)
Irish Cream (page 240)

A few tips: Consider gifting this to Santa's real helpers—the parents—as a little tipple enjoyed just before bedtime or splashed into after-dinner coffee, as dessert.

stockists & sources

EAT BOUTIQUE

Eat Boutique is an online indie food gift boutique. In the shop, you'll find: signed copies of this cookbook, gift boxes, and an array of food for home cooks and gifts, including salt, condiments, cocktail syrups, herbs, tea, chocolate and confections, baking ingredients, coffee, snacks, and preserves. You can also purchase some of the gift-wrap supplies used throughout this book.

www.eatboutique.com

FRESH INGREDIENTS

Chilmark Coffee: coffee beans
www.chilmarkcoffeeco.com

Dufour: puff pastry
www.dufourpastrykitchens.com

Island Creek Oysters: oysters
www.islandcreekoysters.com

Lemon Ladies: Meyer lemons
www.lemonladies.com

Sweetbrook Farm: maple syrup
www.sweetbrookfarm.com

The Orange Shop: Seville oranges, other citrus varieties
www.floridaorangeshop.com

PANTRY INGREDIENTS

Atlantic Spice Company: juniper berries and other spices
www.atlanticspice.com

Bellocq Tea: loose leaf tea
www.bellocqtea.com

Penzeys Spices: paprika and other spices
www.penzeys.com

Preston of Dry Creek: wine, olive oil, figs
www.prestonvineyards.com

Whole Spice: spices and herbs
www.wholespice.com

GIFT-WRAP SUPPLIES

Here are some of my favorite sources for four key categories of food gift-wrap supplies: Paper (the items that hold and/or wrap your food gifts); Pencils (items to identify your food gifts); Tape (items to label your food gifts); and Twine (items to secure and adorn your food gifts).

"Paper"
(items to hold and wrap gifts)

Ball Canning: jars
www.freshpreserving.com

Bormioli: jars
www.bormioliroccousa.com

Ebay: antiques and used items
www.ebay.com

Joann Fabrics: fabric, ribbon, yarn, crafts
www.joann.com

Le Parfait: jars
www.leparfait.com

Paper Mart: boxes, bags, tape, tins, ribbon
www.papermart.com

Paper Source: stationery, tags
www.cutetape.com

POS Paper: butcher paper, craft paper
www.pospaper.com

SKS Bottle: bottles, jars, vials, tins
www.sks-bottle.com

Specialty Bottle: bottles, jars, tins
www.specialtybottle.com

Uline: boxes, bottles, jars, packing materials
www.uline.com

Weck Jars: jars
www.weckjars.com

Pencils
(items to write labels for gifts)

Etsy: craft supplies
www.etsy.com

Tape
(items to seal and label gifts)

Cute Tape: tape
www.cutetape.com

Etsy: craft supplies
www.etsy.com

Twine
(items to secure and decorate gifts)

Artistic Wire: craft wire
www.artisticwire.com

Blick: art supplies
www.dickblick.com

Burpee: garden supplies
www.burpee.com

Duikelman: kitchenware
www.duikelman.nl

Etsy: craft supplies
www.etsy.com

Ikea: kitchenware
www.ikea.com

Joann Fabrics: fabric, ribbon, yarn, crafts
www.joann.com

Studio Carta: fine stationery, ribbons
www.shopangelaliguori.com

acknowledgments

TO MY PEOPLE

I would especially like to thank:

Heidi Murphy: Thank you, thank you for offering beautiful photography, unwavering friendship, and profound support along this journey.

Catrine Kelty: Your effortless, thoughtful styling and expansive prop closet make this cookbook come alive.

Sally Ekus: You went from charming coffee date to fabulous agent in mere moments. Merci.

Kate Knapp: You are the best head recipe tester, a compadre with whom to dream up the coolest food ideas and, no doubt, the perfect Friday afternoon coffee date.

Dawn Baker: You're the reason I could make the time to write this cookbook, in more ways than one. You keep me going.

Lise Pellegrin: Thank you for helping me pack my very first food gift box and for giving of yourself so generously.

Linda Ingroia, Melissa Lotfy, Stephanie Fletcher, and the Houghton Mifflin Harcourt team: You've been a tremendous support through the making of this cookbook and the very best partners in food gift adventures. Thanks for believing.

None of this would be possible without my Eat Boutique family. So grateful to Amy Feiereisel, you're the bee's knees of editors, and all the folks who have contributed to this mission for so many years: Tara Bellucci, Laura Ciampa, Jill Chen, Lucy Engelman, Laudalino Ferreira, Lauren Keiper, Shelby Larsson, Susan Maynard, Matthew Petrelis, Chloé Matthieu Phillips, Dennis Phillips, Josephine Rozman, Molly Shuster, Sean St. John, Rachel Wilson, and Denise Woodward.

My deepest thanks as well to Marilyn and Tom Felice, Merri Jones, Karen Kirsten, Angela Liguori, Michelle Perry, Yvette van Boven, Sarah Welch, and Marisa McClellan—for helping me in so many different ways that generally involved food, drinks, gifts, and friendship.

Diane and John, I could not ask for more generous neighbors with whom to exchange food gifts and life tips. You are always on my mind.

I am eternally grateful for my amazing family: Jennifer Battista, Norma Battista, Angelina and Ramon Cabrera, Jason Cabrera, Melissa Cabrera, Emiliano Valerio, Vanessa Cabrera, Dan and Jessica Shef, and Don and Jacqueline Cosseboom.

Finally, my life would be impossible without Don Cosseboom. You must know that: "i carry your heart (i carry it in my heart)" – E. E. Cummings

TO MY RECIPE TESTERS

E. E. Cummings wrote, "It takes courage to grow up and become who you really are."

Food Gift Love grew up because of this amazing team of recipe testers. They trusted me in their kitchens and encouraged me with their constructive testing notes. I am eternally grateful for their time, kindness, and support.

Nicole Avenia-Fritzky, Joan Baker, Keli Bell-Cole, Tara Bellucci, Jillian Bernardini, Caroline Betcher, Katie Blais, Rachel Blumenthal, Alyssa Breed, Maj-le Bridges, Ilene and Greg Brown, Adrienne Bruno, Connie Campbell, Liz Canter, Sonja Cantu, Joan Cook, Kelsey Cosgrove, Jenn D'Ascoli, Christine Davis, Gail Davis, Tania DeLuzuriaga, Liz Duncan, Mariah Elliott, Ursula Ernst, Molly Farrar, Sarah Finerghty, Jaclyn Fishman, Annie Foy, Amber Gillis, Leslie Goldenberg, Alison Gordon, Megan Graziano, Jessica Grosman, Lena Hanson, Carol Harlow-Carlson, Sophie Hays, Alexandra Holbrook, Katie Homan, Susan Jackiewicz, Jessica Johnson, Nancy Kaiser, Lindsey Lambert Gordon, Sara Lindquist, Tie Lewis, Elizabeth Madden, Davelen McHenry, Jean Mier-Bölinger, Lee Montgomery, Nicole Nacamuli, Tracey Neret, Michael O'Connor, Emily Olson, Leslie Olsson, Jenna Pelletier, Lauren Piro, Erin Rellosa, Penelope Roberts, Lori and Patrick Rohleder, Natalie Roizman, Anna Shipley, Elizabeth Shovers, Alyson Snelling, Julie Stanton, Patricia Starkey, Christine Tobin, Dan Tudor, Debbie Van Hees, Meg Jones Wall, Deanna Welborn, Nancy White, Peggy Witter, Rachel Wilson, Eliza Winograd, Kathy Zoetewey, Renee Zublic, and Mary Zulauf.

TO THE MAKERS

The people behind artisanal small-batch foods make magic every day. They have inspired me with their talent, delighted me with their company, and encouraged me in my kitchen. These are just a few of the many makers who have made me want to eat better and cook well.

Bellocq Tea, Big Picture Farm, Big Spoon Roasters, Blue Chair Fruit Company, Chilmark Coffee, Dave's Coffee, Didi Davis Foods, EH Chocolatier, Evy Tea, Fat Toad Farm, Fox Hollow Mustard, Jacobsen Salt Company, Lark Fine Foods, Liddabit Sweets, Marge Granola, Mike's Hot Honey, Morris Kitchen, Q's Nuts, Quince and Apple, Rare Bird Preserves, Royal Rose, Spoonable, Sqirl, Sweetbrook Farm, Tatte Bakery, Treat Bake Shop, We Love Jam, and Whimsy and Spice.

index

Page numbers in *italics* indicate illustrations

"There's nothing quite so personal and heartwarming as giving a gift of food you've made. But if, like me, you fall back to your default cookie, candy, or bread . . . fear not. Maggie Battista offers us a pantry full of ideas that will delight every hostess, graduate, friend, boss, or Secret Santa. My only gripe with the book is I keep asking myself, 'Why didn't I think of that?'"

—DAVID LEITE, publisher, LeitesCulinaria.com

"Maggie Battista's book, *Food Gift Love*, inspires on every page with lush photography, approachable recipes, and beautiful packaging ideas. It's the next logical step for the do-it-yourselfer."

—CATHY BARROW, author of *Mrs. Wheelbarrow's Practical Pantry*

"Maggie leads us into her delicious world of mixed cocktail nuts and rhubarb vanilla jam and the brown sugar rub . . . oh, the pleasure, the delight of all these choices! The writing is inspiring, the recipes tempting—maybe we just have to make them all. The beautiful, generous Maggie Battista is wonderful in person; with her book, you have the next best thing."

—KATIE WORKMAN, author of *Dinner Solved!* and *The Mom 100 Cookbook*

"DIY fans, this book is for you! Delicious recipes and creative gift ideas are spread through the pages. Maggie's enthusiasm for small-batch food makers will turn you into one."

—ANA SORTUN, chef, Oleana, Sofra Bakery, and Sarma